THE
Literacy
Center

THE
Literacy
Center

CONTEXTS FOR READING AND WRITING

SECOND EDITION

Lesley Mandel Morrow
Rutgers University

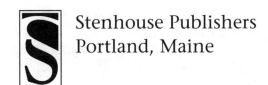
Stenhouse Publishers
Portland, Maine

Stenhouse Publishers
www.stenhouse.com

Credits
Page 78: Lesley Mandel Morrow, "Motivating Reading and Writing in Diverse Classrooms," NCTE Research Paper No. 28. Copyright © 1996 by the National Council of Teachers of English. Reprinted with permission.
Page 120: *Harold and the Purple Crayon.* Copyright © 1955 by Crockett Johnson, copyright © renewed 1983 by Ruth Krauss.
Pages 131–132: "Stories Good Enough to Eat," from *Organizing and Managing Literacy Centers.* Copyright © 1983 by Lesley Mandel Morrow. Reprinted by permission of *Instructor Magazine,* August 1983. Scholastic.

Library of Congress Cataloging-in-Publication Data
Morrow, Lesley Mandel.
 The literacy center : contexts for reading and writing / Lesley Mandel Morrow.
 p. cm.
 Includes bibliographical references (p.).
 ISBN 1-57110-350-3 (alk. paper)
 1. Language arts (Elementary) 2. Language arts—Correlation with content subjects. 3. Classroom environment. 4. Group work in education. 5. Motivation in education. I. Title.
LB1576.M797 2002
372.6—dc21   2002017593

Illustrations by Phyllis Pittet

Manufactured in the United States of America on acid-free paper
06 05 04 03 02 9 8 7 6 5 4 3 2

To my mother, Mary D. Mandel, whose love, guidance, and friendship have been so important to me, and whose strength, wisdom, and wonderful sense of humor I have learned to appreciate all the more in recent years.

Contents

Acknowledgments

This book is a result of my many years of teaching children as well as pre-service and in-service teachers. It is the practical application of the research I have carried out over the years. The ideas come from the work I have done with others involved in my teaching from pre-school through college, and in staff development programs.

I am indebted to the hundreds of children, teachers, administrators, and parents who allowed me to teach their children and collect information to share with others. I would like particularly to thank Jerilyn Bier, Donna Fino Eng, Diane Huggard, Ami Levin, Lisa Lozak, Elizabeth Minnick, Dana Pilla, and Karen Price for their work on the first edition of the book. The following teachers helped with second edition of this book. These individuals made the completion of this manuscript possible: Kristen Fahey, Susan Gallagher, and Karen Lombardy.

An extra special thank you to the following teachers for their dedication and loyalty, intelligence, and commitment to helping me get the job done: Amy Sass, Taylor Holt, Allison Poro, and Jessica Temlock-Fields.

Motivating Independent Reading and Writing

Ms. Johnson's third graders were participating in Writing and Reading Appreciation Program (WRAP) time. (The phrase is credited to Gloria Lettenberger, a first-grade English as a Second Language (ESL) teacher in the New Brunswick public schools.) Steven and Rashaan were sitting on a rug in the literacy center, resting against pillows. They were engaged in partner reading using copies of the same issue of *Ranger Rick* magazine. "Look at all those spiders on page 22!" Steven said. "Aren't they neat?" Rashaan looked over at Steven's copy, then turned to the same page in his magazine. The boys were engrossed as they read and talked about the spiders. "Look!" Rashaan exclaimed. "It says here, spiders have eight legs. I didn't know that. We gotta write this stuff down on the KWL sheet. Let's write what we *know* about spiders in the K column first, and I already have one thing for the L column for what I *learned*." Steven said, "Hey, wait, we gotta write what we *want* to learn in the W column before we write what we learned."

Tamika and Alexis were squeezed into the same rocking chair, each of them reading her own book silently. Larry was sitting in a beanbag chair by himself, reading a novel. When they had finished their reading, they recorded the pages they had read, and what they liked most and least about the reading, on a form prepared by the teacher for recording independent reading that had been completed.

At the listening station, four children were listening to a tape of *Ming Lo Moves the Mountain* (Lobel). When it had ended, Jonathan said to the others, "You know, I don't think Ming Lo is very smart. He kept doing silly things just because the wise man told him to do them." That statement started a lively discussion about whether Ming Lo should have done the things that the wise man told him to do without any questions. After the discussion, each student filled out the listening station accountability form, answering the questions Who are the main characters in the story? What is his or her problem? How was the problem solved?

Yassin, Michael, and Howard in the author's spot. They are working together on their own episode of a favorite television show.

Yassin, Michael, and Howard were in the author's spot. They were working together at the computer, writing and illustrating their own episode of a favorite television show. When their story was complete, they planned to make it into a roll movie and present it to the group as if it were on television.

Colleen, Shakiera, Keisha, Kelly, and Brian were practicing a puppet show they had created from the book *Arthur's Eyes* (Marc Brown). They had made stick puppets and were going to present the story to the class at sharing time, which is held after WRAP time. Sharing time is for students who want to perform or talk about the work they are doing. Ms. Johnson sat and watched as they performed the story. She congratulated them on a job well done. Keisha asked Ms. Johnson if she thought the characters in the puppet show had acted the way the author of the story would have wanted them to. Ms. Johnson replied, "If Mr. Brown, the author of *Arthur's Eyes,* walked into our classroom right now, he would think that he had directed this puppet show himself. I think the characters acted just as he would have wanted them to."

These children are motivated to participate in independent literacy activities in their classroom.

Its physical and social contexts have been designed to foster independent participation that is social, collaborative, and cooperative. In this book I discuss strategies that have been successful in motivating independent reading and writing activities in school and at home. For many years I have been researching ways to motivate children to read and write for pleasure and for information. My work has taken me to classrooms in suburban communities and urban settings, and I have worked with children from diverse backgrounds. In applying principles of motivation to classroom practice, I have found that classrooms need to provide children with certain elements: choice, challenge, social interaction, and success.

In the pages that follow, I outline how to create rich literacy environments through the design of literacy centers that are engaging. Teachers can be seen as architects who design the environment to support strategies for learning. I describe how the teachers I've worked with model pleasurable and skill-oriented literacy activities, such as reading to children and storytelling, so that children will engage in these activities themselves. After the teacher models activities, students form groups and work collaboratively to use the materials and do the activities modeled by the teacher. They then create their own materials for books they have read and stories they have written, which they present to peers and parents. Most of the materials require the students to practice skills learned and to be accountable for activities they work on by handing in products or doing presentations.

This book is filled with practical suggestions from the teachers, children, and parents who participated in the different programs we were involved in together. Suggestions for activities, materials, and accountability forms are provided to help teachers design their own literacy centers, model activities and the use of materials for students, and initiate literacy center time for children to interact with each other while engaged in literacy activities. Literacy center time can be used for recreational reading or for practicing skills learned. It occurs

- after other work is completed,

- during a special time set aside for recreational reading,

- during guided reading periods, when the teacher meets with small groups for direct instruction and the other children work independently at literacy center activities.

During literacy center time, children function with peers or alone but almost always independently of the teacher.

Research about learning and literacy development points to the need for certain physical and social elements to be present in classrooms to help motivate children. This book reflects several learning theories and relates them to practice.

Learning Theories Reflected in This Book

Integrated Language Arts Perspective

The integrated language arts perspective suggests that children learn literacy from a series of meaningful and functional experiences with reading and writing, using varied genres of children's literature. These types of experiences take place within a rich environment created specifically to encourage collaboration and cooperative learning during periods set aside for independent reading and writing. Instruction includes a conscious effort on the part of the teacher to integrate literacy learning within the different content areas (social studies, science, math, art, and music). Equal emphasis is placed on reading, writing, listening, oral language, and viewing because all help to create a literate individual. Skills are taught in a meaningful context; for example, when studying dinosaurs, the teacher may focus on the letters and sounds of the initial consonants found in the names of dinosaurs. The integrated language arts approach emphasizes self-regulated learning. Teachers and children together are responsible for deciding instructional strategies, organization, activities, and materials (Bergeron 1990; Short, Harste, and Burke 1996).

Theory of Developmental Literacy Learning

Don Holdaway's (1979) theory of developmental literacy learning places equal emphasis on teaching and learning. In addition to teaching lessons in literacy, for example, teachers should provide guidance and models of literacy activities for children to practice. According to Holdaway, there are four processes that enable children to acquire reading ability. The first is *observation* of reading behaviors—being read to, for example, or seeing adults read. The children should also have the opportunity to observe the teacher model directly behaviors they should engage in. The second is *collaboration* with an individual (a teacher or peer) who interacts with the child, providing encouragement and help when necessary. The third is *practice*. The learner independently tries out what has been taught. Practice gives children opportunities to evaluate their performance, make corrections, and increase their skills. In the fourth process, *performance,* children share what has been learned and are accountable for their learning by producing a product. There is adult and peer interaction as children observe others engage in literacy acts and as they interact in literacy experiences. There is the opportunity for peer tutoring and collaboration in active literacy experiences. In classrooms such as these, projects are both process- and product-oriented because students need to show accountability for what they have accomplished (Holdaway 1979; Short, Harste, and Burke 1996).

A Balanced Approach to Literacy Instruction

In this approach to literacy instruction, the strategies selected are based on the learning styles of individual children. According to a position paper by the International Reading Association (IRA 1999), there is no single method or single combi-

nation of methods that can successfully teach all children to read. Therefore teachers must have thorough knowledge both of multiple methods for teaching reading and of the learning styles of their students. This means using some explicit skill-based instruction as well as constructivist techniques, including teaching problem-solving strategies. A report by the National Reading Panel (2000) presents the most effective approaches to teaching children to read according to scientifically based reading research. The report discusses a balanced approach to reading by including the following in a program of instruction: phonemic awareness training, phonics instruction, development of vocabulary, comprehension, and fluency.

Guthrie and Alvermann (1999), based on work from the National Reading Research Center, discuss engaged readers as strategic readers who possess multiple skills that enable them to read independently and comprehend what they read. Engaged readers use prior knowledge to gain new information from text read. They also have the ability to transfer and apply acquired information into new contexts. Engaged readers are motivated to read voluntarily and independently, both for pleasure and for information (Morrow 1992). (See Figure 1.1.)

With the current perspectives in mind it is suggested that teachers provide students with the following experiences in literacy instruction (Morrow 2001; Routman 2000):

Figure 1.1 Qualities of Engaged Readers

Strategies, Structures, and Materials in Balanced Literacy Programs

- Reading and writing aloud by teachers and children

- Shared reading and writing by teachers and children

- Teacher-guided reading and writing activities

- Independent reading and writing activities

- Collaborative reading and writing with peers

- Performance of completed reading and writing activities

- Content connections for reading and writing

using the following materials:

- Pencil and paper
- Literature
- Instructional texts
- Manipulatives
- Listening materials (tape recorders, cassettes)

and in the following settings:

- Whole group
- Small group
- One-on-one
- Teacher-directed
- Literacy center
- Social (with adults and peers)

with the following types of instruction:

- Spontaneous
- Direct
- Explicit
- Systematic
- Construction of meaning
- Problem solving

Motivation Theory and Literacy Development

Motivation is defined as an intrinsic desire to initiate, sustain, and direct one's activity. Motivated students return to and continue to work on tasks. The following elements are found to motivate children:

- *The opportunity to have and make choices.* Choice gives children a sense of control and promotes motivation. Providing children with choices suggests that the classroom has a variety of literacy materials, spaces, and activities that students can decide to participate in.

- *Social collaboration.* Collaboration facilitates children's engagement in a task, but fostering collaboration requires time. The teacher needs time to guide literacy activities, and the children need time to practice literacy activities with peers, independent of the teacher. Collaboration can take many forms.

- *Challenging tasks.* Challenges promote goal attainment. Tasks must be challenging but able to be accomplished.

- *Success.* Success gives students a sense of being competent. It is important for them to feel successful when completing tasks. Part of the success experience is sharing completed tasks with peers and teachers (Ford 1992; McCombs 1991).

When students have some control over their activities and feel challenged, competent, and successful in the performance of these activities, they are more likely to participate (Spaulding 1992). Therefore, our goal is to establish classroom contexts that will enhance motivation, provide environments where students have choices of activities they are expected to participate in, where they feel competent to handle the activities, and where, on completing an activity, they feel a sense of accomplishment and success. This combination helps to create motivated readers and writers.

The Value of Social and Physical Contexts for Learning

Social Contexts

When children work independently of the teacher, in collaboration with others, there is movement in the classroom, and more noise than when a teacher plays the traditional, dominant role of leading a lesson. Teachers wonder if learning can really take place in such an environment. They worry about how to get started, how to manage the situation, and how to help children learn to function independently in productive ways. A review of the literature on cooperative learning—that is, students working in small groups to help one another learn through discussion and debate—makes it clear that this type of learning context has many benefits. Researchers have found that interaction and collaboration among small groups of students promotes achievement and productivity (Johnson and Johnson 1998; Sharan and Sharan 1989/90). In addition, the interaction allows children to explain material to each other, listen to each other's explanations, and arrive at joint understandings.

Cazden (2001) found that peer interaction allows students to try out many roles that they would otherwise be denied in the traditional student-teacher structure. In a cooperative learning setting more capable peers observe, guide, and correct while the student performs a task (Forman and Cazden 1985). Students are able to accomplish more together than they could alone. The peer interaction offers the same learning opportunities as tutoring.

According to Dewey (1966), children engaged in task-oriented dialogue with peers can reach higher levels of understanding than when teachers present information to them. Piaget (1959) suggests that peers serve as resources for one another in cognitive development. In addition to fostering greater productivity and achievement, social settings seem to promote in students an intrinsic desire to learn because they become less dependent on the teacher (Wood 1990).

During literacy center time Dharmesh and Imran read a newspaper article entitled "Cartoons Help Fight Drugs." They point out, discuss, and then record on a form cartoon characters who are helping to solve the drug problem.

Physical Contexts

Preparing the physical environment of the classroom is often overlooked in planning. Teachers may concentrate on varying presentation strategies and interpersonal factors without considering the physical context in which teaching and learning occur. When program and environment are not coordinated, "setting deprivation" can result, a situation in which the physical environment fails to support teaching and learning activities (Weinstein and Mignano 1997).

Rather than serving only as a background for classroom activities, the physical environment has an important influence on teaching and learning. For example, rooms partitioned into smaller spaces improve verbal interaction and cooperation among students, and attractive literacy centers with a variety of materials increase use of such materials during free-choice periods (Morrow and Weinstein 1986). When teachers purposefully arrange space and materials in classrooms, the physical environment can motivate children to learn.

Children's Literature as Motivation

Children's literature is also an important source for motivating readers and writers. Experts in the field of children's literature stress the importance of planned programs that encourage pleasurable experiences with literature (Cullinan 1992). Such programs, they say, create interest in and enthusiasm for books. Teachers should read narrative and expository text and fiction and nonfiction trade books to children daily and discuss what they read and what students read. Children should be encouraged to read to each other and to tell stories to the rest of the class. Books should be borrowed from school and taken home, and books from home should be brought to school and shared. Students' exposure to trade books should be frequent and integrated with teaching in content areas. In addition to the motivational factors surrounding the use of children's literature, studies have revealed that students who use literature as a major part of their reading program tend to develop sophisticated language structures, enhance their vocabulary, and improve their reading comprehension and writing ability in both expository and narrative pieces (Morrow 1996).

Well-designed literacy centers provide an inviting area for children to read, write, and appreciate children's literature.

The Importance of Creating Independent Readers and Writers

Educators agree that reading is both a practical activity and a cherished and joyous privilege in life, yet not enough attention has been given to developing children's voluntary reading. In a report to the U.S. Congress entitled *Books in Our Future* (1984), Daniel Boorstin, Librarian of Congress at the time, warned that aliterates—individuals who can read but choose not to do so—constitute a threat at least equal to that of illiterates in a democratic tradition built on books and reading. The practice or absence of independent reading, he wrote, "will determine the extent of self-improvement and enlightenment, the ability to share wisdom and the delights of our civilization, and our capacity for intelligent self-government" (iv). Aliteracy can be as devastating as illiteracy; as Mark Twain said, "Reading ain't no more use to him who don't read than him who can't."

Unfortunately, substantial numbers of children read neither for pleasure nor for information, although they have the cognitive ability to read (IRA and NAEYC 1998). Some studies, which found that children do not spend a lot of time involved in voluntary reading, reveal a strong relationship between the amount of leisure reading one does and the degree of success in reading one achieves (Cunningham and Allington 1999). In a study by Anderson, Wilson, and Fielding (1988), children recorded the number of minutes they spent reading outside of school. The researchers found a positive correlation between the number of minutes read and reading achievement. For example, children who scored at the ninetieth percentile on a reading test spent five times as many minutes per day reading books as children at the fiftieth percentile and more than two hundred times as many minutes per day reading books as children at the tenth percentile. In other studies, children's independent reading has been found to correlate positively with overall achievement in school (Cunningham and

Stanovich 1991; Guthrie and Greaney 1991; Taylor, Frye, and Maruyama 1990).

Other studies have investigated the characteristics of home environments in which children have demonstrated a voluntary interest in books or have established independent reading habits (Greaney and Hegarty 1987; Morrow 1996). These children were likely to be from small families, and their parents usually had educations beyond high school. Their homes had rich literacy environments. Parents provided reading models for their children by reading often in their leisure time. They read a variety of materials—novels, magazines, newspapers, and work-related documents. Books were placed in many different rooms, including the playroom, the kitchen, the bathroom, and children's bedrooms. Parents of voluntary readers read to and with their children often. These children were in settings where interactions between the adults and the children were socially and emotionally conducive to literacy growth (Clay 1998). Some of these home characteristics can be adapted for school.

Voluntary readers score well on reading tests at school (Morrow 1996). Anderson, Wilson, and Fielding (1988) found that children who were in classrooms that promoted independent reading did more reading at home than children from classrooms where there was little emphasis in this direction.

Despite these studies, reading programs are judged only by reading achievement based on scores on reading tests, and personal reading habits do not enter into these scores (Morrow 1996). According to the influential book *Becoming a Nation of Readers* (Anderson et al. 1985), learning to read requires having the motivation or desire, and practicing to achieve proficiency. In addition, to maintain fluency, reading should be a lifelong pursuit.

A survey of educators, most of whom were classroom teachers, indicated that creating motivation for or an interest in reading is of major importance in teaching children to read. Those surveyed, a random sample of International Reading Association members, felt that more research was needed in the area of motivating

readers (O'Flahavan et al. 1992). Since children's reading habits develop early in life, schools must deliberately attract children to reading during the early years, or voluntary reading may never become a lifelong habit.

Format of This Book

In this book I provide practical ideas on motivating children to become independent readers and writers. These ideas are based on research that was carried out over several years and that involved children, teachers, and parents. The students ranged from preschool through sixth grade, and from high to low socioeconomic status; they came from diverse cultural and racial backgrounds (Morrow 1982; 1983; 1992; 1996; Morrow, O'Connor, and Smith 1990; Morrow and Weinstein 1982; 1986). The research was designed to discover elements in classrooms that promote children's interest in reading and writing and to demonstrate the ability to create motivated students who choose to read and write independently of adults both in and out of school. The motivating activities that students participated in are described in this book.

I focus on the social and physical contexts that foster independent reading and writing:

- Physical layouts that encourage literacy instruction in the classroom, in particular the design of literacy centers

- Teacher modeling activities that provide guidance, develop children's skills, and encourage independent use of materials and strategies

- Specific time for collaboration during independent reading and writing

These contexts give children a feeling of competence about their literacy ability and put them in control of decisions about literacy tasks they would participate in.

These contexts foster the processes of socially interactive literacy activity during

- special periods set aside for independent reading and writing,

- guided reading periods, when teachers take small groups for direct instruction,

- free time, when all other work is done and students may engage in independent reading and writing.

These processes in turn result in the following outcomes:

- Enhanced appreciation for reading and writing

- Improvement or mastery of print recognition, phonemic awareness, and phonics and other word study skills as well as reading comprehension, vocabulary development, oral reading fluency, and good writing

- Voluntary participation in cooperative reading and writing by all children, including those with special needs

In the many classrooms in which I have worked, teachers and children gave different names to independent reading and writing periods: recreational reading period, rec reading time, voluntary reading period, independent reading and writing period, Drop Everything and Read (DEAR) time, reading and writing workshop, writing and reading appreciation program (WRAP), and literacy center time, the two favorites being the last two. In this book I refer to cooperative periods of independent recreational reading and writing as WRAP time. When referring to literacy center time, I mean the time that students engage in independent reading and writing when teachers take other students into small groups for guided reading instruction. This is a time when students practice skills learned and must be accountable for work accomplished.

Designing a Literacy Center

The comments that follow were made by third graders who participated in cooperative activities with their peers in their classroom's literacy center (Morrow 1992):

- "The literacy center is the best part of the classroom. You get to read with your friends, and they help you and you help them."

- "I like using the literacy center because you can choose the books you want to read. You can choose fat books, skinny books, story-books, or information books. It's cozy there; you can lean on the pillows or sit in the rocking chair to read."

- "There are so many fun things in the literacy center that it makes you want to read and write. My favorites are the felt stories, tape stories, and roll movies."

- "You get to read a lot when you have your own classroom library because the books are right there. I'm reading so much and practicing so much, which will help me get better at it."

- "The only thing the literacy center needs to make it better is a snack bar where you can get some food, so you can eat and read."

The following are comments by teachers who created a literacy center in their classroom:

- "Children who would never read are reading in the literacy center. They enjoy the choice of all the materials there."

- "I think the carpet is a magic carpet; I'm going to call it the reading rug. Kids who never read before will sit on that little piece of rug and read."

- "My children have a sense of pride about the literacy center. They helped to create it and contribute their reading and writing materials to it. It is indeed a special spot in our classroom—a splash of color, a ray of light, and a place for happiness."

"The literacy center is the best part of the classroom. You get to read with your friends, and they help you, and you help them."

But what does such a classroom look like? What does the teacher do to motivate students to pursue literacy activities in a social setting? The following describes a classroom in the process of developing a dramatic play center that integrates play, literacy activities, and the content area theme.

With each thematic unit, Ms. Millson helps her children design the dramatic play center to reflect the topic being studied and to enhance the opportunity for meaningful experiences with reading and writing. When learning about animals, the students in her combination first and second grade decided to create a veterinarian's office. The class had the opportunity to visit a veterinarian to help with their planning. They began redesigning the dramatic play area by creating a waiting room with chairs and a table filled with magazines and books. Ms. Millson suggested hanging posters and pamphlets about good health practices for pets, which she had obtained from the veterinarian. The children made a poster that listed the doctor's hours, and added signs that said "No Smoking" and "Check in with the Nurse When You Arrive." The nurse's table contained forms for patients to fill out, a telephone, telephone books, appointment cards, and a calendar. The veterinarian's office also contained patient folders, prescription pads, white coats, masks, gloves, cotton swabs, a doctor's kit, and stuffed animals. Blank paper, a stapler, pencils, markers, colored pencils, and crayons were placed in the area as well. The classroom computer was taken from the math center and relocated into this area for keeping patient records and other files. The center design was a collaborative effort by the teacher and children.

After preparing the environment with the children, Ms. Millson modeled the use of various materials. She suggested to them, "While you're waiting for your turn to see the doctor, you can read to your pet in the waiting area and the nurse can ask you to fill out forms. The receptionist might like to talk to people on the phone about problems their pets are having, schedule appointments, and write out appointment cards. You can write bills for visits, accept payments, and give receipts. The doctor can fill out prescription forms and write up patient reports." Later, Ms. Millson joined the children in the dramatic play area, pretending to be the nurse, then the doctor, so that she could model the types of literacy behavior for children to try.

A week later, the children were fully engaged in this center. Jonnell sat in the waiting room reading the story *Caps for Sale* (Slobodkina) to her pet monkey. Damien joined her with his pet rabbit and listened. He took a turn reading. Katie, who was taking the role of the nurse, called Jonnell to answer some questions about her monkey's problems. When Jonnell finished filling out forms, she watched Damien's pet while he spoke with the nurse. Josh was acting as the doctor, examining a stuffed teddy bear that was brought in by Tim. Josh wrote the animal's name and the owner's name on a file folder, and then picked up the prescription pad. He told Tim, "You see this? Now this says to make sure that your teddy bear takes ten pills every hour, until he feels better. This teddy bear needs to stay in bed, keep warm, and get lots of rest until his cold is gone." Then he wrote "10 PLS EVRY HOUR" on the pad.

Let's look more closely at what's going on here. The teacher, along with the children, prepared the

In the thematic play area designed as a veterinarian's office, Josh, acting as the doctor, examined Tim's teddy bear and said, "This teddy bear needs to stay in bed, keep warm, and get lots of rest until his cold is gone." Then he wrote the prescription "10 PLS EVRY HOUR."

physical environment. She described and modeled the use of materials in the literacy-enriched role-playing area; after this initial guidance, she helped students in need of direction. As the children became more involved, the teacher allowed the play to take place on its own, and she participated in the children's activities. The social collaborative setting provided opportunities for purposeful communication. The dramatic play theme allowed for the integration of play, literacy, and content. During their role playing, children pursued real-life behavior that involved meaningful and functional literacy activities. The teacher in this classroom was aware that a classroom environment that encourages children to communicate in varied ways helps motivate them to read and write (Morrow 1990).

Positive Effects Related to Planned Physical Environments

Students' behavior and interactions are influenced by the classroom environment, and classroom design is a critical factor in the success of instruction (Loughlin and Martin 1987). Historically, physical environment has played an important role in fostering learning. Montessori, for example, featured a "prepared environment" as the central part of her educational program (Morrow 2001). She prepared special materials for learning and carefully designed appropriate child-sized furniture where manipulatives were easily accessible and visible. Montessori planned the placement of items in the classroom to be sure optimum learning could take place in a self-directed, independent manner.

Research has shown many ways in which the physical design of the classroom affects children's behavior. Rooms partitioned into smaller spaces help to increase verbal interaction and cooperative activities among children more than rooms with large open spaces. Literacy-enriched dramatic play areas based on themes stimulate literacy activities and the enhancement of literacy skills (Morrow 1990; Morrow and Rand 1991; Neuman and Roskos 1990; 1992). Dramatic play with story props improves story production and comprehension, including recall of details and ability to sequence and interpret. Enhancing the physical setting of literacy centers increases children's use of this area. The increased use results in their doing more reading and writing, thus improving their literacy achievement (Morrow 2001).

The physical environment also influences teachers' behavior. When instruction takes place in good-quality spaces, teachers are more sensitive and friendly toward children. They are more apt to teach students to consider the rights and feelings of others and encourage them to choose activities. Teachers in poorer-quality environments are less involved and less interested, are more likely to teach arbitrary social rules, and are more restrictive (Weinstein and Mignano 1997).

Given these findings, a classroom designed to promote optimum literacy development will offer an abundant supply of materials for reading, writing, and speaking. While most of these materials are concentrated in the literacy center, literacy materials are also provided in content area learning centers. Materials and settings throughout the classroom simulate real-life experiences and make literacy meaningful and functional for children so they can see the purpose for becoming literate.

Physical Environments That Motivate Reading and Writing

Instead of viewing the physical environment as background or scenery for teaching and learning, teachers can purposefully arrange the space and materials, thus acknowledging and using the physical environment as an active, positive, and pervasive influence on instruction (Loughlin and Martin 1987; Morrow 1990).

Classroom Layout and Materials

A literacy-rich classroom usually contains centers dedicated to particular activities or content areas appropriate to the grade level, such as social studies, science, math, art, music, dramatic play, block play, and language arts. Each center contains materials pertinent to the content area in general and materials specific to topics currently under study. Resources are primarily devoted to the content area but are designed to develop literacy skills as well. The materials are manipulative and activity-oriented, and designed so children can use them either independently or in small groups. Figure 2.1 shows a typical floor plan for preschool through first-grade classrooms, and Figure 2.2 shows one for second- through fifth-grade rooms. Because of space limitations and the fact that older children may change classrooms for different subjects, it is sometimes more difficult to have multiple centers beyond the early childhood grades. However, a literacy center can be used to house materials that might ordinarily be found in other centers. A box or shelf can also serve as a center. Centers can simply be places to house materials. The center activities can be done in other parts of the classroom, for example, at a cluster of desks or in a corner of the room.

The following are suggestions of various kinds of classroom centers, with materials that could furnish each center. Of course, teachers should adapt these suggestions to suit their own needs and preferences and those of their children.

Figure 2.1 Classroom Floor Plan for Pre-K Through First Grade

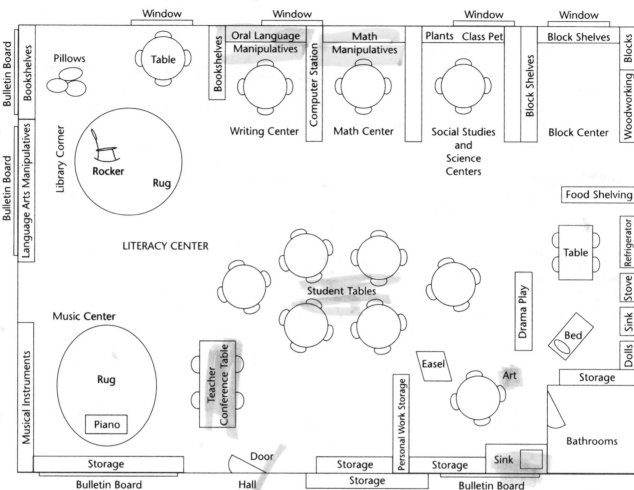

- *Science center.* The science center could include such items as an aquarium, a terrarium, plants, a magnifying glass, a class pet, magnets, a thermometer, a compass, a prism, shells, rock collections, a stethoscope, a kaleidoscope, a microscope, expository and narrative children's literature that reflects topics being studied, and blank journals for recording observations of experiments and scientific projects.

- *Social studies center.* The social studies center could contain maps, a globe, flags from other countries, posted materials on current events, artifacts from other countries, informational books and expository and narrative children's literature that reflect topics being studied, writing materials to make class books, and personal books about themes being focused on.

- *Art area.* The art area could contain watercolor paints, brushes, colored pencils, crayons, felt-tip markers, various kinds of paper, scissors, paste, pipe cleaners, scrap materials (bits of fabric, wool, string), clay, play dough, food and detergent boxes for sculptures, books about famous artists, posters of artists' work, and directions for making crafts.

- *Music area.* The music area could house a piano, a tape recorder with varied musical tapes, rhythm instruments, songbooks, songs that have been made into books, books about famous composers and singers, sheet music, and charts containing song lyrics.

- *Mathematics area.* The math area could contain scales, rulers, measuring cups, movable

Figure 2.2 Classroom Floor Plan for Second Through Fifth Grade

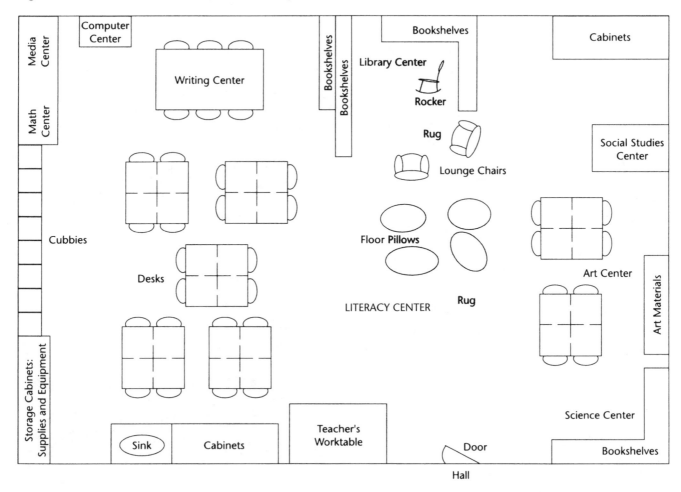

clocks, a stopwatch, a calendar, play money, a cash register, calculators, dominoes, an abacus, a number line, a height chart, an hourglass, numbers (felt, wooden, and magnetic), fraction puzzles, geometric shapes, math workbooks, children's literature about numbers and mathematics, writing materials for creating stories, and books related to math.

• *Block area.* The block area would contain, of course, blocks of different sizes and shapes, but it could also contain figures of people and animals, toy cars and trucks, items related to themes being studied, paper and pencils to prepare signs and notes, and reading materials related to themes.

• *Dramatic play area.* Items promoting dramatic play include a telephone, food cartons, plates,

silverware, newspapers, magazines, books, a telephone book, a cookbook, note pads, cameras and a photo album, and a table and chairs. The dramatic play area can be transformed into settings for theme-related role playing, such as a grocery store, a pet shop, a gas station, or a restaurant. Materials for reading and writing related to the theme should also be available.

Furniture that is part of a center can also serve as partitions to separate centers. Center materials may be stored on tables or shelves, in boxes, and on bulletin boards. These materials, as well as the center itself, should be accessible and labeled. Each piece of equipment in a center should have its own designated spot so that the teacher can direct children to specific items, and children can find and return them easily. Typically, at the beginning of the school year, most centers hold only a few items; new materials are added as the year progresses. Before new items are placed in centers, the teacher introduces and models their purpose, use, and placement (Montessori 1965).

The room design should support whole-group, small-group, and individual instruction. The teacher can hold large-group lessons when the children are sitting at their desks or tables, or sitting on the floor. If possible, the literacy center should be large enough for the entire class to meet there. A teacher conference table can provide space for small-group or individualized instruction. This table can be used for skill development, such as guided reading instruction that is directed by the teacher. The conference table should be placed in a quiet area of the room to facilitate the kind of instruction that occurs around it, but it should also be situated so as to allow the teacher to see the rest of the room where children are working independently. The various centers offer settings for independent and self-directed learning. In general, as can be seen from the classroom floor plans in Figures 2.1 and 2.2, centers are positioned so that areas where quiet work is typical (the literacy, math, social studies, and science centers) are away from the more noisy, active centers (dramatic play, blocks, art).

Having enough space for centers is always a problem. In small rooms, centers are often just storage areas for materials that are used outside of the area. For example, materials may be in boxes, on a bulletin board display, or on a door to a closet. During center time, furniture in the classroom can be moved to provide working space. Not all classrooms will have all centers mentioned, especially in the upper grades. Teachers may need to collaborate and share centers by creating different centers in different rooms, which students can use when they change rooms for different subjects.

Functional Environmental Print

Literacy-rich classrooms are filled with visually prominent functional print, such as labels on classroom items and areas. Signs communicate

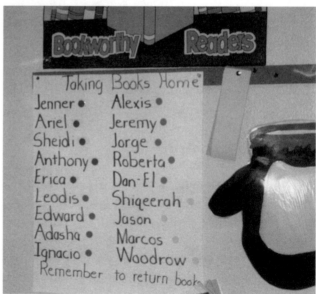

Literacy-rich classrooms are filled with visually prominent functional print, such as labels on classroom items and areas. Signs communicate information and directions.

functional information and directions, such as "Quiet Please" and "Please Put Materials Away After Using Them." Charts labeled "Helpers," "Daily Routines," "Attendance," and "Calendar" can simplify classroom management (Morrow 2001; Schickedanz 1993). A notice board placed prominently in the room can be used to communicate with children in writing and for children to communicate with the teacher and other children. Experience charts and word walls display new words generated from themes, recipes, and science experiments. A word wall often features high-frequency words that are posted under the appropriate letter of the alphabet. The words are used in various ways, for example, if the teacher wants to work with short vowels, he can point to a word such as *map* on the word wall and say, "The word I am thinking of has a short vowel sound like the *a* in *map*." There are activities that students can do independently with the word wall as well. The environmental print needs to be used with the children, or it may go unnoticed. Children should be encouraged to read and copy it, and to use words from the labels in their writing. (See Resource 3.4.)

Creating the Literacy Center

Much of what we know about the contexts of early literacy development emerged from research on the home environment of children who read early without direct instruction (Taylor and Strickland 1986; Teale 1986). Even though the home setting cannot be replicated in school, the classroom environment can be adapted to reflect the physical and social contexts that affect home literacy experiences. For example, one feature of a rich home literacy environment that can be easily incorporated into classrooms is to have a large variety of literacy materials: novels, magazines, newspapers, work-related papers, picture storybooks, blank paper, pads, crayons, and other writing instruments. In fact, the overall goal of creating a literacy center is to provide a homelike environment in which reading and writing occur frequently and naturally in a social setting. This is why pillows and rugs are often seen in the literacy center area.

To convey the importance of literacy, and of books as a principal source of knowledge, the classroom library should be the focal area of the room. Although a central school library is vitally important, classroom libraries provide several benefits. For one thing, they offer immediate access to literacy materials. In addition, they prompt children to read more. Children in classrooms with library collections read 50 percent more books than children in classrooms without such collections (Morrow 2001). An increased use of literature also occurs during free-choice periods in classrooms that have well-designed library corners (Anderson, Fielding, and Wilson 1988; Morrow and Weinstein 1986).

Design

When I began working with teachers, it became apparent that the standard classroom design would not promote the types of social, cooperative, and independent behavior we wanted to encourage. To meet this goal and to keep literacy experiences meaningful and functional, we needed an area for the display, storage, and use of literacy materials—the literacy center. Not only would the literacy center hold a variety of literacy-related materials and be a place for children to collaborate when using them, it would also be a symbolic, functional, and motivating factor for fostering literacy behavior.

In the course of many research projects, I spoke with teachers about changing the physical design of their classrooms to incorporate a literacy center. Their immediate concern was having enough space. Some of the comments I heard were, "It will be too much trouble to change everything." "It will be upsetting to the children." "I just can't fit it into my room." It was already difficult fitting in the instructional materials they had, along with the children's desks and the children. How would it be possible to fit one more item into their classroom?

We discussed rearranging desks and other pieces of equipment to find ways to fit literacy centers into their classrooms. Some teachers were skeptical at first, but they began to see the possibilities as we went from one classroom to the next discussing where the center might be placed and how it might be created. I shared photographs illustrating what other classrooms looked like before and after literacy centers were added, and we visited rooms similar to theirs that had centers in them.

In some classrooms we were able to design the entire literacy center in one section of the room. In others, we had to separate sections. For example, in older buildings with few electrical outlets, the tape players and computers that needed electricity were often placed away from the rest of the center.

The size of the room affected the type of literacy center. In very small rooms the center also had to be small. Instead of being a work space, it became a place to house the materials that children took to use in other parts of the room. In some larger classrooms teachers extended the literacy center so that it was not confined to one section but spilled out into other areas of the room.

Various formats were tried in different classrooms to find the elements that were effective for each room and each teacher. Teachers began to think of the classroom as a second home for both their students and themselves, and they decorated it with the same care as their home. Like interior decorators, they would discuss placement of furniture, purchase needed items, and coordinate colors. Bright colors were often chosen for pillows, rugs, bulletin board coverings, and posters. In what were often very drab-looking environments, we wanted the centers to make a statement about the importance of literacy.

Children were consulted about the design of the centers. Together, the teacher and the children decided where the center would be placed, what materials should be included, and what types of books should be acquired. When the children in one class were asked what kind of books they'd like to have in the center, Roseangela immediately replied, "We need a lot of science stuff; that's all Marcel likes to read." Chris said, "I want motorcycle magazines and ones about trains." Mercedes had a special interest in Africa and wanted some informational books and storybooks on that topic. This triggered the children's interest in books about other countries; they eventually added books about Italy, Japan, Mexico, Israel, and Ireland.

The teacher's preferences were a major factor in the way the centers were arranged. Teachers wanted to discuss plans with me, their colleagues, and their students. For example, Ms. Peters collaborated with me concerning the design of her center, but she wanted to put the area together herself. She used most of the materials I suggested, but she also implemented her own ideas, such as a system for checking out books.

The completed literacy centers were attractive and functional additions to classrooms that were often in poor physical condition. After using them for a time, the teachers commented on their success (Morrow 1997):

- "I never thought that I would have enough space in my classroom for a literacy center. I was surprised that so many materials could fit into such a small area."

- "The literacy center became a place where children of all reading and writing abilities mingled. . . . This social context seemed to provide an atmosphere for cooperative learning. The children looked forward to their time there each day."

- "The children were a great help in deciding what to put where and in setting up the area. Because they were a part of designing the literacy center, they were particularly proud of that area."

- "Children participated in the literacy center quite naturally and with enthusiasm. Children read more, wrote more, and took more books home from school than any other group of youngsters I had had in my classroom before. I think it's because the materials were so attractive and accessible. It suddenly dawned on me that while children had the opportunity to use the centers, they were practicing skills I'd been teaching them during direct instruction."

By the end of the school year, the teachers and children had made some changes to all their centers to accommodate their individual needs. I was delighted with the changes because they showed that teachers were taking an interest in the area and responsibility for it. In most cases, teachers added more pillows, stuffed animals, literature manipulatives, new books, and other ideas that we hadn't thought of to make the area unique for them and their students. We were pleased with how well the centers were cared for and how much they were used. Figure 2.3 shows a literacy center.

Furnishings

The literacy center became a focal area in these teachers' classrooms, a spot that was immediately visible and inviting to the children or to anyone who walked into the room. Bookshelves, cabinets, partitions, or freestanding bulletin boards were used to provide a sense of privacy and physical definition to the area. The size of the literacy center varied with the size of the classroom, but generally it could accommodate five or six children comfortably. Equipment was chosen to attract children to the literacy center and to provide a comfortable area to read, write, and collaborate.

An area rug measuring 4 by 6 feet or 5 by 8 feet allowed children to work on the floor. Pillows, beanbag chairs, and stuffed animals added an element of softness.

A table and some chairs in the literacy center provided a spot for reading, writing, and listening to taped stories.

In school, children rarely have any privacy. To meet this need for children to be by themselves to read and think, we created a "private spot." A large, decorated appliance box often became the private spot, but children found spaces on their own under tables, desks, and other such areas in the classroom where they could be alone to read and think.

We used adult-sized rocking chairs in all the centers. These chairs were an immediate hit. The rocker became a special place, which we named "The Literacy Chair of Honor" because the teacher as well as guest readers sat here to read stories to the children. Children cuddled together in the chair to read during literacy center time. The rock-

ing chair provided the opportunity for the children to take the role of the teacher and read their original stories to each other, perform puppet stories they had created, or tell about books they had read. The homelike quality of the rocking chair, along with the rug, pillows, and stuffed animals, set a tone during story reading that reflected Holdaway's (1979) Shared Book Experience, in which story reading is modeled on the best features of the home reading experience before going to bed.

To make the area as inviting as possible, attractive posters that encourage children to read were obtained from the American Library Association. Teachers prepared bulletin boards to promote reading as well. One popular bulletin board featured a hot air balloon that held two children in its basket with the saying "Get Carried Away: Read and Write" (see Figure 2.3). A bulletin board can also be used for students to write notes to each other, to record the title and date of books read, or to feature favorite authors.

At the end of the school year, when children were asked what they liked about the periods of independent reading and writing, materials in the literacy centers were frequently included in their comments. Tara said she especially liked the pillows and teddy bears. Her friend Lauren added, "I like the animals you get to hug when you read." Jason said that what he liked best was "lying down on the carpet and reading a book with my head on the pillows." Teshan said, "I like to sit on the rug in the Book Nook and read, but the rocking chair is the best of all."

The Book Collection

Two kinds of bookshelves were incorporated into the literacy center. The major collection of books was kept on shelves with their spines facing out. Usually shelves already in the classroom were used. Plastic crates were added as needed for extra space. To call attention to featured books about themes being studied, open-faced bookshelves were used that allowed the covers of the books to be seen. Open-faced bookshelves included the floor-standing wooden type and some that sat on a shelf,

Figure 2.3 A Literacy Center

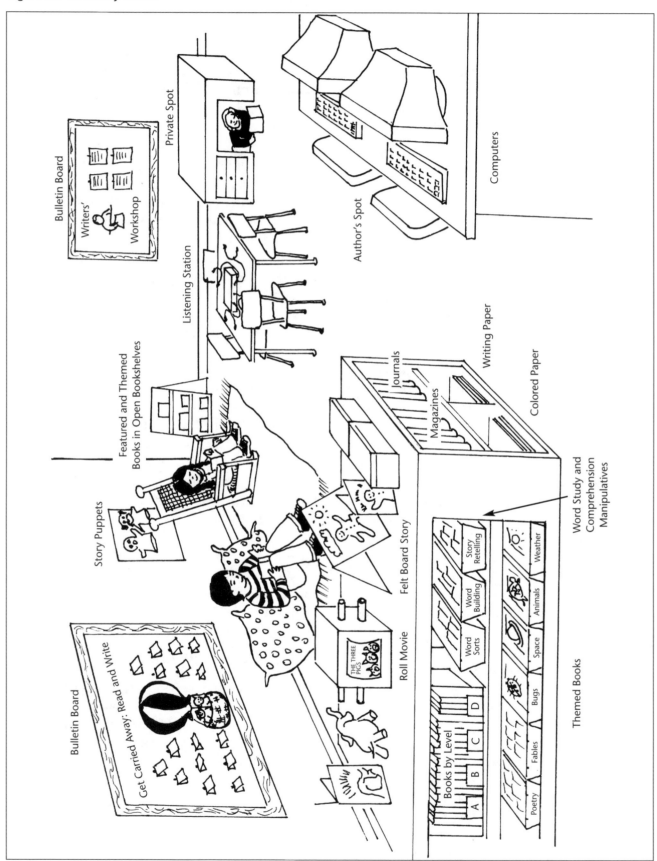

made of wood or corrugated cardboard. We also used wire racks that swivel and stand on the floor and teacher-made shelves of corrugated cardboard.

About twenty-five new books were rotated on and off the regular bookshelves about once a month to stimulate interest. Books on the open-faced shelving were changed with new themes that were studied, holidays celebrated, and so forth. All the books were shelved by category and color-coded according to the type of book. For example, the poetry books were marked with a blue dot and placed on a shelf marked "Poetry." Some classrooms stored all their books by category—animals, poetry, weather—in small plastic crates and labeled the crates. Setting up an organizational system provided a good opportunity to make connections between the school library and the classroom library.

Children were encouraged to check books out to take home. Loose-leaf binders were used for record keeping, with each child's name on a different page. Using different colored binders helps the child identify where her checkout page is and avoid having to wait in line for the book. Some teachers used a sign-out sheet on clipboards. Others used two file boxes, one for books checked out and one for books returned. Cards were filled out and placed in the "out" box when they were checked out of the classroom and put in the "in" box when they were returned. (See Resource 1.2.)

Five to eight books per child were typically included in the literacy center book collection. These spanned three or four grade levels and appealed to a variety of interests. When we found that many children enjoyed reading what a friend was reading, we stocked multiple copies of favorite books. Magazines and current newspapers were also included. To meet all the children's needs and interests, we found it essential to include the following varied selection:

- *Picture concept books* are designed for young children. Each book focuses on a theme through the use of pictures.

- *Picture storybooks* are the most familiar type of children's literature. In these books, text and illustrations are closely associated. Picture storybooks are ideal for reading aloud. These books cover a wide range of topics, and they represent fine literature when at their best.

- *Easy-to-read books* have large print and limited vocabulary. They are designed to help beginning readers succeed on their own. Stories include repetition and rhyme to make the text predictable.

- *Traditional literature* includes fables, folktales, nursery rhymes, and fairy tales. Many of these stories originated in other cultures and thus can broaden a child's experience and knowledge base.

- *Poetry* is too often forgotten in collections of children's literature. Many anthologies have been compiled for children on topics such as holidays, the seasons, foods, animals, and so on. Teachers and families should have poetry on hand to choral or echo read for different occasions. Poetry teaches new vocabulary, knowledge about print, and fluency.

- *Informational books* are usually factual nonfiction and often relate to content areas such as science or social studies. Some books combine fact and fiction, such as the Magic School Bus series (Cole), which includes real facts in a fictional story.

- *Newspapers and magazines* should be included as literacy center selections. Many are created especially for children. For example, *Ranger Rick,* a magazine with a science focus, is published by the National Wildlife Federation. Another popular magazine is *Highlights for Children,* which includes stories, jokes, riddles, crafts, information about all content areas studied in school, and material for many grade levels. Newspapers help make connections from the classroom to real life.

- *Biographies* to include in a classroom library should be of interest to children, such as the lives of sports figures, past presidents, television celebrities, or inventors.

- *Novels* are long books about one topic. Since these books are divided into chapters, they are often called chapter books. They are suitable for children from second grade up.

- *Big Books* are usually large versions of smaller picture storybooks. They can also be original stories. These oversized books rest on an easel to be read. The purpose of Big Books is for children to be able to see the print as it is being read, to make the association between oral and written language, and to notice that the print is read from left to right across the page.

- *Leveled books* are typically small books that have an instructional level assigned to them. They are used in guided reading lessons. It is crucial for instructional material to be at the appropriate level (not too easy or too hard) for the children using it. Books are leveled for difficulty based on criteria (adapted from Fountas and Pinnell 1996) such as

  - length of the book, including number of pages and words,
  - size and layout of the print,
  - patterns, predictability, and structure of language,
  - text structures and genres,
  - phonetic patterns in the words,
  - how well the illustration supports the text (Morrow 2001).

Books can be leveled, or they can be purchased from publishers who have designated levels based on the preceding criteria. (Some publishers known for leveled books are Rigby, Sundance, William H. Sadlier, and the Wright Group.) It is a good idea to have leveled books available to students to read for practice and to enjoy easy material if they wish. Easy reading helps to create fluency. When displaying such books, group them by levels, clearly marked.

In addition to these categories, other books important to include are cookbooks, joke and riddle books, craft books, books made from songs, participation books (which ask children to touch or manipulate features), books about television shows, books made by the class, and books in a series built around familiar characters. (See Resource 4.3.)

One can never tell which children will be attracted to which books. That is why having a varied collection is so important. Yassin, for example, a robust boy who was retained in second grade, attended basic skills classes to help improve his low reading achievement. He often read from cookbooks, which we never would have expected. One day he asked his teacher, "Ms. Peters, you got flour at home?" When Ms. Peters said yes, Yassin asked, "You got eggs?" Ms. Peters nodded. "How about chocolate and nuts?" asked Yassin. "I have those, too," answered Ms. Peters. "That's good," said Yassin. "If you bring that into school we can all bake brownies, 'cause that's the stuff you need. I read it in this book." Yassin came from a home with no parents. His elderly grandmother, who was sick a great deal, took care of him. He read the cookbook to get closer to his vision of home-cooked food.

Manipulatives

The use of hands-on materials that children can see, touch, and manipulate has been a well-accepted educational practice for decades. According to educational theorists such as Pestalozzi, Montessori, Dewey, and Piaget, learning occurs when children have the opportunity to experiment, discover, and manipulate materials (Morrow 2001). The natural potential of a child develops through sensory experiences in which materials are used to learn through hearing, touch, smell, and the use of language. The work of Howard Gardner (1993), dealing with multiple intelligences, stresses the importance of using each child's strength in teaching. He suggests that children need to learn about the same things in different ways according to their learning styles. Kinesthetic learners, for example, learn by actively engaging in manipulative experiences that are both functional and interesting. Beck and Juel (1995) encourage teachers to make experience concrete by letting children manipulate and touch letters as they participate in word-building activities.

Manipulatives increase children's involvement in the literacy center. They can be used for developing both comprehension and word study skills.

Manipulatives to Develop Comprehension

Manipulatives to develop comprehension through storytelling—such as puppets, props, felt board and roll movie characters from children's literature, and taped stories with headsets—motivate children to engage in storytelling, storybook reading, and writing (Morrow and Weinstein 1986). Following are brief descriptions of some of these:

- *Felt board story.* For a felt board story, characters are created out of felt or construction paper, laminated or covered with clear contact paper to protect them, then backed with felt or sandpaper so that they stick to a felt board as the story is told. The felt board can be purchased or made by gluing felt onto a wooden board, a cork board, or cardboard. A felt board should tilt backwards to help the figures stay on. (See Resource Section 2, A2.1.)

- *Roll movie.* The roll movie box is made to look like a television and covered with contact paper to withstand classroom use. Scenes from stories are drawn on a roll of white paper and rotated past the "screen" by means of turning dowels. (See Resource Section 2, A2.2.)

  Teachers who model the use of the roll movie should not be too concerned about artistic quality. In fact, if the teacher's roll story is too professional-looking, it could intimidate the children and make them feel that their illustrations aren't good enough. Not every scene from a story needs to be illustrated; just select those that are crucial for the sense of the story.

- *Prop story.* Prop stories involve collecting appropriate props for telling a particular story. For example, when telling *Strega Nona* (dePaola), a story in which a magic pasta pot bubbles out of control, the teacher can bring in a large pot and pretend to stir pasta with a big spoon while telling the story. (See Resource 2.2.)

- *Puppet story.* Various types of puppets may be used for storytelling, including hand puppets, stick puppets, face puppets, and finger puppets. (See Resource 2.3.)

- *Chalk talk.* Chalk talks are presentations of stories that are drawn as they are told or read. Pictures can be drawn on a chalkboard or on large sheets of easel paper. The main character in a story may be made from oaktag and slipped onto the storyteller's hand with an elastic band, to make it appear that the character is drawing the story. (See Resource 2.4.)

- *Taped story and headset.* Tape recordings of children's literature can provide a model for good reading. Tapes are kept in plastic bags with the original book so the children can follow along as they listen. Commercially produced tapes of books are available from companies such as Scholastic, but it is easy enough for teachers and students to create their own. Teachers, parents, and children can all record their voices onto tapes.

Manipulatives placed in the literacy center often pertain to specific stories and are accompanied by the relevant book. The materials are stored in clear plastic zipper bags in a special spot set aside for them so that they can be easily accessed. Children add to the supply as they make their own manipulatives and come up with new ideas. Resource Section 2 suggests many activities and materials to develop comprehension through storytelling.

We found at first that the manipulatives associated with books were a major attraction, but as time went on, more book reading occurred and the manipulatives were used less. However, they remained a source of ideas for children to create and present their own reading and writing projects.

Manipulatives for Word Study

Manipulatives in the literacy center must also support print recognition, phonemic awareness, and learning print-sound correspondence. We must help children improve their reading by attending to recognized sight words, configuration, context, syntax, and picture clues. Materials in a word study center include magnetic, wooden, foam, and felt letters; color-differentiated letters (e.g., for onsets, rimes, vowels) printed on cardboard; word cubes and word stamps; flashcards; games like Candy Land, Concentration, Bingo, Lotto, Spill & Spell, Boggle, Scrabble, and Jeopardy!; card games and puzzles; word wheels (sliders); a word wall; and pocket charts. They assist word building and sorting; recognition of word patterns, high-frequency words, and sight words; and identification of word parts like onsets, rimes, phonograms, blends, digraphs, rhymes, long and short vowels, prefixes, suffixes, and roots.

Games and materials can be purchased from school supply stores or school supply companies. Materials can be made by teachers cooperatively (see Resource Section 6) or with the help of parents, aides, or upper-grade children. Resource Section 3 contains many ideas for word study activities and materials.

Books with ideas for word study center materials are *Words Their Way* (Bear et al. 1996), *Phonics They Use* (Cunningham 1995), *Making Words* (Cunningham, Hall, and Cunningham 1994), *Developing Literacy Using Reading Manipulatives* (Hill 1997), *What Are the Other Kids Doing?* (Marriot 1997), and *From Phonics to Fluency* (Rasinski and Padak 2000).

The Author's Spot

Because reading and writing are linked (Pappas, Kiefer, and Levstik 1990), each literacy center should include an area for writing. This can be called the author's spot. Materials in the author's spot should provide children with the opportunity to experiment with writing and later to edit and publish their work. Children will base their writing on their experiences with environmental print and texts, on their perception of others' modeling, and on their interactions with peers and adults.

The author's spot may include a table and chairs, and writing materials such as colored markers, crayons, pencils (both regular and colored), chalk, and a chalkboard. Various types and sizes of paper may be available, including unlined white paper or newsprint as large as 24 by 36 inches. Index cards allow children to record their "very own words." The word collections can be stored in file boxes, decorated coffee cans, or plastic baggies (one per child). A writing folder for each child holds writing samples over the course of the school year. A computer or several are a must for writing in the literacy center. Children can use programs such as Microsoft Word to create stories or read the newspaper online.

Materials for making books are essential, including paper, a hole punch, a stapler, and construction paper for covers. Blank books prepared by the teacher or children, especially ones keyed to special occasions, such as books in the shape of a leaf in the fall or a flower in the spring, invite children to fill in written messages and stories. Children's literature in the classroom collection is a catalyst for writing.

A bulletin board for children to display their own writing can be useful. Equally valuable are message or notice boards used to exchange messages among members of the class and the teacher. Teachers can use the message board to send messages to individual children as well as to post important information for the class as a whole. Mailboxes, stationery, envelopes, and stamps for youngsters' incoming and outgoing mail may be placed in the writing center for a pen pal program.

One day I was rushing to school when I realized I didn't have the booklets I'd planned to provide for the writing center. I grabbed instead some university blue books used for taking exams. This turned out to be serendipitous. The books have twelve to sixteen pages, come in packs of fifty, and are inexpensive. I called them author's books, and the children used them to write special stories and as journals. Teachers ordered more when the original supply ran out.

Publishing books is a favorite activity, and the materials for binding books (plain white paper, needle and thread, cardboard, contact paper, and glue) are easily accessible. (See Resource Section 5.) Older children can make their own; younger children may need help, perhaps by parent volunteers in the classroom. Children's original books, complete with a title page citing author and illustrator, are catalogued and made part of the classroom library. These original books are often checked out by other children and may become popular choices for reading material. Teachers and children can also make Big Books as class projects.

Acquiring Materials

One of the concerns many teachers I worked with had about creating a literacy center was how to acquire the needed materials. A literacy center can be outfitted at low cost with a little creativity. The most important step is to acquire enough books for a classroom library. Donations from homes can be requested, and a box put in the school hallway for collecting books. One school suggested that children donate a book to their classroom on their birthday instead of bringing in favors for their classmates. Many children's book clubs, such as Scholastic, Troll, and Weekly Reader, award bonus points based on the number of books purchased by the children in a class. These bonus points can be exchanged for free classroom books. Inexpensive books can also be found at flea markets and garage sales. In addition, school and town libraries should not be overlooked. Books can be rotated regularly from the school's collection to supplement the classroom library.

Parents should be involved in school programs and share responsibility for gathering materials for the children's learning environment. Parent-teacher organizations can be asked for help in fund-raising or creating manipulatives. In one school, where I had designed literacy centers in all the second-grade classrooms, parents voiced their concern that children in all grades should have the advantage of such an environment. After discussion, a plan was made to have a graduate assistant from my university coordinate a parent workshop to make materials for all the classrooms. Parents met in the school library for five sessions, once each week, during which time they created felt boards, roll movie boxes, props, and multiple word study games and manipulatives. They made enough materials to outfit forty classrooms! A group of parents in another elementary school set up a publishing center. Once a week parent volunteers came to bind books that the children had written for publication. All the materials were donated by parents and local businesses.

In districts where it is difficult to get the help of parents I have asked the art teacher to help. She in turn enlisted the help of children in sixth grade through high school, who made many of the materials needed to create complete literacy centers for the elementary school classrooms. They delivered the materials they had created and modeled them for the children. This made the endeavor a truly cooperative one.

One teacher asked parents to help make materials for her classroom and to write on the material, for example, "Made by Johanna's Mother," "Made by Mollie's Father," or "Made by Elena's Aunt." When others found out about this, there wasn't a relative who didn't want to participate, and the children urged their families to help as well. They had a sense of pride to see that a family member had contributed to the literacy center.

A Literacy Center Checklist

Figure 2.4 shows a checklist for teachers who are designing literacy centers for their classrooms. They should look in other parts of their classroom for materials to create rich literacy environments. The checklist suggests content area centers and describes basic materials to include in these centers. When studying specific themes, such as animals or plants, teachers should add literacy materials and other items to the literacy center and content area centers. Teachers I have worked with have taken the ideas presented in this chapter and improved on them, adapting them to their own style and needs.

Figure 2.4 List for Evaluating the Classroom Literacy Environment

	Yes	No
The Literacy Center		
1. Children's participation in designing the center (develop rules, select a name for center, develop materials)	_____	_____
2. Area placed in a quiet section of the room	_____	_____
3. Visually and physically accessible yet partitioned off from the rest of the room	_____	_____
4. Rug, throw pillows, rocking chair, beanbag chair, stuffed animals	_____	_____
5. Private spot in the corner such as a box to crawl into and read	_____	_____
6. Uses about 10 percent of the classroom space and can fit five or six children	_____	_____
The Library Corner		
1. Bookshelves for storing books with spines facing outward	_____	_____
2. Organizational system for shelving books	_____	_____
3. Open-faced bookshelves for featured books	_____	_____
4. Five to eight books per child	_____	_____
5. Baskets of books representing three or four grade levels of the following types: picture books, picture storybooks, traditional literature, poetry, realistic literature, informational books, biographies, chapter books, easy-to-read books, riddle and joke books, participation books, series books, textless books, TV-related books, brochures, magazines, newspapers	_____	_____
6. Twenty-five new books circulated every four weeks	_____	_____
7. Check-out/check-in system for children to take books out daily	_____	_____
8. Headsets and taped stories	_____	_____
9. Felt board and story characters with related books	_____	_____
10. Materials for constructing felt stories	_____	_____
11. Other story manipulatives (roll movie, puppets, with related books)	_____	_____
12. System for recording books read	_____	_____
13. Multiple copies of the same book	_____	_____
The Writing Center (Author's Spot)		
1. Tables and charts	_____	_____
2. Writing posters and bulletin board for children to display their writing	_____	_____
3. Writing utensils (pens, pencils, crayons, felt-tip pens, colored pencils)	_____	_____
4. Writing materials (many varieties of paper in all sizes, blank booklets, pads)	_____	_____
5. Typewriter or computer	_____	_____
6. Materials for writing stories and making them into books	_____	_____
7. Message board for children and teacher to post messages	_____	_____
8. Place to store "very own words"	_____	_____
9. Folders in which children can place samples of their writing	_____	_____
10. Place for children to send private messages to each other	_____	_____
Word Study Center		
1. Magnetic letters and phonograms	_____	_____
2. Wooden letters and phonograms	_____	_____
3. Foam letters and phonograms	_____	_____
4. Cards with letters and phonograms	_____	_____
5. Letter stamps	_____	_____
6. Letter cubes and phonograms	_____	_____
7. Prefixes, suffixes, and roots in magnetic, wooden, foam, cards, and felt forms	_____	_____
8. Pocket chart	_____	_____
9. Felt letters and felt board	_____	_____
10. Word wall for high-frequency and other sight words	_____	_____
11. Word wheels for constructing words	_____	_____

Figure 2.4 *(continued)*

12. Slates and markers _____ _____
13. Magnetic boards _____ _____
14. Word-sorting activities _____ _____
15. Word-building activities _____ _____
16. Skill development games (Concentration, Jeopardy!, Bingo, Lotto, card
    games) _____ _____
17. Puzzles for constructing words _____ _____

The Rest of the Classroom
1. Environmental print, such as signs related to themes studied, directions,
   rules, functional messages _____ _____
2. Calendar _____ _____
3. Current events board _____ _____
4. Appropriate books, magazines, and newspapers _____ _____
5. Writing utensils _____ _____
6. Varied types of paper _____ _____
7. Place for children to display their literacy work _____ _____
8. Place for teachers and children to leave messages for each other _____ _____
9. Print representative of multicultural groups present in the classroom _____ _____
10. Content area centers present in the classroom (circle those appropriate):
    music   art   science   social studies   math   dramatic play

3

Modeling Independent Comprehension Activities

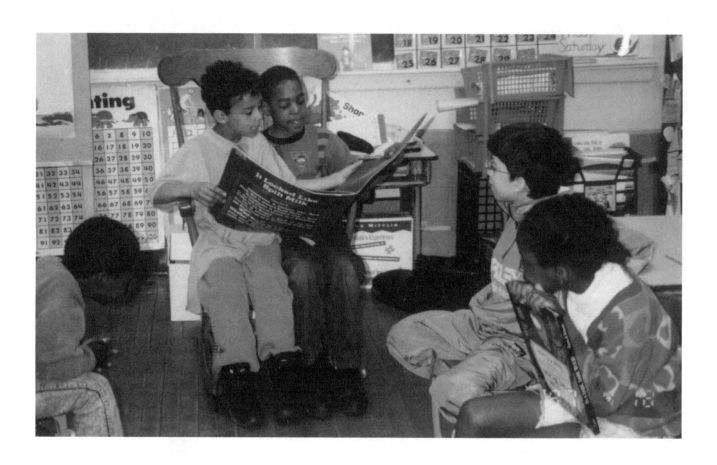

When it was story time in Ms. Davis's first-grade class, the children put aside what they were working on and hurried to the literacy center. They moved around until they were all in comfortable positions on the rug. Ms. Davis sat in the rocking chair, where she always read aloud. She showed the children the caterpillar they had found on the playground, which they kept in their terrarium. The class was studying insects, focusing on what they eat and how they grow. After talking about how the caterpillar moves and eats, Ms. Davis took out the book *The Very Hungry Caterpillar* (Carle) and said, "I'm going to tell a story today about a caterpillar who is very hungry. Listen for the events at the beginning of the story, then listen for the things that he eats and see how many you can remember. Also pay close attention to how the story ends. Finally, what do you think is factual information about caterpillars in this story and what do you think is fiction?" As she talked, she put on a green caterpillar sock puppet that extended from her hand halfway up her arm. In the story the caterpillar eats many things, such as a strawberry, an apple, and a piece of cherry pie. Next to the teacher were cutouts for the food mentioned in the story, with a hole cut in the middle of each. Every child was given a cutout so they could participate in the story reading. As a food was mentioned, the child with the cutout of that food put it onto the teacher's arm as if feeding the caterpillar. After the story, the class discussed how the story began, listed the foods the caterpillar had eaten, and told how the story ended. The children also thought about what was factual information in the story and what was fiction. Then Ms. Davis put the book and story props in the literacy center with an activity card that listed directions for working with the materials. (See Resource 1.4.) In addition, she distributed an accountability form that asked children to

- describe the details at the beginning of the story,

- list five things the caterpillar ate,

- describe how the story ended

- tell what was factual and what was fictional in the story.

During literacy center time the caterpillar puppet and food cutouts were instant favorites. Warren put on the sock puppet, and Michael read the story from the book. Tamika and Mary helped with the food cutouts. A few weeks later Ms. Davis added another activity card for children to create a roll movie story of *The Very Hungry Caterpillar,* and a few weeks after that, for children to write a new version of the story and make it into a felt story. Kevin, Erin, and Kim created a new story, "The Caterpillar Who Didn't Want to Be a Butterfly," and made felt figures. They presented it to the class when it was done.

Mr. Kinsella, a fourth-grade teacher, had just finished reading the short novel *Sadako and the Thousand Paper Cranes* (Coerr) to his class. The novel is about a Japanese girl who develops leukemia as a result of radiation from the atomic bomb that was dropped on the city of Hiroshima in 1945. In the book, Chizuko visits her friend Sadako in the hospital. She has a gold-colored square piece of paper. "Watch!" she says, and she folds the paper over and over, turning it into a beautiful crane. "If a sick person folds one thousand paper cranes," Chizuko says, "the gods will grant her wish and make her well again." Sadako folded 644 cranes before she died at the age of twelve. Her classmates folded the rest.

Mr. Kinsella's objective was to introduce the children to Japanese culture through literature and the art of Japanese paper folding, called origami. He also discussed the consequences of war, an issue that connected with what the class was studying in social studies. Mr. Kinsella guided the discussion of the differences between this novel and stories about children in America. The second part of the discussion revolved around the consequences of war. To help them further understand the culture, at the end of the discussion Mr. Kinsella gave each student an instruction sheet with diagrams for making an origami paper crane (see Resource Section 2, A2.8). Children worked in pairs to help each other. He then placed the storybook, directions for folding an origami crane, and

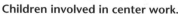
Children involved in center work.

origami paper in the literacy center. There was also an activity card that asked discussion questions: after children had discussed the issues, they were to write about their perspectives on the issues.

After these modeled lessons, during literacy center time Mr. Kinsella's and Ms. Davis's students worked collaboratively using stories, props, and activities the teachers had demonstrated. The children were self-directed and independent. Their motivation came from the engaging activities that were modeled. These teachers had created a climate in their classrooms where reading and writing were pleasurable, collaborative, and challenging, and students could feel successful. The teachers were helping the children to discover the joy in reading, the satisfaction in learning information, and the pleasure in sharing ideas. How did these first-grade and fourth-grade teachers encourage this to happen?

From a theoretical perspective, Ms. Davis and Mr. Kinsella provided support and guidance that enabled children to participate in activities they could not have done on their own (Vygotsky 1978). Gradually, through practice, the children became self-directed, claiming responsibility for their own learning. Modeling the use of materials makes activities more interesting to children. They were also given the opportunity to work in social settings. They had some control in the exploration of

activities and in practicing skills associated with them, such as comparing and contrasting the novel *Sadako and the Thousand Paper Cranes* to stories about children in America. These are the elements that create motivating situations (Csikszentmihalyi 1991; Erickson 1995; Turner 1995).

Using Children's Literature

Using literature with children is an important way to motivate them to become readers and writers. Pleasurable experiences with literature create an interest in and an enthusiasm for books. In addition, studies reveal that children who use literature develop sophisticated language structures, enhanced vocabulary, improved reading comprehension and writing ability in expository and narrative pieces (Dahl and Freppon 1995; Goatley, Brock, and Raphael 1995; Morrow 1992).

Teachers should read every day to children in the elementary grades and discuss the stories read. Children should be encouraged to read to each other and discuss the books among themselves. Books can be borrowed from school and taken home, and books from home can be brought to school and shared with others. (See Resource 1.2.) Exposure to books and stories should be frequent and integrated with teaching in the content areas.

When I began to work with teachers introducing them to activities to motivate reading and writing, they were concerned about the time it would take to add these to all that they already needed to accomplish in their literacy programs and content area subjects. We discussed the fact that the activities I was suggesting would develop skills and teach content; and if children could be motivated to participate in reading and writing voluntarily in and out of school, this would enable them to practice and improve skills taught. Together we decided that the teachers would try to carry out three to five pleasurable literature activities each week. To many it seemed impossible; however, they found many opportunities. The literature activities meshed well with more explicitly taught literacy skills.

The activities that motivate children to read also play a large role in skills development. During these activities the skills development may be implicit rather than explicit. There are other times when we teach children explicitly. In the following sections are strategies that teachers found

motivated children to read and write voluntarily, encouraged social learning, and enhanced literacy skills development (Morrow, O'Connor, and Smith 1990; Morrow 1992; 1996).

The objectives for skills development during these literature activities are for children to

- retell stories,

- identify structural elements in text, such as setting, theme, plot episodes, and resolution,

- respond to text with literal, interpretive, and critical comments and questions,

- know what an author and an illustrator are.

Reading Aloud

Using literature in the school curriculum and reading to children on a regular basis in school helps to enhance literacy skills, including vocabulary and syntactic development, phonemic aware-

Teachers and special visitors read aloud to students.

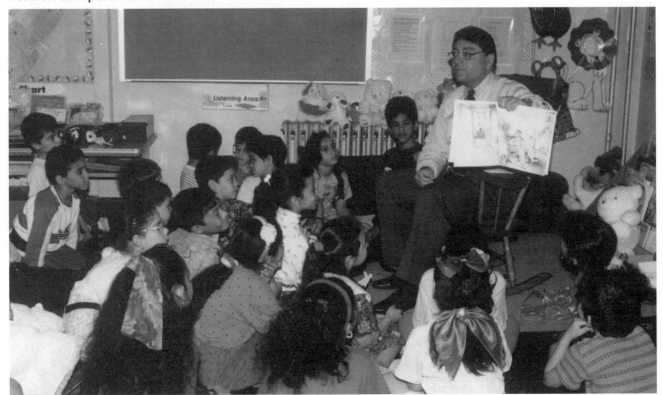

ness, decoding skills, and the ability to comprehend text (Dickinson and Smith 1994; Feitelson et al. 1993; Robbins and Ehri 1994). Reading aloud to children is a daily event that teachers and children find rewarding. It provides an opportunity for children to experience literature pleasurably, discuss ideas about books read, and relate books to content area instruction.

To make the story readings as pleasurable as possible, teachers should read in a relaxed atmosphere and in the same location every day. If there is a rocking chair in the classroom, this is the perfect place for the teacher to sit. Children can sit on a rug on the floor or in chairs, but they should be close to the teacher, who should be in a position to be seen by all. The teacher should always read the material in advance in order to be familiar with the text. If there are illustrations in the book, they should be shown during the reading. Expressive readings, in which different voices are used for different characters, is a good reading strategy. Children also enjoy facial expression and animation on the part of the reader. This helps the book come alive. Other genres should be used in addition to narrative and expository selections. Books selected should be tied to the children's interests and personal experiences, and topics being studied. Books that the children themselves may not be able to read, such as sophisticated novels read a chapter at a time, are good choices, as are books with beautiful illustrations and interesting language. Young children enjoy rhyme, repetitive phrases, and conversation. Narratives selected for reading to children should have a clear plot structure that includes the following elements:

- *Setting*. Descriptions of time, place, and characters

- *Theme*. A problem or goal faced by the main character

- *Episodes*. A series of events that helps the main character achieve his or her goal or solve his or her problem

- *Resolution*. A clear ending to the story, in which the main character accomplishes the goal or solves the problem

Directed Listening or Reading

The Directed Listening (or Reading) Thinking Activity (DLTA or DRTA) is a general strategy teachers can use to guide story readings. When used it should be modeled—presented in a way that prompts students to use it themselves. There are three parts to this strategy:

1. A pre-story discussion that provides background knowledge and sets a purpose for listening or reading

2. The reading of the text, which is mostly uninterrupted except for some comments and questions when appropriate

3. A post-story discussion that relates to the purpose for listening

The DLTA or DRTA can focus on improving comprehension of story elements, a content area theme, or illustrations, or just foster enjoyment of reading. Having a purpose to direct the children's reading or listening is the key for getting them involved with the literature presented. The two examples at the beginning of this chapter demonstrated the method. *The purpose for modeling the strategy when we read to children is to help them learn how to use it when they read on their own, and thus enable them to become critical and reflective readers.*

Conversations and Questions That Engage Students

Conversation about books can vary, but it can begin with the teacher's asking some questions about the book. Questions that deal with *aesthetic* issues provoke responses that can be personalized to children's experiences, feelings, and interests, and therefore motivate engagement. The following aesthetic questions have been found to spark lively discussion:

How does the story makes you feel?

Was anything especially interesting to you in the story? funny? sad? scary? exciting?

If you could change part of the story, what would it be?

If the story continued, what do you think would happen?

Has anything similar to what occurred in the story ever happened to you?

Does the story remind you of another story or TV show?

Have you known people like the characters in the story?

Pretend you are a character in the story. What does it feel like?

What was your favorite part of the story?

Efferent questions usually deal with expository material and the details in a part of a book. They require children to recall and analyze details, main ideas, and cause and effect. Some questions that will elicit efferent responses (Rosenblatt 1988) include the following:

How would you describe the main character?

What new ideas did you learn?

How can you find out more about these ideas?

If you talked to the author, what would you want to ask?

What ideas seemed most important to the story?

The following dialogue shows second graders' responses when they were asked if the story they had just read, *The Legend of the Blue Bonnet: An Old Tale of Texas* (dePaola), reminded them of another story they knew:

Alison: It reminded me of another book.

Teacher: What book was that?

Alison: *The Legend of the Indian Paintbrush* [dePaola].

Suzanne: Me, too, because it kind of relates. *The Legend of the Blue Bonnet* that we read is a folktale and so is *The Legend of the Indian Paintbrush* and Tomie dePaola did both of those books—retold and illustrated—and She-Who-Is-Alone in *Blue Bonnet* wanted something green very badly, and Little Gopher in *The Legend of the Indian Paintbrush* wanted something very badly, too. So they have lots of things alike.

This type of discussion is providing a model for discussions that we want to happen in settings with literature that are independent of the teacher. With adequate modeling, children will be able to initiate and sustain such conversations alone. Literature circles begin with this type of modeling by teachers and then move to children running them on their own.

Efferent discussions are especially appropriate for nonfiction expository texts, which are often related to content area subjects. Asking students to talk about the following is pertinent to efferent discussions:

- Identify details, sequence, and main idea.
- Classify ideas in different parts of the text.
- Paraphrase or retell the texts.
- Make associations.
- Compare and contrast ideas, draw conclusions, apply information in other settings.
- Evaluate for interest level, clarity, and accuracy of content.

K-W-L

K-W-L is a cognitive strategy to enhance comprehension. It is used mainly with nonfiction expository text and elicits efferent responses. K-W-L stands for What We *Know*, What We *Want* to Know, and What We *Learned* (Ogle 1986). With this technique students use prior knowledge to create interest about what they will read. It helps

Figure 3.1 K-W-L Chart

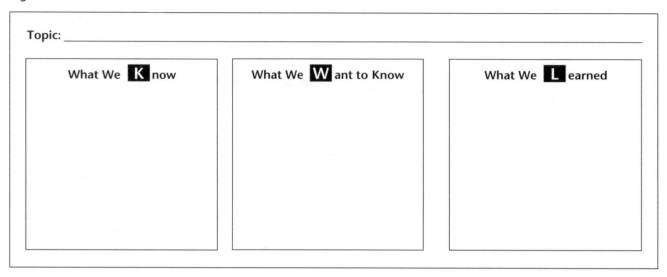

set a purpose for reading, directs thinking, and encourages the sharing of ideas. A K-W-L chart (see Figure 3.1) can be used to list items generated in a K-W-L discussion. The following steps put the strategy into practice:

1. Before reading an expository text, children brainstorm what they think they know about a topic. For example, if the book is about spiders, a list of What We *Know* about spiders is created by the class.

2. Children list questions about What We *Want* to Know as a result of previewing the book.

3. After reading the text, children make a list of What We *Learned* about spiders.

4. Children compare information from the text that they already knew before reading it, what they learned as a result of reading the text, and what they would still like to learn (because it wasn't in the book).

Modeling this strategy will help students to use it on their own.

Small-Group and One-to-One Story Readings

Small-group and one-to-one readings are also useful in fostering interest and comprehension. These

formats allow children to respond more than they can in whole-group reading. The children create the meaning of the story through their participation (Holdaway 1979). For example, during conference time one day, Ms. Johnson read portions of *The Mountains of Tibet* (Gerstein) to Davida, Ryan, and Alison. She asked what they found especially interesting. The kind of in-depth conversation that followed would be difficult in a whole-group setting.

Davida: It was interesting and puzzling when the galaxies talked to him.

Teacher: What do you think was going on then?

Davida: I really don't know. It was puzzling when the animals talked. Animals make their own noises, but they don't talk.

Teacher: Um, let's go back to that galaxy and voice part. There was a voice that talked from the galaxies. What do you think that was about?

Ryan: I think it was God.

Alison: I think it was God, too.

Teacher: What do you think, Davida? You said you're puzzled.

Davida: I don't know, really.

Small groups of children interact with the teacher and each other.

(*Davida was silent while the other children took turns; then she reentered the conversation.*)

Davida: I thought since it was a book, that the galaxies could be speaking to him [the main character].

Alison: Yeah, authors can do what they want. [N. O. Johnson 1995, 60]

Repeated Readings

Reading a book more than once can be a pleasurable experience, like singing a favorite song. As a result of repeated readings, children develop favorite books that they ask for over and over. One class asked for *Strega Nona* (dePaola) so often that the teacher asked me for reassurance that repeating the story could still be a valuable learning experience. The fact is, repeated readings allow children to be more interpretive in their understanding. Their familiarity with the story allows them to predict outcomes, make associations, and form judgments (Morrow 1988; Yaden 1985). Also, as a result of repeated readings of books children become familiar with story structure models. Recently attention has been shifted to the importance of fluency when reading because it is a bridge between the decoding and comprehension of text (Rasinski and Padak 2000). Repeated read-ings help to create fluent readers. When a text becomes well known through being repeated, children's reading becomes more accurate, quick, and expressive. This fluent oral reading demon-strates that the reader understands the text (Rasinski et al. 1994).

The following is taken from a transcription of a kindergarten child's response to a third reading of *The Little Red Hen* (Galdone). For the sake of brevity, this excerpt includes only the child's com-ments and questions and the teacher's responses; most of the story reading has been omitted.

Teacher: Today I'm going to read the story *The Little Red Hen*. It is about a hen who wanted some help when she baked some bread. (*The teacher begins to read the story.*) "Who will help me to cut this wheat?"

Melony: "Not I," said the cat. "Not I," said the dog. "Not I," said the mouse.

Teacher: That was good, Melony. You are read-ing. (*The teacher continues to read, but Melony stops her.*)

Melony: I want to read that part, but I don't know how.

Teacher: Go ahead and try. I bet you can, I'll help you. It starts: "The cat smelled it."

Melony (*chiming in*): "The cat smelled it, and she said, 'Umm, that smells good.' And the mouse smelled it, and it smelled good . . ."

(*After finishing the story the teacher asked Melony if she wanted to say anything else about the story.*)

Melony: I want to find the part where it says that the animals were so bad that they couldn't have any bread. (*Melony searches through the book.*) There it is, almost at the end. She's going to make bread and she'll say "Who's going to bake this bread for me?" And the cat says, "Not I," the dog says, "Not I," the mouse says, "not I." And then when she's cooking it, they smell a good thing and then they wanted some, too, but they didn't have any, 'cause they didn't help with the work.

Teacher: You're so right. They didn't help do the work, so they didn't get to eat the bread.

Melony: Where does it say "Not I"? Show me the words in the book.

Teacher: Here it is. See if you can find it on this page.

Melony: I found it. Oh look, there's the word dog, dog, dog. [Morrow 1996, 210]

This example demonstrates the value of repeated reading for comprehension, word study, and fluency. It is a strategy we teach so children will do it independently of the teacher.

Additional Reading Aloud Activities

There are many more strategies to increase children's enjoyment of literature and to provide good models. Ms. Colon invited guests each week to come to her third-grade English as a Second Language (ESL) classroom and read to her students. Readers included the school principal, the custodian, parents, high school athletes, children from older grades, and a school bus driver, as well as the superintendent, the town mayor, and an author. Not only did this show that people from diverse backgrounds valued reading, it also provided a sense of excitement and novelty to hear many different people read. Ms. Colon took pho-

tos of all the people who had read to her class during the year and created an exciting bulletin board with the pictures.

Children should be encouraged to bring books from home to share with the class and to take books home to share with their family. Books published by the children themselves may be chosen as read-aloud books. These may prove especially popular and can encourage the children to write their own stories for publication.

When books featuring food are read, the class can prepare the food. Ms. Youseff's class made fruit salad after reading *Mister Rabbit and the Lovely Present* (Zolotow), jam sandwiches after reading *Bread and Jam for Frances* (Hoban), and vegetable soup after reading *Stone Soup* (Marcia Brown). In fourth grade, Ms. Tofel's class made chocolate after reading *The Chocolate Touch* (Catling).

Television and film can be powerful tools in drawing children to books. Many fine pieces of children's literature have been adapted for television or movies, from *The Cat in the Hat* (Seuss) for young children, to *James and the Giant Peach* (Dahl) for older children. Be aware of books that are featured on TV, and encourage children to watch such programs. Then use the books for classroom discussion.

Storytelling and Retelling

Storytelling is an effective strategy to get children excited about literature. It establishes rapport between the listener and the teller because of the eye contact that occurs. Long pieces of literature can be shortened to accommodate attention spans. Teachers should first model storytelling and then encourage children to participate in the activity. Storytelling is an art, but it can be mastered by all.

Many of the teachers I worked with had not used storytelling as a specific technique before. We discussed the technique and told stories to each other to gain confidence. The following points are essential in effective storytelling:

- Know the story well but don't memorize it.

- Use catch phrases or important words from the story.

- Be expressive.

- Look directly at the audience.

- The length of the storytelling depends upon the attention span of the audience.

- Encourage audience participation when possible.

- Practice the story before telling it.

- Always have the book present to connect with the printed word.

Story retelling by children offers active participation in a literacy experience and helps youngsters understand language structures and develop vocabulary. Retelling a story, whether orally or in writing, enhances comprehension and organization of thought. It allows for personalization of thinking, as children mesh their own life experiences into their retelling. As children gain experience in retelling, they assimilate the concept of story structure. They learn to introduce a story with its setting. They recount its theme, plot episodes, and resolution. In retelling stories, children demonstrate their comprehension of story details and sequence. They also infer and interpret the sounds and expressions of characters' voices. Initially retelling is not easy for children, but with practice they improve quickly. To help children develop the practice of retelling, it is best to let them know before they read or listen to a story that they will be asked to retell it. Props such as felt board characters or pictures in the text can be used to help students retell the story. The following is a modeling procedure for guiding children's oral retelling (with written retelling, teachers may prefer to have them write the entire story first and then confer with them using the following guidelines).

Ask the child to retell the story: "A little while ago, I read the story [Name]. Would you retell the story as if telling it to a friend who has never heard it before?" If needed, use the following prompts: If the child has difficulty beginning, suggest beginning with "Once upon a time" or "Once there was. . . ." If the child stops retelling before the end of the story, encourage continuing by asking, "What comes next?" or "Then what happened?" If the child stops retelling and cannot continue even with the preceding general prompts, ask a question about the place in the story where the child has paused, for example, "What was Jenny's problem in the story?"

If a child is unable to retell the story, or if the retelling lacks sequence and detail, use one or

Children retell stories using the felt board with story characters.

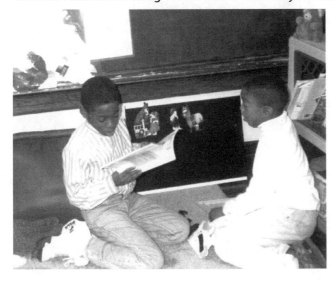

more of the following prompts (Morrow 2001, 221):

"Once upon a time" or "Once there was . . ."

"Who was the story about?"

"When did the story happen?" (Day, night, summer, winter?)

"Where did the story happen?"

"What was [the main character's] problem in the story?"

"How did [he or she] try to solve the problem? What did [he or she] do first (second, next)?"

"How was the problem solved?"

"How did the story end?"

Retelling can be used to develop many types of comprehension. The prompts, of course, should match the goals.

The following excerpt shows the interaction between a teacher and a kindergarten child in a first story retelling:

Teacher: Philip, can you tell me the title of the story I just read to you today?

Philip: I don't know.

Teacher: Let's look at the cover of the book to help you remember. It was about a turtle. Can you remember his name?

Philip: Oh yeah. *Franklin in the Dark* [Bourgeois].

Teacher: That was very good, Philip. You remembered the whole title of the story without my help. Now can you retell the story as if you were going to tell it to your good friend Patrick? Now Patrick hasn't ever heard this story, so you don't want to leave anything out when you tell it to him. Why don't you try and start to tell the story.

Philip: Okay. *Franklin in the Dark.* One time Franklin didn't want to go in his shell. He was too scared. But his mama said, "There's nothin' in there." But Franklin didn't want to go in the shell because there was monsters in there. He didn't like to go in because he was afraid. At the end he went in 'cause his mama got him a night light in his shell. So he turned on a night light and went to sleep. And that's it.

Teacher: You did a fine job, Philip. You remembered Franklin's problem, or the theme of the story, and how Franklin and his mother solved the problem at the end of the story. Let's look at the book and see if there is anything else you could include in your retelling. (*The teacher and Philip look through the book.*)

Philip: Oh yeah, I forgot stuff. Franklin went for a walk and he saw lots of animals who were scared of things. There was a lion who was afraid of loud noise, so he put on earmuffs.

Teacher: Were there any other animals?

Philip: Yeah, well . . . there was this bird who was scared to fly high, so he got a great big balloon thing to help him fly.

Teacher: The thing he used was called a parachute. Did he meet anyone else?

Philip: I don't know, I'm tired.

Teacher: Okay, I'll help you out. There was a polar bear who was afraid of the cold, so he wore a snowsuit to keep him warm; and there was a duck who was afraid of deep water, so he used water wings when he went swimming.

Philip: Oh yeah, that's right.

Teacher: Philip, you did really well today. When you have some time, why don't you take the book and look at the pictures and try to tell the story again.

Suitable Books for Retelling

Story retelling is not an easy task for young children. Books selected should have clear plot structures that make their story lines easy to follow and therefore easy to retell. Other elements, such as repetitive phrases, familiar sequences (days of the week, numbers, letters), conversation, and general familiarity or popularity of the plot or characters can add to a story's predictability and thus aid retelling. Following is a short list of books suitable for retelling:

- Books with repetitive phrases
  The Cat Sat on the Mat (Cameron)
  Brown Bear, Brown Bear, What Do You See? (Martin)
  Polar Bear, Polar Bear, What Do You Hear? (Martin)

- Books with familiar sequences
  The Very Hungry Caterpillar (Carle)
  Ten Bears in My Bed (Mack)
  Chicken Soup with Rice: A Book of Months (Sendak)

- Books with conversation
  The Gingerbread Man (Arno)
  Ask Mr. Bear (Flack)
  Mister Rabbit and the Lovely Present (Zolotow)

- Popular and familiar stories
  The Three Bears (Galdone)
  The Little Red Hen (Galdone)
  Caps for Sale (Slobodkina)

- Stories with good plot structures
  Peter's Chair (Keats)
  Swimmy (Lionni)
  The Tale of Peter Rabbit (Potter)

When children retell together with the use of props, such as a felt board with story figures, often one does the telling and the other manipulates the materials. They will sometimes then switch roles. One child begins, then the other takes over, taking turns throughout a given retelling. As two or more children retell together, they can offer assistance to one another as needed, such as offering prompts about what comes next or correcting mistakes in the retelling.

Following is a retelling of the classic folktale *The Three Little Billy Goats Gruff* (Marcia Brown) by two first graders using a flannel board. Patrick retells the story, while Charlene puts the characters on the board. Charlene offers prompts and corrections, and fills in parts Patrick left out.

Patrick: There was these three billy goats, a big one, a little one and, um. . . .

Charlene: It's the medium one you forgot.

Patrick: The goats had no grass on their side of the water, so the little one goes over the bridge to get some grass. The troll says, "I'm going to eat you up."

Charlene: No, the troll says, "Who's that trip-trappin' over my bridge?" And the little goat says, "It is me, the little one," and then the troll says, "I'm goin' to eat you up."

Patrick: The little one says, "I'm too little, my middle brother's comin'," and the troll said, "Then be off with you." The middle goat comes, and the troll says, "Who's that trip-trappin' on my bridge?" "It is me, the middle one." "I'm goin' to eat you up." The middle one says, "I'm too small, here comes my big brother." Charlene, put up the big goat.

Charlene: Okay, I'm gonna tell some now. The big goat came, and the troll said, "Who's that trip-trappin' over my bridge?" "It is me, the big goat," said the big one. "Come on, come over," said the troll.

Patrick: I'm finishing. Now he knocks him in the water.

Charlene: No, not yet. The troll says, "I'm gonna knock your eyeballs into your ears."

Patrick: And that's what the goat done. He knocks the troll in the water. That's the end.

Charlene: No, it's not, Patrick. You have to say, "And the billy goats lived happily ever after," and now it's the end.

Older children who read novels will not be retelling the entire book as with picture story-books. To retell a novel, children should be asked to summarize the main idea of the book and to retell the chapter they liked best or least. They can retell a very sad part, a scary part, or the most interesting part.

Using Retelling and Rewriting as an Assessment Tool

Story retelling or rewriting can be used to measure a child's comprehension of a story (Morrow 1992). Through analysis of a retelling or a rewriting, one can diagnose a child's ability for literal recall (remembering facts, details, cause and effect relationships, and sequencing of events). Retellings can reveal a child's sense of story structure. For example, does a child's retelling include statements of setting, theme, plot episodes, and resolution? Through retelling, children also reveal their ability to make inferences as they organize, integrate, and classify information that is implied but not expressed in the story. They may generalize, interpret feelings, or relate ideas to their own experiences. Children's story retelling and rewriting can be assessed several times during a school year to evaluate change. When a child's retelling is to be evaluated, the child should be informed of that fact before the story to be retold is read. During the retelling for evaluation, the teacher should not offer prompts. She may, however, encourage children to offer their best by saying when they pause, "Can you think of anything else about the story?" or "You are doing very well. Can you try to continue?"

To assess a child's oral or written retelling for its sense of story structure or inclusion of structural elements, the teacher should first parse, or divide, the events of the story into four categories: setting, theme, plot episodes, and resolution. The teacher then notes the number of ideas and events that the child accurately includes within each of the four structural categories, regardless of their order. A story guide sheet, outlining the parsed text, is used to help tabulate the ideas and events the child includes in the retelling (see Figure 3.2). The child receives credit for partial recall or for recounting the gist of a story event. Having checked off the child's inclusion of elements, the teacher observes sequence by comparing the order of events in the child's retelling with the actual story. The analysis indicates not only which elements a child includes or omits, and how well a child sequences, but

Figure 3.2 Teacher's Quantitative Analysis of a Story Retelling

Child's Name ___Beth___ Age __7__
Name of Story _Jenny Learns a Lesson_ Date_____

Directions: Give 1 point for obvious recall and "gist." Give 1 point for each character named as well as words such as *boy* and *girl*. Credit plurals (*friends*) with 2 points.

Setting
a. Begins story with an introduction. __1__
b. Names main character. __1__
c. Number of other characters named. __2__
d. Actual number of other characters. __4__
e. Score for "other characters" (c/d). __.5__
f. Includes statement about time or place. __1__

Theme
Refers to main character's primary goal or problem to be solved. __1__

Plot Episodes
a. Number of episodes recalled. __4__
b. Number of episodes in story. __5__
c. Score for "plot episodes" (a/b). __.8__

Resolution
a. Names problem solution/goal attainment. __1__
b. Ends story. __1__

Sequence
Retells story in structural order: setting, theme, plot episodes, resolution. (Score 2 for proper, 1 for partial, 0 for no sequence evident.) __1__

Highest score possible: 10   Child's Score: __8.3__

*Use checks instead of numbers to determine elements included and progress over time. Retellings can be evaluated for interpretive and critical comments (Morrow 1997).

also where instruction might be necessary to develop an area where the child's retelling has been particularly weak. A comparison of retellings over a year will illustrate if the child has progressed.

The following outline presents the events, or parsed story, for *Jenny Learns a Lesson* (Fujikawa):

Parsed Story: *Jenny Learns a Lesson*

Setting

Once upon a time there was a girl who liked to play pretend.
Characters: Jenny (main character), Nicholas, Sam, Mei Su, Shags the dog.

Theme

Every time Jenny played with her friends, she bossed them and insisted that they do what she wanted them to.

Plot Episodes

First Episode Jenny decided to pretend to be a queen. She called her friends to come and play. Jenny was bossy and told them what to do. The friends became angry and left.
Second Episode Jenny decided to play dancer, with the same results as in the first episode. (She called her friends to play. She told them what to do. The friends left.)
Third Episode Jenny decided to play pirate, again with the same results.
Fourth Episode Jenny decided to play a duchess, again with the same results.
Fifth Episode Jenny's friends decided not to play with her again because she was so bossy. Many days passed and Jenny became sorry for being bossy.

Resolution

The friends played together, each doing what he or she wanted to do. They all had a wonderful day and were so tired they fell asleep.

Sample Verbatim Transcription, Beth, age 7

Once upon a time there's a girl named Jenny, and she called her friends over, and they played queen and went to the palace. They had to, they had to do what she said, and they didn't like it, so then they went home and said that was boring. . . . It's not fun playing queen and doing what she says you have to. So they didn't play with her for seven days, and she had . . . she had a idea that she was being selfish, so she went to find her friends and said, I'm sorry I was so mean. And

Figure 3.3 Student's Evaluation Form for a Story Retelling

Name _____ Date _____
Name of Story _____

	Yes	No
Setting		
I began the story with an introduction.	____	____
I talked about the main character.	____	____
I talked about other characters.	____	____
I told when the story happened.	____	____
I told where the story happened.	____	____
Theme		
I told about the problem or the main goal of the characters.	____	____
Plot Episodes		
I included episodes in the story.	____	____
Resolution		
I told how the problem was solved.	____	____
I had an ending in the story.	____	____
Sequence		
My story was retold or rewritten in proper order.	____	____

Comments for Improvement
Next time I need to include in my retelling:

said, let's play pirate, and they played pirate and they went onto the pretend boat. Then they played that she was a fancy lady playing house. And then they have some tea. And they played what they wanted, and they were happy. . . . The End.

Children should play an integral part in evaluating their own oral and written retellings. As a teacher evaluates a child's retelling, a child can do the same with his or her own form (see Figure 3.3). The following is an assessment discussion about an oral retelling (Morrow 2001, 222–223).

Teacher: Beth, let's read the transcription of your retelling together. (*They both begin to read.*) Now let's review your retelling and look at the storybook to see how much you remembered.

(*The teacher gives Beth the book and an evaluation form to evaluate her work.*)

(*After the evaluation this discussion occurs.*)

Beth: I have an introduction, "Once upon a time there was a girl named Jenny."

Teacher: Good, Beth, and you also named the main character and talked about her. Can you find that in your retelling?

Beth: (*Searching*) Yup, here it is.

The teacher and the student move through the retelling and use the student assessment form as they find the elements included. They also note what is missing and comment on what to be careful about including when retelling the next story.

Creative Storytelling Techniques

Creative storytelling techniques are a form of retelling stories. Storytelling has all the benefits of retelling that were mentioned in the previous section. Children improve understanding of language structures, vocabulary, knowledge of story structure (setting, theme, plot episodes, resolution), and organization of thought. They demonstrate their knowledge of story details and sequence, they infer and interpret the sounds and expressions of characters' voices. When they select and create techniques that fit stories, they are classifying and interpreting information. Storytelling lends itself to engaging activities to be done in collaboration with others independent of the teacher. Resource Section 2 lists many storytelling activities for students to participate in independently while the teacher is working with guided reading groups.

The teachers I worked with modeled creative techniques to make stories come alive. Such techniques excite the imagination, provide enjoyment to the listening audience, and perhaps most important, get children interested in using the techniques to create and tell their own stories. After telling a story to children, the actual book must be available because children will want to read and enjoy the book presented. Some stories are best told with no props; however, many lend themselves to the use of creative techniques. One can take cues from the content. When a story contains a good deal of dialogue, puppets may be suitable; other stories are perfect for felt board stories. Many stories are suited to several different techniques.

I began this chapter with descriptions of two teachers who were modeling creative techniques in their story readings. The first-grade teacher modeled the use of puppets with props when telling *The Very Hungry Caterpillar* (Carle), and the fourth-grade teacher modeled the use of origami in teaching *Sadako and the Thousand Paper Cranes* (Coerr). That is the best way to start: the teacher models the technique and then encourages the children to try it on their own. Children who are reading novels can summarize the story and then recount the part of the book they liked best, tell about a chapter, describe the introduction, or create a symbol that characterizes the story. Older children create techniques as a form of book reporting and to entice their friends to read the book. When engaged in storytelling, children demonstrate their comprehension of story. The following are some storytelling techniques.

Felt Board Stories

Felt board stories can be told or read while placing felt characters on a felt board to provide a visual representation of the story. Stories that work best with the felt board have a limited number of characters that are introduced one at a time. The well-known folktale *The Mitten* (Brett) is a suitable book for a felt board story. A small boy loses his mitten in the woods. Animals come one at a time and crawl into the mitten to stay warm. To tell the story with the felt board, first a large red felt mitten is placed on the board. As each animal is mentioned, its corresponding piece is placed on the red mitten. At the end of the story, the mitten is so full that it explodes and all the animals come bursting out. To illustrate this, the teacher takes the red mitten off the felt board and shakes the animals onto the table. Children really enjoy this ending. Other books suitable for the felt board include *The Grouchy Ladybug* (Carle) and *Tyrone the*

Horrible (Wilhelm). One fifth-grade teacher engaged her class in a felt board story with the book *Grandfather Tang's Story: A Tale Told with Tangrams* (Tompert). She cut the tangram shapes from felt, and as the story was read to the class, the tangrams were assembled and reassembled on the felt board as they took the different forms of animals in the story. (See Resource 2.1.)

Prop Stories

Another storytelling technique is to use materials mentioned in the story to make it come to life. The props are displayed when needed. A fourth-grade teacher told the story of Gongitsune, a fox named Gon, a Japanese folktale with a sad ending. To set the mood for the unusual experience, the teacher draped a silk Japanese scarf across the front of his desk and decorated the desk top with Japanese artifacts. He put on a kimono, took off his shoes, and sat cross-legged on the desk to tell the story. This set the scene for his presentation. For *The Little Engine That Could* (Piper), a kindergarten teacher collected toy trains and other toys to use at the right time in the retelling. (See Resource 2.2.)

Puppets Stories

Some classroom teachers have a storytelling puppet who tells stories to the children. For example, Ms. Lettenberg had a special monkey puppet that the children named Chatter. The teacher is the only one who is allowed to use Chatter. He tells stories to the class. Other puppets that can be used for storytelling include stick puppets, finger puppets, and face puppets. This technique is especially useful in getting shy children to participate, since they are usually willing to hide behind a puppet when telling a story. Stories that work well with puppets are those with a limited number of characters but a lot of conversation. Some good books for puppet presentations are *Amelia Bedelia* (Parish), *William's Doll* (Zolotow), and *Are You My Mother?* (Eastman). (See Resource 2.3.)

Chalk Talks

The storyteller can draw the story on the chalkboard or on mural paper as it is told. When large boards or spaces are not available, a small easel can take their place, with sheets of paper that can be torn off easily to allow moving from one picture to the next. An overhead projector with a marker can also be used.

It is best to preselect about five pictures of scenes from a book to draw for the chalk talk. The quality of the finished drawings is not important; indeed, the children will feel more secure in their own drawing if your artwork is less than perfect. The focus is on the telling of the story.

Some stories that make good chalk talks are *The Very Busy Spider* (Carle) and the *Harold and the*

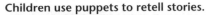
Children use puppets to retell stories.

Chalk talks help children retell stories.

Purple Crayon books (C. Johnson). Teachers can use this technique with older children by having them introduce a chapter in a book or relating their favorite part of a book. Fables are good short stories for older students to chalk talk.

In addition to drawing different scenes from a story, chalk talks can have surprise endings. In this case, a single picture is begun and added to as the story is told, with the completed picture being the surprise at the end. *The Tale of the Black Cat* (Wither) can be used for a chalk talk with a surprise ending; other titles are provided in Resource 2.4. Once this type of chalk talk has been modeled for them, children in grades three through five can be asked to create their own.

Photo Stories

Students can also become the characters in a book. A story that is easy to stage should be tried first; the teacher can help the children enact the main plot episodes. The enactment can be recorded with snapshots, which can be put into an album for the classroom library. A video recorder can also be used. Another alternative is to make a slide show with an audiotape made by the children. Good books for photo stories are *The Snowy Day* and *A Letter to Amy*, both by Ezra Jack Keats. (See Resource 2.5.)

Sound Stories

Sound stories are those in which the storyteller and the audience provide sound effects for a story while it is being told. The effects are often made with one's own voice. Rhythm instruments or some simple props can add to the presentation.

When preparing a sound story, the teacher should first select the places where sound effects will be used, then decide on the sounds that will be made and who will make them. While the story is told, the children chime in with their parts.

Sound stories can be recorded. The tape can be left in a listening center with earphones and the book. Children enjoy following the text of the book, the narration, and the sounds.

Many children's books are filled with references to sound. Good books for this technique are *Too Much Noise* (McGovern) and *Mr. Brown Can Moo! Can You?* (Seuss). (See Resource 2.6.)

Music Stories

Whether you can play an instrument or not, you can create a music story. Select a piece of literature with a limited number of well-delineated characters that appear throughout the story, such as *The Three Little Pigs* (Marshall). If you can play an instrument, select a melody you know that seems appropriate for the character, and play that tune each time the character is mentioned in the story. Different tunes can be created to represent the different characters in the story.

Music can also be used as background. For example, older children can provide classical music to set the mood for novels, and scary sounds for mystery stories.

If you can't play an instrument, try using one anyway. For example, in the case of *The Three Little Pigs,* tinkle your fingers on the top high notes of a piano to represent the pigs when they appear in the story. Pound slowly on the low bottom notes to represent the wolf. Roll your fists back and forth over a series of notes in the middle of the keyboard to represent the huffing and puffing of the big bad wolf. Slide your thumb from the top of the keyboard down to the bottom to represent the straw and stick houses falling down. Rhythm instruments also can be used for creating music stories by those with little or no training. In fact, often the most interesting musical effects are developed in a music story by those who are not trained to play an instrument.

Music stories should always be tape-recorded, especially when children participate. *The Three Little Billy Goats Gruff* (Marcia Brown), *The Three Bears* (Galdone), and *The Little Red Hen* (Galdone) are good stories to read to music. (See Resource 2.7.)

Roll Movie Stories

The teacher should model the roll movie technique for children, with the goal of having them create roll stories themselves. Most younger children's books are appropriate for roll movie stories, as long as they have pictures that can be drawn by teachers. With older children's books, it is usually best to illustrate one chapter or a favorite part of the book rather than the whole. For the book *Tuck Everlasting* (Babbitt), a sixth grader used the prologue, which sets the scene for the book in a mysterious way with five situations. The student illus-

trated each of the five situations on shelving paper to create a roll movie to show classmates. (See Resource 2.8.)

Signing Stories

We sign when we sing songs with motions depicting the words. We can also sign with sign language when storytelling. It is a good activity to foster following directions. Select short simple stories or stories that have a repeated phrase, and learn to sign this phrase every time it appears in a story. Model signing, and have children do it with you. A good story to sign is *The Carrot Seed* (Krauss). You can sign the entire story or just the repeated phrase in the story, "It won't [will not] come up" (see Figure 3.4).

The goal for modeling storytelling techniques is to engage children in independently using the materials the teacher created to retell a story, creating their own materials for stories they read, and creating their own original stories and a technique to suit the theme.

Figure 3.4 Signing "It won't [will not] come up," repeated phrase from *The Carrot Seed* (Krauss).

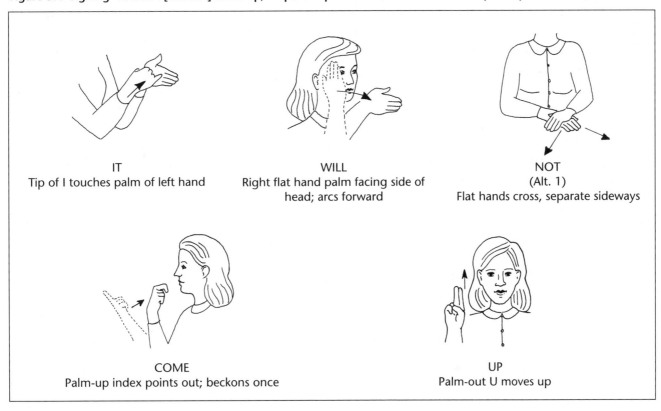

More Comprehension Strategies for Independent Collaborative Work

Think, Pair, Share

The think, pair, share strategy involves teacher-posed questions that students are asked to think about before answering. Children are then paired with peers to discuss their answers to the questions. They then return to a larger group to share the answers they have discussed among themselves (Gambrell and Almasi 1993).

Webbing and Mapping

Webs and maps are diagrams or graphic representations for categorizing and structuring information. They help students see how words and ideas are related to one another. Webs are drawn using a spiderlike effect, and maps use boxes with labels in them that connect in different places. Webbing and mapping strategies build on children's prior knowledge. Children become active learners as they retrieve what they know about a topic, expand their knowledge, and use the information in reading and listening to text. Research has demonstrated that the use of webbing and mapping strategies develops vocabulary and comprehension. It has also shown that these strategies are effective with poor readers (Pittelman, Levin, and Johnson 1985; Pittelman et al. 1991).

When webbing or mapping is used to develop vocabulary concepts and definitions, a word is written on the board or on chart paper. Children brainstorm ideas related to the word. For example, after reading *The Snowy Day* (Keats), the teacher asked children to provide words that describe what snow is like. The word *snow* was written in the center of the chart or chalkboard, and the words given by the children were attached to it.

Another web about the same story could be used to expand ideas about activities to do in the snow. For instance, a first-grade class generated the things that Peter did in the snow in the story

and then added other things that can be done in the snow.

The map provides a format for graphically presenting materials before and after listening to or reading a book. Maps deal with more complex representations; therefore boxes for different categories are needed to present the ideas graphically. Story structures can be mapped to help children learn about the structural elements in the text, such as the setting and theme.

Reading and Writing Across the Curriculum

Reading, writing, and oral language materials and activities are easily incorporated into content instruction, enabling these areas to contribute to literacy learning. Literacy becomes purposeful and takes on additional importance when integrated with other content areas (Dewey 1966).

Subject-specific literacy materials will be found in content areas throughout the classroom, including books, magazines, and newspapers for children to read, materials with which they may write, and activities they can talk about and do. These materials create interest, new vocabulary, and ideas, and in general a reason for participating in literacy activities. With each new theme studied, additional books, posters, artifacts, music, art projects, dramatic play materials, and scientific objects can be added to create new interest.

Themes help to motivate reading and writing if the chosen topics are of interest to children. Content area materials should be coordinated with themes. For example, Ms. Mitchell's third-grade class carried out an extended study of plants. As a science activity the class used a "Do-It-Yourself Science" book called *All About Seeds* (Berger) to carry out experiments about what plants need to grow. They planted seeds, withholding water, soil, and warmth in various combinations and making predictions about the growth of the seeds. Each day they wrote their observations in the class science journal.

Other activities grew out of the plant topic. A gardening center was set up to make a window box garden for the classroom. The class referred to the book *Kidsgardening* (Raferty) as a resource for how to prepare the soil, what seeds to plant, and how to care for them. Ms. Mitchell also read a story to the class about the rain forest. In this story the treasures of the rain forest, along with the dangers of deforestation, are discovered and discussed. The children created a large mural to show the types of plants and animals that live in the rain forest. To find out what was appropriate to include, they used nonfiction informational books such as *Rain Forest Secrets* (Dorros) and *Life in the Rain Forests* (Baker), which were placed in the art area. As a final project, the class wrote a letter to their congressional representative to voice their ideas and concerns. Ms. Mitchell took this opportunity to teach the children the form of a business letter. During literacy center time, Tara wrote a story about what the world would be like if there were no more rain forests. She titled her book "The Day the Forest Died." After the final editing was done, the book was published and became part of the classroom library.

In another third-grade class that was involved in science, where the teacher integrated literature with content area teaching, it was difficult to determine whether what was going on was a literacy lesson or a science lesson. The class had just completed a unit on animals and was about to begin one on "The Changing Earth." When the science period began, Ms. Scifflette, the teacher, called the children to the literacy center. They sat on the rug, and Ms. Scifflette sat in the rocking chair. With her she had the rack that held the science trade books. It was filled with stories about animals. She said, "Since we have completed our animal unit, I will put these books in the science section of our classroom library. I'm going to change the sign on the science book rack to 'The Changing Earth,' since that is our next topic." She asked the children if they could predict what they might be studying about with the topic "The Changing Earth." Dominick said, "Maybe how the rocks change from years of wind and rain on them." Ms. Scifflette agreed that was a good idea.

Stacey said, "Hurricanes can change the earth when they blow down trees and wash away the sand from the beach." Ms. Scifflette agreed with her about that. She then introduced five books and read their titles: *Volcanoes* (Branley), *How to Dig a Hole to the Other Side of the World* (McNulty), *Time of Wonder* (McCloskey), *The Magic School Bus Inside the Earth* (Cole), and *Bringing the Rain to Kapiti Plain* (Aardema). She explained that these stories, along with their textbook, would help them learn about the changing earth. She said that she'd be reading them during the unit and that she would leave them in the special featured science book rack for them to read during their free time. She asked if anyone had any more ideas about what "The Changing Earth" unit might be about as a result of hearing these book titles. Tiffany said, "I guess volcanoes, since they change the earth with all that hot stuff that pours out of them." Tim added, "We're probably gonna learn about what's inside the earth, from the titles of those books you told us about." "I know that *Bringing the Rain to Kapiti Plain* is about drought," said Alex. "The dry land causes the ground to change."

Ms. Scifflette was teaching science and at the same heightening her students' interest about the topic to be studied through the use of children's literature.

Later, after they had been studying "The Changing Earth" for a while, the class assembled in the literacy center for the science lesson. The teacher sat in the rocking chair while the children sat on the rug. Ms. Scifflette picked up a book about the changing earth and wrote the title on a chart: *How to Dig a Hole to the Other Side of the World*. She underlined the title and asked the children why she had done that. Bernice replied, "When you write the name of a book, you are supposed to underline it." "Good," said Ms. Scifflette. She continued, "We've been studying the changing earth and what the earth is made up of. This book is factual and it also has fictional information. While I'm reading, try to remember the facts we come across. After I finish we'll record those facts. After that we'll retell the story together, and emphasize the facts." Ms. Scifflette read the name of the author and illustrator and began the story. After reading, the class discussed the facts and Ms. Scifflette wrote them on the chart. This discussion followed:

Teacher: What is the first thing that you hit when you dig a hole in the earth?

Tyrone: Loam. It is like topsoil. Then we could find clay.

Teacher: Good. Then what?

Adelise: Next comes bones, rock, and limestone.

Joseph: Isn't rock the same as limestone?

Teacher: Yes. Now what do we find?

Children: Crust and then water.

Teacher: What else?

Kevin: I think oil is next. I guess that's what people mean by "filthy rich." When you find oil you get rich, but you also get dirty from digging.

Teacher: There are geysers with scalding hot water and basalt. Who can tell me more about basalt?

Tyrone: Well, when it's in the earth it's black, and when it's melted, it's called magma. When it comes out of the earth through volcanoes, then it's called lava.

Jennifer: The next part is fictional; the book talked about going through the layers of the earth in a jet-propelled red submarine.

Teacher: Good. I'm glad you can tell the difference. Who can finish up?

Damien and Dan: Well, next they came to mantel, which is hot. (*Ms. Scifflette wrote that on the chart.*) Then there is the outer core made of melted rock and iron and the inner core at the center of the earth. After the center he goes back through all the other stuff again till he came out on the other side.

Teacher: That was great. Now would someone retell the entire story with the facts listed on the chart?

April volunteered and began with, "Once upon a time there was a boy who wanted to dig a hole to the other side of the world." She followed the facts on the chart to the end. When she had finished, everyone clapped.

Encouraging writing about science topics was also stressed in these integrated language arts classrooms. For example, Ms. Scifflette's class brainstormed words about the topic being studied by filling in a web entitled "What Changes the Earth?" Using the words generated by the web, such as *hurricane, volcano, lava,* and *drought,* children wrote stories about the science theme. Some students found this activity difficult at first, but after a while they got the idea. They wrote their science stories and used many of the storytelling techniques outlined earlier in this chapter to present them to the class.

After a brainstorming session about vocabulary and concepts related to the changing earth, Ms. Scifflette guided her students as they wrote a class story.

The Treasure Hunt

My friends Amber, Alex, and Kevin found a map of a buried treasure. We decided to look for it. We followed the map to hunt for the treasure. It said go to a stream and find waters that get rough that made the rocks strange shapes from banging up against them. We walked for hours and then Kevin shouted, "Look, there are the rocks." We looked for the next clue. Amber found it carved in the rock. It was hard to read from the wear of the wind and water. It said, "Go to the forest and find the clearing with the colored flowers." We walked for hours. It was hot and dry, the ground was hard, it hadn't rained for months, the grass was brown, the flowers were dead with no color in them from the drought. Then the sky got dark, the wind blew 100 miles an hour, the rain came down in buckets, we ran into a cave. This was a hurricane. When the storm ended it looked like a different place. Trees fell, the lake washed away the beach, but colored flowers were growing. We had found the spot. We saw a note that said go to the mountain. We saw it ahead. We ran toward it. The earth began to shake, the mountain rumbled. It wasn't a mountain, it was a volcano. Red hot lava ran down the side. We ran for cover. When the volcano finished erupting, the earth was covered with ash. When it was safe we came out to look for a clue. I saw a paper. It said go to the forest and you will find it. When we got there, the leaves were green, the flowers were pretty, the sky was blue, there was a breeze, there was fruit to eat on the trees, and birds were singing, and the sun was warm. Alex said, "This is it." "What?" we said. Alex said, "We saw changes in the earth that were scary, like jagged rocks from wind and water, and a hurricane that blew down trees, and a volcano burned up the ground. Now we can see the beautiful part of the earth. This is the treasure." We all agreed and enjoyed the pretty earth.

In a first-grade classroom that was using an integrated language arts approach to motivate reading and writing in content subjects, the teacher, Mr. Gravois, extended the theme—the study of animals—to all the learning areas in the classroom. To encourage literacy skills development, he added the following materials and activities for students to participate in at each of the centers.

Art Center

Printed directions for making play dough were written on a chart for the art center. After following these directions, and making the modeling clay, children created real or imaginary animals for a pretend zoo they had designed in the block area. The children named their animals and wrote their names on index cards as they placed them in the zoo. Children practiced literacy skills such as reading, writing, and following directions.

In the art center, children read the recipe for the play dough. They practiced sound-symbol relationships when writing the animal names on index cards, and they voluntarily engaged in reading and writing.

Music Center

Children sang animal songs, and Mr. Gravois wrote the words to new songs on chart paper that was displayed in the music center. Children were encouraged to read or copy the charts. In the music center, vocabulary was enhanced and the relationship between oral and written language strengthened.

Science Center

Mr. Gravois borrowed a hen whose eggs were ready to hatch. The class discussed the care of the hen. They started an experience chart when the hen arrived and added to it daily, recording the hen's behavior and the hatching of the eggs. They listed new vocabulary words on their thematic word wall and placed books about hens in the science area. Children kept journals of events concerning the hen. Index cards were available in the center for children to record new "very own words" relating to the hen. The science center was rich in opportunities for children to develop early writing, vocabulary, and recognition of sight words.

Social Studies Center

Pictures of animals from different countries were placed in the center along with a map highlighting where they come from. Children matched the animals to the appropriate places on the map. They made books about animals around the world and focused on correct punctuation.

Math Center

Counting books that feature animals, such as *Count!* (Fleming) and *1, 2, 3, to the Zoo* (Carle), were placed in the math center along with math manipulatives such as Unifix cubes. The children developed math and literacy skills by matching the right number of manipulatives to the number names and number symbols in the books.

Dramatic Play Center

The dramatic play area became a pet store. There were (empty) boxes of pet food and other products for animals, marked with prices. A pet supply checklist was available for customers to decide what things they needed and how much they

Figure 3.5 Teacher-Modeled Literature and Comprehension Activities

1. Read and tell stories to children.
2. Discuss stories read in many different ways.
3. Have a 30-minute literacy center period a few times a week that includes the use of books and all other literature-related materials in the library corner.
4. Allow children to check out books from the classroom library.
5. Encourage children to read during their spare time and keep track of books read.
6. Have children keep the literacy center orderly.
7. Read poetry to children and have children read and recite poetry.
8. Share books read at home or at school.
9. Invite the principal, custodian, nurse, secretary, a parent, and others to come to school to read to the children.
10. Discuss authors and illustrators, and write to them.
11. Have children read to younger children and to each other.
12. Show videos, DVDs, or movies of stories.
13. Use literature across the curriculum in content area lessons.
14. Relate art activities to books (draw a mural related to a book, create a picture using the technique of a particular illustrator of children's books).
15. Tell stories using creative storytelling techniques such as felt boards, roll movies, puppets, sound stories, music stories, chalk stories, prop stories.
16. Have children tell stories with and without props.
17. Have children act out stories.
18. Prepare recipes related to stories.
19. Read TV-related stories.
20. Make class books and "very own books," bind them, and store them in the library corner.
21. Sing songs that have been made into books and have the book on hand.
22. Make bulletin boards related to books.
23. Have children write advertisements for good books they have read.
24. Discuss the proper way to care for and handle books.
25. Feature and introduce new books in the open-faced bookshelves.
26. Introduce new books in the literacy corner.
27. Circulate 25 new books every two weeks.
28. Provide booklets for children and parents for selecting books to read in and out of school.
29. Have a bookstore in the school where children can buy books regularly.
30. Give each child a book or bookmark as a gift.
31. Have a young author's conference (share books children have written, bind books, invite authors).
32. Have a book fair for children to purchase books.
33. Have a book celebration day (dress up as book characters, tell stories to each other, show book videos and movies, have stories told creatively).
34. Have children order books from a book club.
35. Provide a newsletter a few times a year about book-related activities in school.
36. Ask parents to participate in literature-related activities at school (reading with children, helping with book binding, raising money to buy books, participating in literacy center time).
37. Have a workshop for parents that describes the purpose and activities of the school literature program.
38. Have a workshop for parents describing how they can participate in a home recreational reading program.

would cost. There were sales slips for writing orders, receipts for purchases made, and a calculator to help figure totals. Animal magazines and pamphlets that discussed pet care were present in the store, and pet posters labeled with animals' names hung on the walls. Other materials included a sign that said "Open" and "Closed," with store hours posted. Stuffed animals were used as the pets for sale. They were placed in boxes that served as cages, labeled with the animals' names. There were appointment cards for grooming pets and a checklist for owners to record activities necessary for maintaining a healthy pet. The environmental print and writing materials in this center provided meaningful ways for children to practice literacy skills.

Block Play Center

The block area became a zoo, housing animal figures, stuffed animals, and play dough animals created by the children. Children used the blocks to create cages and made labels and signs for each animal and section of the zoo, such as "Petting Zoo," "Bird House," "Pony Rides," "Don't Feed the Animals," and "Don't Touch Us, We Bite." There were admission tickets and play money to purchase tickets and souvenirs. This simple addition of markers, paper, and index cards resulted in children's participation in literacy activities.

Literacy Center

Books and magazines about animals were highlighted on the open-faced bookshelves of the literacy center. The author's spot had animal-shaped blank books for writing animal stories. Many of the activities from other centers spread into the literacy center, and it became a central resource for information and materials.

Resource Section 2 contains activities to promote comprehension through storytelling. Figure 3.5 provides a checklist of teacher-modeled literature and comprehension activities.

The School Library or Media Center

The school librarian or media specialist is a valuable resource in establishing a program for self-directed and collaborative literature experiences (see Lamme and Ledbetter [1990] for many suggestions). Librarians can guide the selection of books for the classroom library because they are the most familiar with the current literature and can also gauge the likely popularity of books. Librarians can also give presentations to update teachers and students about new literature. They help coordinate read-aloud book lists for different grade levels to ensure that students are exposed to a variety of literature as they progress through school.

Librarians are also a resource for children's learning to read and tell stories. They can serve as role models for classroom teachers; can conduct workshops on storytelling, puppet making, and reading aloud; and can visit classrooms to read to children. They can help set up a coding system for books in the classroom library. They can make connections for the children between the classroom and the school library collections and coding systems. In an ideal situation, the librarian coordinates schoolwide thematic units, which are kept on file. These units contain activity plans, teaching strategies, and lists of annotated bibliographies of children's literature for classroom use.

Modeling Independent Word Study Activities: Phonemic Awareness and Phonics

From the rich collection of ideas and word study materials in her literacy center, Ms. Abere assigned the following activities for students to work on while she took small groups for guided reading instruction.

Four children were to make little words from the big word *Thanksgiving*. The word was selected because that holiday was coming up soon. The individual letters of *Thanksgiving* had been cut out for each child and placed in plastic baggies. In addition to manipulating the paper letters to create little words, the children were to record the words they had made on an activity/accountability form. (See Resource 3.13.)

Another group of four, also using the big word *Thanksgiving,* was to create word ladders with magnetic letters and individual magnetic slates. Starting with one-letter words, then two-, three-, and four-letter words, each child was to arrange the magnetic letters into words and write a ladder of the created words on an activity/accountability form. A partner was to check the words. (See Resource 3.13.)

The next group of four children was to work with ending phonograms, or chunks, by varying onsets, or initial consonants, to make different words. Ms. Abere had prepared sliders (e.g., word wheels)—two oaktag circles, one with ending phonograms written on it and one with onsets written on it. (See Resource 3.11.) Children were to move the sliders around to create words and then write them (and any similar words that came to mind) on 5-by-8-inch index cards.

Finally, another group was to create sentences with word stamps. The stamps had familiar words for the children to combine into sentences.

All these activities were manipulative. They involved children's working independently with words, from individual letters to letter chunks to beginnings and endings of words to whole words to sentences. They also required children to work together and check each other's work. All children had the opportunity to do at least three of the four activities during this period. Children changed activities each time Ms. Abere finished with one guided reading group and began another.

Developing word study skills and knowledge about print involves teaching strategies that will help children to figure out words and become independent readers. Word study skills include the use of context and syntax to figure out an unknown word, developing a sight vocabulary, using the configuration or shape of a word to recognize it, and structural analysis (attending to different parts of words, such as syllables, prefixes, suffixes, and roots to decode). The best-known word study strategy is making phonics connections, that is, associating the *sounds* of letters and combinations of letters (phonemes) with their corresponding printed *symbols* (graphemes). One of the problems with learning correct print-sound correspondence is that the English alphabet has at least forty-four sounds, and print-sound correspondence is not consistent—there are many irregularities and exceptions to many rules. Phonemic awareness—understanding that words are made up of individual sounds that can be segmented from the rest of the word and blended to form words—is considered by some to be a precursor to learning phonics skills and learning how to read. The purpose of phonics instruction is to build independent readers. Understanding phonics connections has received a great deal of attention as an important skill for reading success to a greater or lesser extent over the years. There is no doubt that research has demonstrated its importance. However, it is the concurrent learning of several of the word study skills mentioned that will create the most proficient reader.

To become proficient readers, children need to learn the language codes. There is considerable evidence from experimental and longitudinal studies in many countries that phonemic awareness and knowledge of print-sound correspondence are necessary for success in learning to read and write alphabetic languages (Adams 1990; Juel 1994). According to Juel (1989), the precursors to learning to read proficiently are (1) alphabetic understanding (knowing that words are composed of letters), and (2) phonemic awareness (knowing that words are composed of a sequence of spoken sounds and being able to hear those sounds).

There are concerns in literacy education about word study practice, such as exactly what skills should be taught, when they should be introduced, how they should be taught, and how much time should be spent dealing with them. We don't have definitive answers to all these questions, but we have found that teaching these skills in a variety of ways seems best. For example, we should include explicit, systematic instruction to be sure we can account for objectives being accomplished, spontaneous instruction that takes advantage of unexpected teachable moments, and arrangements for allowing the skills to be practiced in meaningful, contextually based settings.

Objectives for Word Study

Some objectives for word study to enhance literacy development are for children to be able to

- capture messages from environmental print (signs, logos);

- recognize high-frequency and other sight words;

- identify rhyming words and make up rhymes;

- identify and name uppercase and lowercase letters;

- blend and segment phonemes in words;

- associate letters with their corresponding initial and final consonant sounds including varying sounds of the same letter (*cat, city, goat, George*);

- associate letters with corresponding long and short vowel sounds (*acorn, apple; eagle, egg; ice, igloo; oats, octopus; unicorn, umbrella*);

- blend initial consonants (*bl, cr, dr, pr, fl, gl, st, str, spr*);

- identify consonant digraph sounds (*ch, ph, sh, th, wh*);

- use context, syntax, and semantics to identify words;

- divide words into syllables;

- attempt reading by attending to picture clues and word configuration;

- predict words based on a knowledge of print-sound correspondence;

- identify different structural elements of words, such as prefixes, suffixes, roots, and inflectional endings (*-ing, -ed, -s*), and contractions;

- apply the following generalizations:
  - In a consonant-vowel-consonant pattern, the vowel sound is usually short (*bat, bet, but, bit*),
  - In a vowel-consonant-*e* pattern, the vowel sound is usually long (*cake, cute*),
  - When two vowels come together in a word, the first is usually long and the second is usually silent (*train, receive, bean*);

- identify common word families (rimes or phonograms) and build words by adding initial consonants (onsets) to word families (*-it, -an, -am, -at, -ite, -ate*);

- read fluently and at grade level.

Spelling is also learned as sound-symbol correspondence patterns are acquired. As you teach word study skills and strategies, be sure to have children practice these word patterns by using them in their writing to help with spelling.

Activities for Teaching Word Study Strategies

Instructional activities designed to help youngsters learn about the function, form, structure, and conventions of print should involve many types of learning experiences. Children need to be socially interactive when they are learning about print; they need models to emulate; and the learning must be through experiences that are meaningful and connected with real life. If children see a skill as useful, it is more likely to be learned. In addition, children learn from direct skills instruction.

When developing word study skills, teachers explain what is being taught, model the activity, and let children practice and apply new skills.

In direct, systematic approaches, lessons need to teach strategies for children to use. In these lessons the teacher does the following:

1. Begins with an explanation to let children know what is being taught and why

2. Models and demonstrates how and when to apply what is taught

3. Gives students the opportunity to practice what is taught

4. Encourages students to apply what is taught

Developing Sight Words

In the classic book *Teacher* (1963), Sylvia Ashton-Warner describes "very own words" as a method for developing sight vocabulary. She encourages children to write their favorite words from a story or content area lesson on 3-by-5-inch cards, each word on a separate card. Such words are often drawn from the child's home life or what they are studying in school, and they often have emotional connections for the child. The words are recorded on index cards and stored in a child's file box, coffee can, plastic baggie, or loose-leaf book. Then, during literacy center time, children read them to friends or to themselves, copy them, or use them in sentences and stories. The words can also be alphabetized, studied for letter patterns, and so on.

Environmental Print

Research has found that children as young as two can recognize familiar environmental print (Goodman 1980; Harste, Woodward, and Burke 1984). The initial recognition may come from

Environmental print helps to develop and reinforce recognition of sight words.

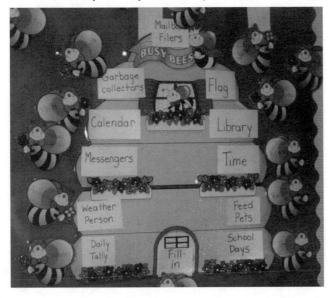

the logo, but the children simultaneously learn that the accompanying group of letters (e.g., McDonald's) makes up a word that can be read to obtain information. Reading environmental print often receives positive reinforcement from adults and gives children a sense of accomplishment.

Be sure to make children aware of environmental print in school, in their homes, and outside. Point out road signs, food boxes, and well-known restaurant signs. Fill your room with environmental print that is functional, for example, by labeling materials or putting up signs ("Wash Your Hands Before Snack"). Reading environmental print is a form of sight word development. Children should be encouraged to trace or copy the print. Make flash cards for them to practice the words alone or with a partner. Use the print as a center activity, Read Around the Room (see Resource 3.4), in which children walk around the room with a clipboard copying words. Older children can use the words in sentences.

The Morning Message

Post messages and assignments daily for the children. Select a permanent spot for the morning message and use it for writing about themes being studied in school and writing about children's experiences and families. Use words with different spelling patterns. Model letter writing, showing

the appropriate format for corresponding with someone. Make mistakes on messages by using incorrect punctuation or spelling, and see if children will pick up on them and correct them. As a center activity, children can search the message for skills that were stressed in a whole-class lesson. (See Resource 3.5.)

High-Frequency Words

Words that are found frequently in reading materials for young children need to be learned as sight words for quick recall. They are usually words that don't carry concrete meaning but rather hold sentences together. They are often difficult to decode because they have irregular spelling patterns. It is helpful if children do not have to spend time segmenting these words as they read but can just read them easily by memory or sight.

High-frequency words are most often taught in a systematic, explicit manner. The teacher selects a few for the children to learn each week using the following activities:

- Words are said aloud and used in a sentence.

- The sentence is written on a chalkboard or flip chart, and the word is underlined.

- Features of the word are discussed, such as the letters, similarity to other words, and any regular or irregular pattern.

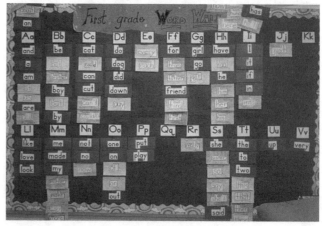

The morning message and word wall develop recognition of sight words and high-frequency words.

- Children are asked to spell the word aloud, trace the word with their fingers in the air, and write the word on paper.

- Children chant the letters as they spell the word.

- The words can be put on an index card, as in the "very own words" activity, and stored with a child's "high-frequency words" or in a "sight words" box.

- The word can be written down and its shape cut out.

- Children can write the word on a slate and outline the word's letter patterns, or use magnetic letters to spell the word (see Resource 3.16).

Word walls can be used to reinforce high-frequency words. A word wall typically has letters of the alphabet posted across it. As high-frequency words are featured, they are taped under the letter where they belong. A word wall can be used as a center activity. For example, if the teacher wants children to work with rhymes, she can point to *went* or *look* and say, "The word I am thinking of rhymes with *went* but begins with *b*" or "The word I am thinking of rhymes with *look* and begins with *c*." Word wall words can also be sorted by those that have prefixes or those with similar phonograms, and so on. The teacher provides activity cards in the word study center for using the word wall independently. The difficulty of words and activities is based on grade level (Cunningham 1995; Moustafa 1998).

Using Context and Syntax to Figure Out Words

Help children to use the context and syntax of a sentence in order to decode words. Encourage students to use these elements of written language by stopping your oral reading at points in a story and asking them to fill in words. For example, when reading *The Carrot Seed* (Krauss), first read the entire sentence, "It won't come up"; the second time say, "It won't come _____"; the next time,

"It won't _____ _____"; and last, "It _____ _____ _____." More difficult passages are used with older children. For center work, prepare activity sheets to fill in with the words left out. With practice, children will acquire the ability to thoughtfully predict the missing word or words, based on context, syntax, and clues from the print. This technique is called the cloze procedure.

In addition to the preceding suggestion, other techniques can be introduced, so that students have different strategies for using context to figure out words. A common way to figure out words from context is through the meaning of the text. For example, in the sentence that follows, it is apparent that the missing word is Queen. We need to show children how to use the meaning of the text to figure out a word that might be unknown to them.

The King and _____ lived in the castle together.

Another context clue exercise involves a series of related words. To help with this exercise or other context clue exercises, the initial consonant can be included. For example,

My favorite kinds of fruit are apples, bananas, p_____, and oranges.

A context clue exercise that involves the use of scrambled words is the following:

I am always on time, but my sister is always _____ (alte).

When working with the cloze procedure, teachers can choose to leave out structural elements in sentences, such as nouns or verbs, and then explain that the missing word makes sense based on its placement in a sentence.

Learning the Alphabet

Much practice with varying activities is needed to learn the alphabet. Children need exposure to letters daily in both explicit and constructive situations. They need to explore letters by using manipulative materials.

Create an alphabet center with the many different alphabet materials such as magnetic letters with magnetic boards, wooden letters, felt letters and a felt board, sandpaper letters matching letter games, alphabet puzzles, alphabet stamps, alphabet flashcards. Provide for accountability with activity/accountability forms or other types of assessment materials.

Be sure to have a plentiful supply of alphabet books. Some recommended ones are *Calypso Alphabet* (Agard), *Animalia* (Base), *A Is for Angry: An Animal and Adjective Alphabet* (Boynton), *Alphabet Times Four* (R. Brown), *ABC Discovery* (Cohen), *Jambo Means Hello: Swahili Alphabet Book* (Feelings), *Alphababies* (Golding), *Alphabet City* (S. T. Johnson), *Amazing Alphabet* (Jordan), and *Miss Spider's ABC* (Kirk).

Center activities for learning and reinforcing what is known about the alphabet include

- Listening on headsets to the alphabet song and having an activity sheet or alphabet book for pointing to the letters as they are sung. Encourage children to write some of the letters they hear.

- Playing Letter Bingo with Bingo cards filled with letters and markers to cover them. Call a letter and hold up a card with the letter on it to help children with identification. When a child has covered one row of letters on the card, he gets Bingo. Children should write down the letters they covered on an accountability form. (See Resource 3.1.)

- Alphabet journals with a letter of the alphabet on each page. On the different pages children can trace the letter, write the letter, or find words in a magazine that use the letter and paste them on the page. (See Resource 3.6.)

Developing Phonemic Awareness

Phonemic awareness is the knowledge that words are made up of individual sounds that can be segmented and then blended again. Phonemic aware-

ness is considered by some to be a necessary precursor to phonics instruction.

The simplest level of phonemic awareness is to become aware that words are made up of sounds that we are able to hear, identify, and match in "similar word" patterns such as rhymes. In doing so, children are developing auditory discrimination.

Because developing phonemic awareness depends on oral language instruction, this skill is fostered in teacher-led activities with small groups or the entire class, not practiced independently in a word study center. Phonemic awareness is so important in the development of early reading, however, that activities to promote it are described here. Later, when the objective is to manipulate printed letters in connection with sounds, some of the same activities, such as rhyming and identifying distinct sounds within words, can be done independently in centers.

One of the ways that young children acquire knowledge about the sounds in words is through exposure to rhymes and jingles. Reading books that contain rhymes, such as *Green Eggs and Ham* (Seuss), *Goodnight Moon* (M. W. Brown), and *The Missing Tarts* (Hennessy) help with the skill. Teachers can take words from the books—some that rhyme and some that don't—and recite them to children, who are asked to differentiate between rhyming and nonrhyming words. For additional practice with rhyme, children can say words (real or pretend) that rhyme with their names, sing songs and separate out the rhyming words, or act out well-known nursery rhymes such as Jack and Jill or Itsy-Bitsy Spider.

Segmenting and blending words is more difficult for children. If this is done with the word *man*, the child would be guided to say "mmm" for the onset /m/ and then "annn" for the rime /an/. After segmenting the word, the child blends the segments back together and says the entire word, "man." Eventually we would like children to be able to identify each sound within a word, know the number of sounds heard, and be able to blend the word back together. The following are some teacher-led activities that will help children learn to segment and blend:

- Sing the song "Bingo." In the song each letter is chanted and then they are blended. Change the words from "There was a farmer had a dog, and Bingo was his name" to "There is a girl (or boy) I know so well, and Jenny is her name-o, J-e-n-n-y, J-e-n-n-y, J-e-n-n-y, and Jenny is her name-o."

- Play a riddle substitution-of-onsets game. Say, "I'm thinking of a word that sounds like *head* but begins with the /b/ sound" or "I'm thinking of a word that sounds like *fat* but has an /m/ sound at the beginning."

- Select a word and draw square boxes next to each other that represent the word. Have chips for children to put into the squares. Say a word such as *tree* and have the children put the number of chips in the boxes that represent the number of sounds they hear. For *tree*, three chips would be placed into the boxes, for /t/, /r/, and /ee/ (Fitzpatrick 1997; Johns, Lenski, and Elish-Piper 1999).

  Example: Let's figure out how many sounds are in the word *bell*. I'm going to say it again, /b/, /e/, /l/. Put a chip in the squares for each sound you heard in the word *bell*. How many chips did you use? Now look at the letters in the word *bell*. How many do you count? A word can have different numbers of letters and sounds.

For a word center version of this activity, see Resource 3.3.

Learning Print-Sound Correspondence

Phonics instruction should occur in meaningful contexts as well as with some systematic presentation of skills in a more explicit manner. We know that children need continual practice in order to learn print-sound relationships; rarely is a single lesson sufficient. Therefore provide several experiences with phonics elements through different modalities, review frequently, and allow for practice often.

Phonics Activities in Context

Children can be helped to recognize sound-symbol relationships of consonants and vowels in meaningful contexts. Science and social studies themes lend themselves to featuring letters and letter patterns in words used in units of study. For example, when studying farm pets and zoo animals, feature the letter *p*, because it is used frequently in this context. The following activities are meaning-based and help teach phonics skills. They can be done alone or with other children independently of the teacher during literacy center time.

- After having read *The Pig's Picnic* (Kasza), *Pet Show* (Keats), and *The Tale of Peter Rabbit* (Potter) during the unit, and pointing out words that begin with the letter *p* in these books, have children find the words and write them on an activity sheet provided in the center.

- Make a list of animals whose names begin with the letter *p* and another list of animals whose names have a *p* anywhere in the name. These words are listed in separate columns on an activity sheet.

- Children choose words beginning with *p* that they would like on "very own word" cards. For a center activity, they write these words into a story using all the words.

- Providing magazines with lots of pictures in them, have children search for objects or people whose names begin with *p* and then create a collage of these.

- Ask children to write a nonsense poem that features words beginning with *p*, such as
  My name is Penelope Pig.
  I pick petals off petunias.
  I play patty cake and
  Eat pretzels with pink punch.

As another example, in a unit on food, Ms. Taylor, a first-grade teacher, featured the letter *b* and read *Blueberries for Sal* (McCloskey), *Bread and Jam for Frances* (Hoban), and *The Berenstain Bears and Too Much Birthday* (Berenstain).

Children's literature is a good source for featuring letters attached to themes, but don't spoil the children's pleasure in the stories by overemphasizing the sound exercises.

Explicit Phonics Activities

Based on research about how children learn, it is clear that activities with word families, or phonograms, to build words and sort words into different patterns helps children to learn print-sound correspondence and consequently to independently decode unknown words. Word building and sorting with onsets (the initial letter or letters before the first vowel) and rimes (the vowel and

Figure 4.1 Word Study Center Activities

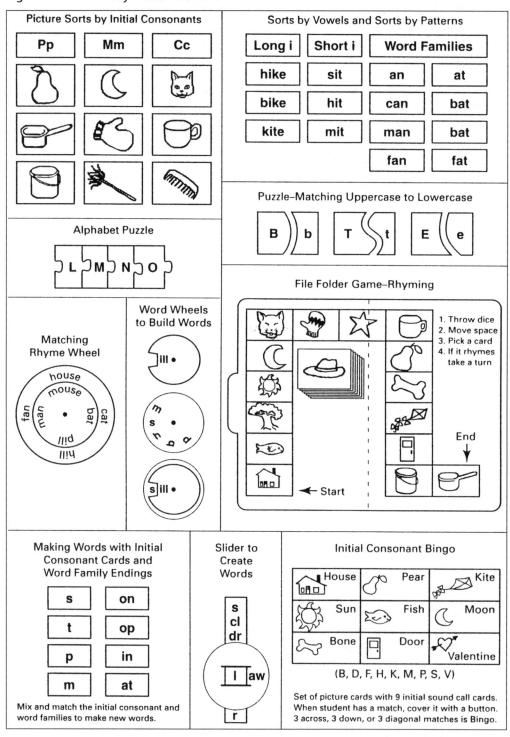

Source: Adapted from *Words Their Way* by D. R. Bear, M. Invernizi, S. Templeton, and F. Johnston. © 1996 by Prentice Hall. Used by permission.

what follows) allow children to look at bigger chunks of words. When children learn some words and how to figure out new ones by using patterns in words, they develop a strategy to do the same with new words. According to research, the brain looks for known patterns when it is learning new ones. It takes what is known and tries to apply it to the unknown. Recognizing patterns such as familiar word endings helps children to deal with unknowns (Adams 1990; Goswami and Bryant 1990).

Making Words Making words is a gamelike activity in which children look for patterns in words and try to make new words by changing one letter or more. For instance, the teacher asks children to make little words from a big word that includes letters for the desired patterns. The big word could be selected because a holiday is coming up (e.g., Thanksgiving), from a story, from new vocabulary, from a unit theme, and so on. The big word is usually spelled out correctly but could be presented in scrambled form. At centers, this activity can be done with magnetic letters or cut paper letters. When words have been created, children write them on index cards or as "word ladders" on an activity sheet that has places for two-letter words first, then three-letter words, then four-letter words. (See Resource 3.13.)

Building Words Building words is done with onsets and rimes. With younger children, the teacher provides a few well-known rimes such as -at, -an, and -in and asks the children to make as

many words with these endings as they can think of by adding different initial consonants or consonant blends. With the rime -at, for example, children could create the following words: *cat, sat, mat, rat, hat, fat, nat, pat,* and *bat.* Words can be built with magnetic letters, cardboard letters, letter cubes, and similar materials. When the words have been created, they are recorded on an accountability form. (See Resources 3.8 and 3.9.)

Sorting Words Words made in the "making words" and "building words" activities can be sorted in different ways. For example, if children make little words from the word *Thanksgiving,* such as *thanks, giving, sing, sang, sin, gang, hang, sting, king, thanking, having,* they can be asked to sort them by listing all those that have an *-ing* ending, that rhyme, that end with the consonant *g,* that begin with the consonant *s,* and so on. Sorting words for blends, digraphs, or number of syllables can help students see patterns. Words can be sorted for meaning by categories such as colors and types of food.

As with all center activities, the teacher models the activity first so children understand what to do. Then an activity card with directions can be placed in the center for independent work. An accountability form is prepared for listing sorted words. (See Resource 3.7.)

Pocket Chart Activities

A pocket chart is a must in a literacy center. Pocket charts can be used in many center activities for

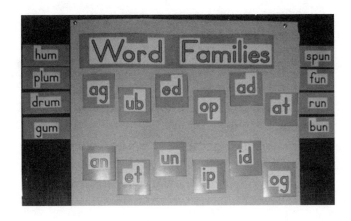

Word family phonogram and vowel word wall charts help children to sort, classify, and build words and segments and blend them.

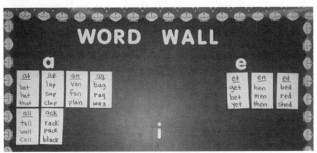

A pocket chart can be used to construct and match words, such as opposites, homonyms, and synonyms.

many of the skills discussed. They are associated with sequencing sentences from short stories, poems, and songs. A short story, for example, is printed on sentence strips that students chant together. The sentence strips can be scrambled and sequenced, or each strip can be cut up for children to sequence the words back into a sentence.

When studying a unit on food and featuring the consonant *t* in all parts of words, Ms. Albury selected the book *Potatoes on Tuesday* (Lillegard) for her kindergarten class. The text of the book is as follows:

> On Monday, cabbage,
> On Tuesday, potatoes,
> On Wednesday, carrots,
> On Thursday, tomatoes,
> On Friday, peas and green beans, too—
> On Saturday, a great big pot of . . .
> Stew! Mmmm.

Ms. Albury wrote the text on chart paper and then on sentence strips. She cut a second set of sentence strips into individual words. This provided the children with activities to practice sequencing whole sentences into a story, building sentences from individual words by using the syntax and semantics of the text, identifying the consonant *t* within the context of words and a story,

and rehearsing new vocabulary. Children can use these materials to practice the skills independently during center time.

In addition, pocket charts can be used in sequencing the letters of the alphabet, in constructing words using cards with letters, phonograms, prefixes, roots, suffixes, and so on. The pocket chart can also be used to match opposites, homonyms, and synonyms. Teachers provide the materials, activity cards, and accountability forms. (See Resources 3.7, 3.12, and 3.14.)

Oral Fluent Reading

We ask children to read orally for practicing skills, for accountability, and for assessment. We can determine reading level, the types of strategies children have for decoding text, the types of errors they make, and the strategies they need to develop. Oral reading tells us about fluency in reading, which is determined by the rate of reading, accuracy, expression used, and phrasing. Fluent readers use verbal expression and intonation that convey the meaning of the text. They also attend to punctuation.

We have found that children who read fluently are better able to comprehend text. There seems to be a relationship between the two skills. With this information we can plan appropriate instruction. Some strategies to develop fluency are

- children's participating in repeated readings of stories,

- children's practicing reading with material that is easy,

- teachers' modeling shared read-aloud experiences.

- children's practicing echo reading by repeating the sentences the teacher reads.

- children's practicing choral reading by reading together orally.

The accuracy with which children read particular passages determines their reading level. Reading level indicates which materials should be

Children become fluent readers when they practice reading the same story over and over again.

used for instructional purposes and which for independent reading, and which materials will be too difficult.

When children read orally, we can also find out if they monitor their own reading. For example, when they make an error, do they correct it on their own? Do they search back and forth through the text to figure out words?

As an independent center activity, oral reading can be practiced with a partner. For accountability, the children can tape-record each partner reading. For assessment, the teacher can listen to the tapes and evaluate the fluency of the reading. Good expression, fluency, and attention to punctuation are characteristics of high-quality oral reading.

Resource Section 3 contains activities to promote independent and collaborative word study. Figure 4.2 provides a checklist of teacher-modeled word study activities.

Figure 4.2 Teacher-Modeled Word Study Activities

1. Involve children in word sorting, word building, finding little words in big words.
2. Involve children in games created for practicing word study skills.
3. Involve children in word study activities when the opportunity arises.
4. Involve children in word study in content area subjects.
5. Use the word wall for high-frequency and sight word activities.
6. Use environmental print in your classroom.
7. Involve children in cloze procedure activities.

Organizing and Managing a Literacy Center

In Ms. Taylor's third grade the children are engaged in literacy center time. The teacher has reviewed the choices of activities and decided that the emphasis for the day would be to read traditional tales, those handed down over the years from one group of people to the next. Among the books the class has discussed are *Little Red Riding Hood* (Grimm), *The Gingerbread Boy* (Galdone), and *The Three Billy Goats Gruff* (Asbjørnsen and Moe). Children were to compare the themes of the story to see the similarities in style. Ms. Taylor asked the children to form groups and make decisions about what they would do. They would record their decisions on sign-up sheets before going off to work together. The students knew that during this period they would be working on something for which there needed to be an outcome. Children could choose to read an original folktale they had written, tell about the different versions of a particular folktale, do a felt board presentation of a story they had read, or choose any other available center activity to rehearse the idea of traditional tales. They would have about a week to complete their projects, depending on the progress made.

Once the children had made choices concerning with whom they would work and what they would do, they began their activities.

John and Tasha were reading several versions of *The Three Little Pigs* (Brenner; Izawa and Hijikata; Marshall; Scieszka) as they relaxed on soft pillows, both holding stuffed animals as they read. When they finished reading, they discussed and wrote down the differences among the versions. Christopher read to James while the two of them were inside the box called the private spot. After reading they filled out an accountability form to document their reading. Jacki and Jerome used a felt board to tell the story *The Three Billy Goats Gruff* (Asbjørnsen and Moe; Marcia Brown). One manipulated the felt characters as the other read the book. A group listened with headsets to a taped story of *The Little Red Hen* (Galdone). When they had finished listening, they answered questions provided on an activity card.

Tyrone and Jessy were writing letters about their work with fairy tales to pen pals in another classroom. The teachers in the two rooms were coordinating programs: the two classes were working on the same project so that the students could correspond about their common work. A few children were checking out books to take home, and others were looking in their logs, comparing the number of books they had read and the literacy tasks they had accomplished.

At the beginning of the period Ms. Taylor walked around to make sure that children were involved. She helped a group that was having difficulty getting started on a roll movie they wanted to create for the story of *Cinderella* (Perrault). Then she observed a few youngsters acting out *The Three Bears and Fifteen Other Stories* (Rockwell) with finger puppets. After that she sat down with a novel and read, modeling her own interest in books. The room was generally quiet, but one could hear the buzz of activity. Not only were the children's activities productive, they were also relevant—each child or group of children had interpreted for themselves the concept to be focused on during this independent reading and writing period. All were doing different activities, but all were using folk and fairy tales.

When all the children were settled into literacy center activities, Ms. Taylor sat among them with a professional book and read, modeling her own interest in books.

Literacy centers are especially useful because they provide students with opportunities for collaborative learning and promote motivation for reading and writing. But what are the benefits of collaborative learning experiences? What types of collaborative settings can children be involved in? And how does a teacher organize and manage collaborative literacy settings—literacy centers—where children work productively in social groups, independently of the teacher?

Benefits of Collaborative Learning Experiences

The aim of collaborative, or cooperative, learning is to bring children together so they can teach and learn from each other through discussion and debate. Social interaction and collaboration within small groups of children promote achievement and productivity (Johnson and Johnson 1999; Salomon and Perkins 1998). According to researchers, cooperative learning succeeds because it allows children to explain material to each other, to listen to each others' explanations, and to arrive at a joint understanding of what has been shared. In the collaborative setting, more capable peers support others in the group. For example, they may observe, guide, and correct while the others perform a particular task (Forman and Cazden 1985). Children are able to accomplish together what they could not do alone. Such peer interactions offer the same learning opportunities as tutoring.

In collaborative settings children form friendships and develop greater acceptance of differences. High and low achievers are able to work together, as are children from varied racial and ethnic backgrounds. Children with special needs (physical disabilities, emotional handicaps, learning difficulties) and social isolates are more likely to be accepted in cooperative learning settings than in traditional classroom structures (Augustine, Gruber, and Hanson 1989; Johnson and Johnson 1998; Slavin 1994).

Collaborative Literacy Settings

There are several collaborative literacy settings. They involve children working in pairs or groups of three or four. Following are descriptions of some of these settings.

Buddy Reading and Writing

Buddy reading and writing involves pairing a child from an upper grade with a child in kindergarten, first, or second grade. The child in the upper grade is instructed on how to read to children and participate in other literacy activities as well. With their teacher, the older students plan activities for each buddy reading and writing session. At specified times buddies get together for reading and writing. Both older and younger children benefit from these interactions. The younger children's literacy is enhanced from the mentoring they receive. The older children are learning how to teach, discovering in the process that the teacher often learns as much as the student. Wonderful social relationships are also formed in this learning structure. Buddy reading and writing can take place during literacy center time by prearrangement with the children's teachers.

Partner Reading and Writing

Partner reading and writing involves pairs of students from the same class who have chosen (or been designated by the teacher) to read and write together. Activity sheets or cards guide the students on how to proceed. Questions that prompt conversation about texts can be used (see Chapter 3). Directions for a typical project for partner reading and writing are as follows:

1. Select and read a book of your choice.

2. Discuss the parts you liked best and write them down.

3. Prepare a roll movie story illustrating one of the parts you chose.

Partner reading and writing involves peers who are paired by the teacher or by their own choice.

Although partner reading and writing typically includes students with similar skills, it can also pair a more capable child with one who could benefit from peer tutoring.

Literature Circles

Literature circles can be formed for children to discuss books they have all read. Teachers need to model literature circles so that children can carry them out successfully without the teacher. The teacher begins by leading the discussion in the circle. Children are encouraged to place Post-it notes on spots in the book that they want to talk about. They all turn to the same page when discussing a particular part. A set of questions for discussion, adjusted by grade level, can help make circle conversations productive (see Resource 1.4, A1.3).

Children can be given different roles in the literature circle, such as the leader, who indicates who will speak when, and the recorder, who writes down important responses. In addition, students can be assigned specific questions to pose to others. Harvey Daniels' book *Literature Circles* (1994) provides useful information about this form of collaboration.

Writing Conferences

Writing conferences can be held between teachers and students or independently between students themselves. During peer conferences, children share pieces of their own writing for the purpose of hearing others' reactions to their writing or seeking guidance. Teachers need to model this activity to help children discuss others' writing constructively and in a supportive manner (Atwell 1987; Calkins 1994). Questions for discussion can help make the conference productive, such as

What are the good points about the piece of writing?

What could be improved?

Is the setting stated?

Is there a main character?

Does the main character have a problem to solve or a goal to achieve?

Are there episodes that help the main character solve the problem or attain the goal?

Does the story end with a resolution of the problem or attainment of the goal?

Is there an end to the story?

Organizing and Managing Collaborative Literacy Settings

Chapter 2 described how to design literacy centers in the classroom, and Chapters 3 and 4 suggested teacher-modeled, skills-oriented, pleasurable literacy center activities that engage children and motivate them to read and write. This section focuses on the organization and management of collaborative literacy settings in which children can work independently of the teacher.

Scheduling Literacy Center Time

When instituting literacy center arrangements in their classrooms, teachers hope to provide children with the learning opportunities that allow for social interaction, collaborative peer learning, self-direction, and practicing skills.

During literacy center time teachers model an activity or skill, and then children select whom they will work with. When groups have been formed, children choose the tasks they will undertake from among the available center activities (those that have been modeled that day or previously). They share what they have accomplished when the activities are completed.

During this time children can *choose* activities on which to work, alone or with others; *observe* literacy center activities by seeing peers and teachers engaged in them; *collaborate* with peers and be supported by more literate others; *practice* what has been learned; and *share* their accomplishments with peers and adults.

Literacy activities need to be integrated with content area studies, and subjects such as social studies, science, math, and art can provide the topics for practice of literacy skills.

To participate in literacy centers, children need to know the *choices* they have for activities; the *rules* that guide selection of materials and groups and what is to happen in those groups; the *guidelines* for cooperating with other members of the group; and some *accountability* expectations as a result of taking part in the group work. Independent collaborative settings require a strong, preplanned underlying structure that provides children with freedom within limits.

The literacy center arrangements described in this book are meant to fit within a total school program that provides students with more traditional explicit instruction as well. Typically, literacy center activities cannot take place throughout the whole school day. Also, the suggestions for managing such activities should be adapted to suit individual teaching and classroom needs.

We ask children to use literacy centers

- at special times designated during the school day, to promote independence, motivation, and process learning,

- in their "free time," when children have finished assigned tasks early,

- while teachers are working with small groups in guided reading instruction (see the later section Using Literacy Centers During Guided Reading).

Teachers should schedule literacy center time a few times per week for about thirty to forty-five minutes each time. During each period children choose an activity and decide with whom they will work.

Books and other materials placed in the centers by the teacher usually reflect a content area theme being studied or a literacy skill to be practiced. If children are learning about animals in science, for example, some of the books and materials would concern animals. Or if the class has discussed character study during storybook reading, an activity sheet or card might ask children to talk or write about characters in books they have read.

Structuring Literacy Center Activities and Groups

Learning How to Work in Groups

The rules for children to follow during literacy center time are reviewed before each session and posted (see Figure 5.1). In addition, guidelines for

Figure 5.1 Rules for Literacy Center Time

1. Decide whom you will work with or if you will work alone.
2. Choose a reading or writing activity.
3. Do only one or two activities in a period.
4. Materials can be used in or outside of the literacy center.
5. Be sure that what you do includes reading and writing.
6. Handle the materials carefully.
7. Speak in soft voices—people are working.
8. Put materials back in their place before taking another.
9. Try activities you haven't done before.
10. Try working with people you haven't worked with before.
11. Be ready to share your completed tasks with the class.
12. Record completed activities in your log.
13. Keep the literacy center neat.

Figure 5.2 Guidelines for Cooperating During Literacy Center Time

---

Helpful Things to Do When Working in Groups
Select a leader to help the group get started.
Select a recorder to write down what the group does.
Select a reporter to share the accomplishments of the
    group.
Give everyone a job.
Take turns talking.
Share materials.
Listen to your friends when they talk.
Stay with your group.

Helpful Things to Say When Working in Groups
Can I help you?
I like your work.
You did a good job.

Check Your Work
Did you say helpful things?
Did you help each other?
Did you share materials?
Did you take turns?
Did you all have jobs?
How well did your jobs get done?
What can we do better next time?

Figure 5.3 Group Activity Sign-up Sheet

Date group formed _____
Activity selected _____

Circle how long you think the activity will take to complete.
1 day   3 days   1 week   1 1/2 weeks   2 weeks

Members in the Group and Assigned Jobs
Leader _____
Recorder _____
Reporter _____
Other job assignments (list job and name):
_____
_____
_____

---

cooperation within groups, including helpful things to do and say, are taught and posted (see Figure 5.2). Both aids to working well in literacy centers can be photocopied and enlarged on colored sheets of paper, laminated, and displayed in centers for children to refer to.

Selecting Groups and Activities

Ideally, children decide with whom they want to work; then, once a group has been formed, they collectively decide what they would like to do. Or, children may select an activity from among those available and join a group based on that activity.

Sometimes, for various reasons, teachers assign children to groups but allow them to choose tasks from a specified array of activities. Or, teachers assign children both to the group and to the activity that they want children to participate in. Teachers have sometimes found it best to begin the school year with a more structured setting, where they assign groups and tasks. As children become familiar with center work and learn to function independently, they are given more opportunity for decision making. In addition, a teacher may want certain children to work/not work together or may want to group heterogeneously for practice of particular skills.

However groups and activities are chosen, it is helpful for children (in late first grade and up) to record on a group activity sheet the activity they will participate in and the names of the members in their group (see Figure 5.3). Children may also check items on a list activities they might like to do (see Figure 5.4). This sheet can be used at all grade levels, though teachers with kindergartners and early first graders often use pictures along with the words to depict activity choices. Photocopies of one or both sheets may be given to each child to fill out at the beginning of center time. As children arrive at a center, they sign up on a generic sign-up sheet, headed with Name and Date, that is posted in each center. A number posted at each center indicates how many children may use the center at one time, for instance, six at the author's spot. If the maximum number of children are already signed up and using the center, others will have to find alternative activities. For each center, there is a place to work, a sign-up sheet, and a number indicating how many students may participate at once.

Figure 5.4 Checklist of Activities to Do During Literacy Center Time

Name _____ Date _____

❑ 1. Read a book, magazine, or newspaper.

❑ 2. Read to a friend.

❑ 3. Listen so someone read to you.

❑ 4. Listen to a taped story and follow the words in the book.

❑ 5. Use the felt board with a storybook and felt characters.

❑ 6. Use the roll movie with its storybook.

❑ 7. Write a story.

❑ 8. Draw a picture about a story you read.

❑ 9. Make a book for a story you wrote.

❑ 10. Make a felt story for a book you read or a story you wrote.

❑ 11. Write a puppet show and perform it for friends.

❑ 12. Make a tape for a story you read or a story you wrote.

❑ 13. Record activities completed in logs.

❑ 14. Check out books to take home and read.

❑ 15. Use activity cards with directions for activities you do.

Roles Within Groups

With children in late first grade and up, once groups are formed and activities decided on, the role of different individuals within the group needs to be decided. There must be a leader, who will outline the tasks to be accomplished and help delegate assignments (e.g., who will write the story, who will draw the pictures for the roll movie) so that everyone has a job. There must also be a recorder, who will write down the jobs to be done and who is doing them. A reporter will share the accomplishments of the group. When working together, all the children must remember to take turns talking, to stay on task, and to be sure that everyone has a job related to the project.

Choosing Activities

A checklist like the one in Figure 5.4 can help children select activities. In addition, activity cards of varying levels of difficulty, which list steps for car-

rying out individual literacy activities, help children organize their work. Teachers of kindergarten and early first-grade children make activity cards with drawings for beginning or emergent readers. Activity cards are printed on colored paper, laminated, and placed in the centers for children to select and use.

Children's choice of activities may be determined by the materials and the space available. For example, they can't all choose to listen to taped stories if there are only five headsets. Teachers must devise systems to ensure that an appropriate number of children use each center at once. Besides posting a number in the center, as mentioned previously, this can be done by requiring each child to have an activity card for the center to be used, with the same number of activity cards printed as there is room in the center. For example, if there are only five headsets in the listening center, only five cards are printed. When the activity cards are in use, others must go to an alternative activity.

Practicing Participation in Collaborative Settings

One of the purposes of literacy center time is for children to read and write collaboratively. Children need time to practice the different behaviors necessary to function in social settings. Initially, the children's goal in the literacy center should be learning how to cooperate rather than to complete particular tasks. At first, some children may move from one activity to the next without completing any. As time passes, children will spend more time on projects, some of which may extend over several days or weeks. When literacy center time ends for the day and children haven't completed an activity, the project is stored for them to pick up later. Thus, teachers need to allow for storage space for unfinished activities.

Recording, Performing, and Evaluating Projects

When children work independently, they must learn to select goals and accomplish tasks. To provide encouragement, recording individual stu-

The bulletin board displays rules on how to participate in literacy center time and index cards hung on rings for recording books read. Cards in the file boxes on the table record books checked out of the classroom library.

dents' accomplishments is a good idea. The groups will record their accomplishments, but it is also useful for individual children to keep records of what they have done. There are different methods for doing this, for example, children can have a collection of index cards on which they record their accomplishments (e.g., titles of books read). The cards may be punched and hooked onto a ring that is hung on a bulletin board, or stored in file boxes. Students can maintain individual logs

After completing a literacy center task, Adasha records it in her log.

for recording completed tasks. Younger children and those who don't know English well can be given logs with pictures for them to circle activities in which they participated.

Children should also collect their original stories, poems, activity sheets, and other creations in individual manila folders or large envelopes. Just looking at what they have completed provides children with intrinsic rewards. These folders can also be shared with others in the class.

Sharing Completed Tasks

Children should share their accomplishments and can do so through a number of ways—book talks, demonstrations, reading what they've written, presenting an original puppet show, and so forth. Children evaluate their own projects, peers evaluate each other's, and teachers prepare evaluations as well. A few times a week, time is set aside for sharing accomplishments. The chance to show what they have done gives students an added reason for pursuing literacy activities.

The Role of the Teacher During Literacy Center Time

In addition to preparing the environment and modeling literacy activities, the teacher interacts with the children during literacy center time, in the following ways:

- Facilitates or initiates activities when children cannot get started alone.

- Guides or scaffolds literacy behaviors when help is needed.

- Participates in activities with children at their request.

- Observes activities and provides positive reinforcement for jobs well done.

To increase their supply of materials, teachers in different classes can share manipulatives and books. The children can also make materials for the literacy center, such as taped stories for the listening center and books, felt stories, and roll movies for others to use. Their original stories can be bound and made part of the classroom library. Participating in these activities increases students' motivation because they will feel an increased sense of partnership and respect for the area. Parents and older students can prepare materials. Teachers should work together in preparing materials.

Using Literacy Centers During Guided Reading Periods

Teachers conduct guided reading with small groups for specific instruction based on children's needs. For this to happen, the other children must be working, alone or collaboratively, independently of the teacher. The literacy center setting is ideal for meeting this need. Literacy center activities are engaging and relatively quiet, allow practice of skills, and require accountability for work done. The literacy center arrangements and activities that have been suggested can be just as successful while the teacher is occupied with guided reading as when center time has her full attention. If children have been introduced to center activities and rules, and are accustomed to them, they will work in centers independently and willingly when given the opportunity to do so. Nevertheless, some teachers have felt uncertain about assigning independent center work during guided reading periods: How should I organize center time? How can I be sure my students are on task? they ask. As with centers at all times, careful planning of activity choices and preparation of materials (including activity sheets and cards) as well as clearly stated expectations for accountability are essential.

During guided reading, center activities may be more structured than at other times. Activities that are available in centers may be limited to less active ones. Children may be assigned both to particular activities and to particular heterogeneous groups by the teacher. Each center group stays with an activity only as long as the teacher meets with one guided reading group. When the teacher changes to a new group for guided reading, the center groups all move to another designated center activity.

Teachers are often concerned that children who are in guided reading instruction miss out on center activities. But these children can be assigned to missed activities the next day. Because guided reading groups are based on need, usually only two or three children leave the heterogeneous center groups to attend guided reading for each instructional period.

A visit with Mr. Sass, a second-grade teacher, will provide a look at the organization of literacy center work during guided reading periods. The activities that Mr. Sass models for his class at such times are often skills- and theme-related. They are always familiar activities and in familiar places in the room. At the beginning of the school year, Mr. Sass spent time gradually introducing children to the centers and the types of activities they could do. He offered them opportunities to practice working on different activities at different centers. Early in the year, Mr. Sass did not conduct guided reading during literacy center time. He helped the children in the centers so that eventually they would be able to work independently.

Now, while Mr. Sass conducts guided reading, the children have some tasks they must do and others from which they can select. The tasks engage the children in reading and writing that will help their skills development. Activities 1–4 in the following list must be done by all. Activity 5 or 6 may be chosen by children after they have finished their required tasks.

Required Activities

1. *Partner Reading.* Children pair off and read the same book together. They may also read separate books and tell each other about the story they read. Since they are studying animals in the science unit, they are to select stories or expository texts about animals from the open-faced bookshelves. Discussion about what is read is encouraged. Each child must fill out an index card with the name of the book read and one sentence about the story.

2. *Writing.* Children are to rewrite the story that Mr. Sass read at the morning meeting, called *Ask Mr. Bear* (Flack). In their rewriting, they

are to include story elements discussed, such as setting, theme, plot episodes, and resolution. They may consult copies of the book from the classroom library. Each day a writing activity is assigned that is related to the story read; however, the writing assignments vary.

3. *Working with Words.* Children are to find words in signs around the room that have the *sh* and *ch* digraphs in them. They then classify these words by writing them on a sheet of paper under appropriate digraph headings. They may look through books to find these digraphs as well.

4. *Listening Center.* Children listen to taped stories about animals. For each story, there is a sheet of paper with a question to answer about the story. Two titles on tape for this unit about animals are *Is Your Mama a Llama?* (Guarino) and *Arthur's Pet Business* (Marc Brown).

Optional Activities

5. *Art Center.* Children may create animal collages with pictures from the many magazines in the center.

6. *Computer Center.* Children may play math or literacy games.

Figures 5.5 and 5.6 show the rules made up by Mr. Sass and his students for children to follow

Figure 5.5 Rules for Using Materials and Completing Work

1. Do all required jobs before you do the optional jobs.
2. Speak in soft voices—people are working.
3. Put materials back in their place.
4. Take care of the materials so they are in good condition for others.
5. Put your completed work in a designated place.
6. Record completed work on contract form or in a log.
7. Use "Ask Three and Then Me" rule if you have questions. Ask students designated as helpers before asking the teacher when he is in a guided reading group.

Figure 5.6 Rules for Cooperating in Groups

1. Share materials.
2. Take turns.
3. Listen to your friends when they talk.
4. Offer help to others you are working with if they need it.
5. When you complete an activity, ask yourself if you were helpful to others and if you shared materials.

when working in literacy centers during guided reading periods. He also provides a checklist of activities to do during guided reading, similar to the one shown in Figure 5.4 except that the first five of the eight activities listed are required and must be finished before starting optional work. Mr. Sass uses a center chart to rotate groups of children through the centers (see Resource 1.5). The rotations occur in coordination with guided reading periods: when the latter change, the center groups move on to another center. If children finish a required activity before rotation time, they may start one of the optional activities or go on to the next required task if there is space at the center. There is a basket for completed work, and every center requires some type of accountability in the way of sign-up sheets and a finished product to be handed in.

Ms. Holt, another second-grade teacher, also assigns children to center activities when she is occupied with guided reading instruction, and the center groups rotate in coordination with the guided reading periods. Her students sit at "pods" of four desks pushed together. Each pod group is heterogeneous and moves from one center activity to another as indicated on a center chart. From time to time, Ms. Holt changes the pod groups so that children have a chance to work with various others. The pod groups often give themselves names. Later in the school year, children may select activities from a designated list in any order they wish, and when they have finished an activity, they may go on to the next.

Both teachers know that the management of center time is crucial to its success. Students must be clear about the choices before them, the activities in which to participate, the rules that guide participation and use of materials, and what is expected of them.

Assessing the Literacy Center Program

Evaluating the success of the literacy center program should be done regularly. Teachers need to discuss with each other the physical design of their centers and how they could be improved. They need to share new ideas for using literature to develop comprehension and word study skills. They need to talk about issues concerning collaborative settings, for example, how to help children who are not on task, how to encourage different children to work together, how to help children try different tasks, and how to make sure that everyone has a leadership role at some time. When teachers meet, they gain a cooperative support system and an opportunity to learn from each other. Meetings give teachers the chance to experience firsthand what it feels like to participate in a cooperative setting, so that they can better understand how their children feel and the help they may need.

Teachers are very concerned about on-task behavior during center time. We can more easily see when children are off-task during this time than when they participate in whole-group lessons. We need to keep reinforcing rules and varying activities children may choose. Centers can be changed to increase the productivity of the students. For example, teachers often move literacy centers from one area of the room to another because they find a space that is bigger, brighter, or quieter. They add materials, such as books and manipulatives, to give children more choices. When necessary, changes can also be made in how literacy center time is managed.

Children's progress can be documented by recording anecdotes of activities, collecting writing samples, and audiotaping or videotaping groups at work and performances of completed

activities. Children should be involved in self-evaluation. They can evaluate how they cooperated and the quality of their completed tasks. When finished projects are presented to the class, peers can offer constructive criticism. Children should be given the opportunity to make suggestions for improving the program and to identify books and other materials they would like added to centers.

Families and Literacy Center Time

In previous chapters we discussed literacy-rich home environments where children are motivated to read and write by parents who provide models by doing so themselves. These parents read to their children and discuss issues related to literacy in their daily routines. They provide literacy materials in the home—books, magazines, newspapers, pencils, crayons, markers, and paper of all kinds.

Families should be an integral part of children's literacy learning in school as well. Teachers should keep families informed about classroom

All family members are welcome at the literacy center. Eight-week-old Cody and his mother are visiting here.

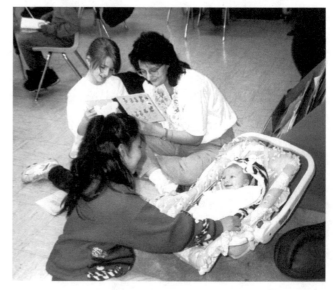

activities and invite them to take part in literacy center time. All family members are welcome—parents, brothers, sisters, aunts, uncles, grandparents, and friends. They can come to watch, to participate as the children do, or to read to the class. They can share their cultural heritage by telling stories about the countries they come from or by reading stories from that culture. Children take pride in having family members participate in classroom activities, and family members enjoy the time they spend in the centers and learning about their children's literacy activities in school. Figure 5.7 shows a sample invitation to families to take part in literacy center time.

Figure 5.7 Sample Invitation to Families for Literacy Center Time

HELP WANTED   HELP WANTED   HELP WANTED   HELP WANTED

Dear Families,
   We want to invite you to come to school to participate in our literacy center time. This is a time when children read and write together, choosing materials and activities they would like to do. We want you to read and write with them, and you can take part in many ways. Below is a form listing the types of things you could do during literacy center time and a space for you to let us know the time of day and date that you can attend. We are flexible and will arrange our time for literacy center activities when it is convenient for you to come. After you visit once, you will want to come again, and we want you to come as often as possible. All family members are welcome—younger brothers and sisters, babies, aunts, uncles, grandparents, and friends as well as parents.
   Please come, get involved in your child's education, and help us form a true home and school partnership.
   Sincerely,
   Ms. Tofel and her fourth-grade class

Please fill out the following form and send it back to school with your child.

Come and Visit School During Literacy Center Time
Your name _____
Your child's name _____
The days I can come during the week are _____.
The time of day I can come to school is _____.

When I come to school I would like to do the following:
   1. Just watch what the children are doing. _____
   2. Participate with the children in literacy center time. _____
   3. Read to a small group of children. _____
   4. Read to the whole class. _____
   5. I am from another country and would like to tell the children about my country and show them clothing, pictures, and books from there. _____
   6. I have a hobby and would like to share it with the class.
      My hobby is _____.
   7. I have a talent and I would like to share it with the class.
      My talent is _____.
   8. I'd like to tell the children about my job. My job is _____.
   9. Other ideas about what you would like to do? _____

6

Scenes from the Literacy Center

atrick had several copies of the story *Franklin in the Dark* (Bourgeois), which he handed out to the other children. He also had a Big Book of the story. He asked his friends to sit in a circle and took the role of leader or teacher. He began to read. After a while, he asked if anyone would like to have a turn, and Lisa volunteered. When Lisa had trouble with a word, Patrick helped her. Later Tiffany asked to be the leader teacher, and Patrick agreed to let her have a turn. When they had finished reading the story, Tiffany started a discussion about it. She asked if any of the children were afraid of the dark and if they would tell the group about something they were afraid of. A serious and enthusiastic conversation about what the children were afraid of then took place. Each child then wrote down on an activity sheet something he was afraid of.

During literacy center time, interactions such as this one occur frequently. Over the years I have collected hundreds of hours' worth of field notes and videotapes of classrooms that used literacy center time and other collaborative strategies to motivate children's reading and writing. My purpose was to see firsthand the nature of the activities that took place and their results. I also wanted to determine the processes involved in cooperative literacy activity that promoted independent reading and writing. In addition to the field notes and videotapes, interviews with teachers and children also helped me better understand the literacy activity that occurred during literacy center time (Morrow 1992; Sharkey 1992).

My classroom observations and videotapes revealed a variety of collaborative literacy behaviors occurring during literacy center time, self-directed activities that involved children in decisions about what to do and how to carry through with their plans. Whether reading, writing, or working on word study activities, most students worked in groups of two to five that involved both peer collaboration and peer tutoring. Overall, groups were friendly and mixed in gender, race, ethnicity, and ability, and included children with special needs. Children took charge of their own learning. They read orally and silently, they wrote, they worked with words, and they demonstrated literal, interpretive, and critical comprehension. The best way to describe the processes that occur during literacy center time is to present anecdotes recorded during classroom visits. The observations include choices made by students, choices made by teachers, and choices made by both students and teachers.

Collaborative Activities During Literacy Center Time

How Groups Formed

When making decisions about whether to work alone or with others, and if with others, with whom, children tended to observe groups before joining them. For example, Kim, Alexandria, and Tarene were reading joke and riddle books in a private spot sectioned off for reading. They snuggled together as they read. Damien stood nearby and watched for a while, listening attentively as the jokes and riddles were read. Once he understood the nature of the group's activity, he asked to be included. The three allowed him to join them.

Some groups formed according to gender. At various times there were all-boy groups and all-girl groups, but overall 41 percent of the groups I

Patrick had his friends sit in a circle and took the role of teacher. He began to read and asked the others if they'd like a turn.

Children formed groups, some according to gender. At various times there were all-boy and all-girl groups, but 41 percent of groups observed were of mixed gender.

observed were mixed-gender groups. When groups formed by gender, their members often carried out activities that one could call sex-stereotyped. The activities of mixed-gender groups were not sex-stereotyped. Here are some examples (Morrow 1996, 60):

> Amber and Jessica searched the index of a cookbook and read out the foods they liked. Jessica pointed to the phrase "chocolate chips" and said, "Look, Amber, on page 42 they have something with chocolate chips. Let's look at that." When they found the page, Amber said, "Wow, it's chocolate chip cookies. They're my favorite. Let's see how you make them."

> Matthew, Scott, and Andre worked on a roll movie for the story *Kick, Pass, and Run* (Kessler). Matthew said, "Yo, you guys! Scott, you draw the football field, and Andre, you do the stands. I'll do the goal post."

> Mary, Tina, Jason, and Kevin were writing an original story and created felt figures to use on the felt board to present it to the class. When they finished, they decided to tape the story. The group designated Mary as the reader. Tina and Jason read silently as they

followed along with her. Kevin followed the story and placed the felt characters on the felt board as they were mentioned. Tina and Jason made sound effects as needed for the story. After the taping, they played it back. They all listened and giggled.

As mentioned earlier, groups ranged in size from two to five; however, groups of two were the most common. Groups larger than five seemed to have trouble dealing with conflict. When groups had more than five, one child would often leave on her own. Girls tended to form groups of two most of the time, whereas all-boy and mixed groups were typically larger. The number of children in self-selected groups suggests that when teachers form groups they should keep the maximum number at five.

Although working cooperatively in groups was quite common, many children also chose to work alone. They usually read silently, but some did felt stories and chalk talks by themselves. Equal numbers of boys and girls chose to work alone.

Rules and Leadership Roles

Once formed, whether by the teacher or the students, groups established their own rules and leadership roles. The rules involved decisions about the work that was to be accomplished, the responsibilities of the members for that work, and the quality of work that was acceptable. For example, Tesha and Cassandra decided to work together with a felt board story of *The Gingerbread Boy* (Galdone). They decided that they wanted to work on the floor. Cassandra told Tesha to carry the book and the felt characters and said she would bring the felt board. Tesha said, "We need to work together to do this, and we have to hurry in order to finish because we don't have much time." Cassandra said, "You read first and I'll put up the felt characters. When we are halfway through the story, then I'll read and you put up the characters." The girls began the story, and halfway through, they switched roles. When they came to the rhyme "Run, run as fast as you can; you can't catch me, I'm the gingerbread man," they read together, laughing and saying how much fun they were having.

Within most groups, leaders emerged who were respected by other children. Ryan, Alex, and Gabe were working on the illustrations for a story they had written called "The Golden Sword." They spread out a large picture of a castle, and Ryan began to outline it in black marker.

Ryan: Alex, go get a black marker and help me outline this.

Gabe: Where should I start?

Ryan: Right over here. (*Alex returns with the marker.*) Alex, go get a red crayon.

Alex: Why, Ryan?

Ryan: Because we forgot to color this.

Alex: Will a red pencil do?

Ryan: I guess so. But Alex, we also need a blue crayon.

Alex: What do we need it for?

Ryan: We forgot to color in the water over here.

Gabe: What color should I do the sky?

Ryan: Blue will look good. (Morrow 1996, 61–62)

Collaboration Within Groups

When groups formed, their members collaborated by helping each other, taking turns, sharing materials, and offering information. For example, Adasha and Tiffany decided to do a felt story together. Adasha said, "I want to do this one, *Cloudy with a Chance of Meatballs*" (Barrett).

Tiffany said, "Let's do *Animals Should Definitely Not Wear Clothing*" (Barrett).

"I know," said Adasha, "We'll do them both. They both have the same author and illustrator."

The girls decided to read *Cloudy with a Chance of Meatballs* first. Margaret and Tracey joined them but sat quietly while Adasha moved the felt figures on the board and Tiffany read. When the story was finished, Margaret asked if she and Tracey could read. Everyone agreed but decided that they would read the other book, *Animals Should Definitely Not Wear Clothing*. Margaret read and Tracey moved the felt figures, and Adasha and Tiffany listened.

Peer Tutoring

Peer tutoring was frequent, with one child offering guidance and assistance to a peer who needed help. Children often whispered words and hints to help each other with words, spelling, or decisions about literacy projects. The help was often reciprocal: students would offer equal amounts of help to each other. They sought each other's opinions and offered positive reinforcement to each other. For example, Esther and Charo were reading a book of rhymes. Although both children also attended basic skills classes, in this situation Charo was able to take the typical teacher's role and help Esther with words she didn't know. Charo opened the book and selected a rhyme. Esther looked at the page and started to read, "'Old Mother . . .' What does that next word say?" Charo said, "That says 'Hubbard.' Now you read the rest." Esther continued, "'She went to the . . .'" She paused and Charo helped again: "It says 'cupboard.' See, it rhymes with 'Hubbard.'" "Oh, yeah," said Esther, and she continued to read, "'to get her poor dog a bone.'"

Children tutor each other as they work together writing stories by hand or on the computer.

Charo said, "Wait, Esther, we forgot. You gotta read it again, and this time start with the title of the poem first."

Conflicts

Although cooperation was more evident than conflict during group activities, conflicts did occur. Many involved selecting specific activities, sharing materials, and taking turns, and most were easily resolved. Other conflicts concerned specific questions within the activities themselves—deciding how to spell a word, identifying a word from the printed page, determining how to write a story cooperatively. Such conflicts were usually settled by discussion, by looking up words in a dictionary, or by seeking help from others. Learning theories suggest that learning occurs when conflict arises and those involved figure out how to settle it (Piaget and Inhelder 1969). The following episode demonstrates one such incident.

Zarah and Shakiera were writing a story together that they called "A Fish Called Wanda." Zarah wrote the title, "A Fish Called Wander." Shakiera looked at it and said, "That's not the way you spell *Wanda*. It's W-A-N-D-A, not W-A-N-D-E-R." Zarah looked at her title and disagreed. "I'm right," she insisted. "I wrote a story about how I wander around my house and that is the way I spelled it, and it was right."

Shakiera then said, "You've got the words mixed up. *Wanda* is a name, and *wander* is when

you walk around, do you understand?" Reluctantly, Zarah agreed that Shakiera must be right, and she changed the spelling of the word.

Zarah continued writing while Shakiera dictated: "A fish called Wanda was a talking fish who had magic."

Zarah commented, "She had more than magic. She had magic powers."

"But that's what *magic* means," said Shakiera. "It means you have powers, so you don't have to say it."

"I think you do," said Zarah, "so that people really know how strong she was."

"I guess that's okay," said Shakiera. "You can write that she had magic powers."

Literacy Behaviors

Students' collaborative behaviors centered on literacy activities during literacy center time. The activities they engaged in were active and used manipulatives. The activities fell into five categories: oral reading, silent reading, writing, comprehension development, and word study.

Oral Reading

Oral reading was a common practice during literacy center time. Oral reading provides practice with pronunciation, intonation, pacing, fluency, and performance. It also provides the teacher with evaluative information concerning reading proficiency. During literacy center time children read aloud in pairs, in small groups, and alone. They shared books, magazines, and newspapers. For example, Larry took the book *The Magic School Bus Lost in the Solar System* (Cole) from a bookshelf in the library corner. "I gotta read this book again," he said to Bryan. "It's neat." The boys sat down on the carpet. Shon, who was standing nearby, asked if he could read too, and they agreed. Larry began reading, then Bryan took a turn and so did Shon. They listened attentively to each other. When they finished, the boys chose another book to read together (Morrow 1996, 64).

Children selected narrative stories to read as well as expository texts associated with content areas they were studying. Mercedes and Patricia selected a book that was featured in their science unit on the changing earth: *Bringing the Rain to Kapiti Plain* (Aardema). They decided to read it and use felt figures to illustrate the story. Patricia got the book, and Mercedes brought over the felt board and story characters. Patricia said she would read, and Mercedes agreed to place the figures on the board at the right time. Patricia read aloud, and Mercedes followed along in the book. When they finished reading, they discussed the story. They agreed that it was good that it finally rained because there was a drought in the jungle and all the animals were thirsty and would have died, and all the plants were brown and dying.

With many children in classrooms, the opportunity for oral reading is limited and often tedious for those who are made to listen. In the literacy center, children choose to read orally often and others may choose to listen or not, making the oral reading experience both productive and pleasant. Asking children to read orally in front of others can be unpleasant and threatening, yet during literacy center time children willingly participate in oral reading without being asked.

Silent Reading

Research has demonstrated a relationship between the amount of time spent reading and reading achievement (Anderson, Wilson and Fielding 1988; Morrow 1990; Taylor, Frye, and Maruyama 1990).

Silent reading was apparent in many observations of literacy center time. Children read alone and sometimes together. They would curl up on a rug, leaning against pillows or each other, holding stuffed animals as they read. They read at their desks, in the closets, and under desks and tables. One child read silently while walking slowly around the classroom. One group I observed was typical: Jon was sitting in the rocking chair with Jenny, reading. Ben was leaning against a pillow reading the newspaper, and Jessy was leaning against him so he could read from the newspaper, too. Doreen and Kelly were in the coat closet reading the same book together, and David was sprawled on the rug with *Space Rock* (Buller and Schade).

In interviews both children and teachers said that the reading children were doing during literacy center time—both oral and silent reading—was improving their ability as readers and writers, especially since they were doing so much of it. They also said that the help with reading that was readily available from peers and their teacher during literacy center time made them better at reading.

Children also chose to do silent content area reading during their time in the literacy center. For example, one group of children decided to continue their study of plants, a science unit they were studying. As they were looking for books to read, Jovanna said, "Hey, you guys, I have an idea. Let's all read a book about plants." She went to the featured plant books, which were displayed because plants was the topic being studied in science, and distributed them to group members. "Who wants *The Poison Ivy Case* [Lexau]?" Phillip took that one. Next Jovanna held up *A Tree Is Nice* (Urdy). Tyshell asked for that one. The next book was *Johnny Appleseed* (Moore). Adasha raised her hand, and Jovanna gave that one to her. There were two left: *Discovering Trees* (Florian) and *Cherries and Cherry Pits* (Williams). Jovanna said, "Josh, I think you'll like *Discovering Trees*, and Kendra, you take *Cherries and Cherry Pits*." They took their books, found a spot on the rug, and began reading. When they finished, each took a turn telling about the stories.

Writing

Initially literacy center time was simply to be a time for independent reading. But children either asked for writing materials or found them on their own and began writing. They used the materials in the literacy center for writing as well as reading. They wrote new episodes for Harold in *Harold and the Purple Crayon* (Johnson). They wrote stories about the puppets and felt characters. Their writing was based on their interest, experiences, current events, and fiction they had read. Stories were written about news events, sports, and topics being studied in class, such as plants or dinosaurs. Children made up episodes for popular television shows. Others created computer games with illustrations and dialogue. Still others wrote biographies about popular rock stars with illustrations cut from magazines.

Children wrote in pairs and small groups more often than alone, and their writing projects sometimes lasted for an entire period or longer. Such projects often became performances presented to the class in the form of puppet shows, roll movies, stories with musical backgrounds, plays with scenery, and so forth. The projects were self-sponsored and self-directed by the children. Here is an incident related to narrative writing: Paul and Kevin are writing together. Paul said, "I'm writing a series of stories. Each book is a different part but about the same character. I have 'The Horse Named Jack,' 'Jack Becomes a Police Horse,' and now I'm on the third, called 'Jack Enters a Horse Race.'" Kevin asked, "Can I read the one where he's a police horse?" Paul answered, "Okay, but you really should read 'The Horse Named Jack' first since they go in order" (Morrow 1996).

As with reading, writing occurred all over the classroom. In one case, the table at the author's spot could fit only about three children, so students wrote sitting on the floor and at their desks.

Children collaborating on writing projects selected topics from their content area studies, such as dinosaurs, space, and the changing earth.

They often moved their desks together to make a large work surface at which they all could write together.

In interviews teachers and children said that the children's writing was improving because they did so much of it. Teachers expressed surprise that children who would never write before were now choosing to do so. They were also amazed at the variety of topics children wrote about.

Comprehension Development

Understanding what is read is the goal for proficient reading. Comprehension occurs at literal, inferential, and critical levels. Typically it is taught by posing questions for children to answer after they have read a passage. This activity is actually more of a test than a teaching approach. It does not involve the child actively in constructing meaning from text. During literacy center time, however, children were actively involved in constructing meaning, and they demonstrated comprehension at literal, inferential, and critical levels.

Literal comprehension requires the ability to remember and demonstrate an understanding of the facts, sequence, and structural elements of a story. Christopher and Albert, for example, demonstrated this level of comprehension when they decided to retell *Amelia Bedelia's Family Album* (Parish) using a roll movie. Chris told the story as Albert rolled the paper in the box to the appropriate scene. Chris retold the story using the dialogue from the book and included details of the story as he went along.

Inferential comprehension requires children to think beyond the text and involves understanding the characters' feelings, predicting outcomes, or putting oneself in the place of a character to determine another course of action—in other words, going beyond the simple facts and explicit statements of a story. For example, Darren decided to retell *Frog and Toad Are Friends* (Lobel). He retold the story with puppets, changing his voice and inflection as he interpreted the different characters.

Critical comprehension requires hypothesizing, analyzing, judging, and drawing conclusions.

This level of thinking entails making comparisons and distinguishing fact from opinion. Corey and Michael decided to listen to the taped story of *The Mitten* (Brett). As they listened with headsets, they read along and shared a copy of the book. When they finished, Corey said, "You know, that story is a total fantasy. Does that author really expect us to believe that all of those animals fit into that little boy's mitten?" Michael said, "Well, you know, this is a folktale and lots of those have stuff in them that isn't true, except I think they want you to believe it is." Corey continued, "Well, maybe little kids would believe that this really happened, but I don't." Corey demonstrated critical comprehension in his discussion with Michael about whether the story of *The Mitten* could possibly be true.

In self-directed activities during literacy center time, children demonstrated their comprehension of stories in almost every incident recorded. None of these incidents involved the presence of a teacher or a lesson prepared by the teacher with questions for children to respond to. Interview data revealed that children were aware that their comprehension was being enhanced during literacy center time. When asked, "What do you learn during LCT?" half the children responded that you learn to understand what you are reading and you learn a lot of new words. All the teachers mentioned that children were enhancing their comprehension, their sense of story structure, and their vocabulary development in the literacy center.

Word Study

Word study is a necessary part of reading development. Children must be able to decode in order to comprehend. Ability in the following skills will help with decoding: phonemic awareness; knowledge of print-sound correspondence, structural analysis, and syllabication; recognizing sight words; and using picture clues and the semantics and syntax of text to help decode words (Adams 1990).

Children engaged in these activities readily. Most were carried out using manipulatives and gamelike materials, and were reinforced by completing an activity sheet. A common scene was two children working with onset and rime letter cards to create as many words as they could for a particular phonogram. Tim and Brad worked next to each other with their own cards. They created a contest to see who could come up with the most words ending in *-ight*. Each had five words when time was up. Tim had *tight, right, bright, night,* and *light.* Brad had *right, night, light, sight,* and *kight.* Tim said he didn't think *kight* was a real word because he knew that the kite one flew was spelled with *-ite* and not with *-ight.* They decided to look in the dictionary. They found out that Tim was right. Both children then wrote the words they had created on an activity sheet prepared for that activity. Brad thought of the word *flight* to fill in for the one that wasn't correct.

Appreciation for Reading and Writing

The ultimate goal of reading instruction is to develop the student into a person who has a positive attitude toward reading, appreciates and enjoys reading, and therefore will read. Children must associate reading with pleasure in order to read more and improve their reading ability. The fact that children engaged in literacy activities independently and in a self-directed manner was evidence of their positive attitudes toward literacy. There were few discipline problems during literacy center time, and few children were off-task. The interview data consistently reflect positive attitudes. Children interviewed said such things as, "Reading and writing is fun. During this time it makes you happy, it makes you like to read and write because you can choose what you want to do and where you want to do it. You can get to decide if you want to read or write alone or with others. If you choose to work with others, you can decide who you will work with." Teachers agreed with the children; they said their students liked the element of choice—of activity, of place and space to work, and with whom to work.

One episode in particular seems to encapsulate the pleasure children felt during literacy center time. Yassin was leaning on a pillow on the carpet reading a story. When he finished reading the

book, he sat up, raised the book over his head, and exclaimed out loud but to himself, "This is such a lovely story, it makes me feel so good, I think I'll read it again." He settled back down to his former position and began to read (Morrow 1996, 69).

Voluntary Participation by Children with Special Needs

The ability to participate voluntarily and in a cooperative fashion during literacy center time was a positive outcome for the children I observed. They enjoyed the literacy center a great deal, and they were able to stay on-task. An important finding I made while working with the literacy center program over the years is the response of children who have difficulty learning. Many children with special needs were in classrooms where this program took place. A large percentage attended basic skills classes because their development in reading and writing was considered below grade level. There were also children

Corine, who is designated as learning disabled, takes a lead role when reading a script for a puppet show she wrote.

who attended English as a Second Language classes and children with social or emotional problems. All these children participated in literacy center activities as much as the children in the class without specifically designated learning problems. In fact, classroom observers often did not know which students fell into these groups until the teachers pointed them out. These children often emerged as leaders and found activities in which they excelled, and their special needs were often not obvious during this time.

All children were welcomed as group members. Individual differences did not seem to be an issue in the cooperative learning environment. For example, when Anita entered class in late fall, she spoke only Spanish. Unsurprisingly, she did not initially participate in literacy center activities. A few weeks later, however, she began to participate in activities, though always alone. One day, she selected a book from the literacy center and sat down on the rug to look at it. Lindsay sat down next to her and asked if Anita would like her to read the story to her. Lindsay understood Anita's smile to mean yes. She read, at the same time pointing to items in the illustrations and naming them for Anita, who after a while began to repeat the words. Lindsay seemed proud of herself for helping Anita, and Anita was proud of the fact that she was learning some English. But most of all, she was happy because she had found a friend. The two read together often during literacy center time.

Yassin was repeating second grade and receiving basic skills instruction. Yet he emerged as a leader during literacy center time, frequently organizing and carrying out projects with other children. One time he decided to make a taped story. He stimulated the interest of James, Roseangela, Tamika, and Tara. He selected the story and delegated responsibilities, deciding who would read which pages, when the group would choral-read certain parts, and where they would include musical background in their tape. With completion of the tape several days later, it was presented to the class and placed in the literacy center for further use.

Jonathan had been classified as an "elective mute": he never spoke. During literacy center time, he often sat on the rug and silently read books about sports. Other children sometimes sat next to him, looked on, and seemed to read from the same book with him. On several occasions, from recording on videotapes and reports by observers and his teacher, Jonathan was observed discussing the books with classmates around him—the only time anyone had seen or heard him speak during the entire school day.

During interviews teachers commented that there seemed to be something for everyone in the literacy center. Children lacking in basic skills found literacy activities they could enjoy and succeed at. ESL children found ways to participate, and the literacy center appeared to be an excellent environment for enhancing language development. Children with emotional problems who tended to be withdrawn or disruptive became productive participants. Children with special needs participated in conventional reading and writing activities, though reading and writing using manipulatives occurred more often and was a motivating factor for these children.

Family Participation

During guided reading instruction, adult family members can help to supervise independent work in centers by making sure children stay on-task, helping with problems that arise, and providing explanations so that teachers can work without interruption in guided reading groups.

When no small-group instruction is occurring, family members can become an integral part of literacy center activities. Their involvement starts slowly and catches on with time. They sit on the rug and read to small groups of children, or they sit in the rocking chair and read to the entire group. They share their special talents, hobbies, interests, and cultural backgrounds, tied to what students are studying. In a unit on immigration to the United States, several family members who were immigrants themselves came during literacy center time to discuss their experiences and show artifacts from their countries.

For a unit on immigration to the United States, several family members came to the literacy center to tell about their experiences and show artifacts from their countries. Often their children translated from their language to English.

Teacher Participation

In most classroom settings both students and teachers experience constraints (Bossert 1979). In conventional recitation settings, teachers control how long a child may talk and on what subject, and students' opportunities to speak are limited (Sirotnik 1983). The teacher is also limited. Giving too much attention to one student reduces instructional time for others and may cause the group to lose focus.

The role of the teaching during literacy center time differs depending on the goal. When the teacher is meeting with groups for guided reading, it is the teacher's job to teach children how to work independently at the center so she can work with individuals and not be interrupted. The class practices working with center activities before the teacher is able to meet with groups.

During literacy center time, when there is no guided reading instruction or conferences being held by teachers, they can respond to the questions of one student or group without affecting the productivity of the others. In fact, the multitask structure of the literacy center, with its emphasis on collaborative learning, changed the teacher's role from information giver to "guide on the side." For example, as their teacher, Ms. Pelovitz, circulated near where Sarah and Kim were writing a story, Kim asked Ms. Pelovitz how to spell *suddenly*. She spelled the word and then asked "Okay, suddenly what?" She then worked with Kim and Sarah to develop the story further. After Sarah had read a portion of the story, Ms. Pelovitz asked, "Since you talk about your sister making you mad, why not write about why she makes you mad?" Sarah said, "Okay, let's see, well she sits by the phone all day waiting for it to ring for her and when it does, it is always her friends." Ms. Pelovitz smiled and said to Sarah, "That would make me angry, too."

During literacy center time the teacher acts as a participator and a facilitator, and offers positive reinforcement. For example, Ms. Pelovitz sat down by Patrick, Lewis, James, Tiffany, and Shani to look at a roll movie they had just finished for *Mister Rabbit and the Lovely Present* (Zolotow). She congratulated the group for a job well done. She then became the audience as the students performed the roll movie story again for her. She commented at the end that the pictures were very vivid. James said he didn't know what *vivid* meant, so Ms. Pelovitz defined the word for him. Before leaving the group she said, "If Maurice Sendak, the illustrator of this story, were to walk in the door of our room right now, he would think that he had drawn the pictures for the movie. Your work looks as good as his."

Although the teacher's being able to respond spontaneously as events unfold in the literacy center benefits both the children and herself, independent center work can still go on without it. If, during the first part of the school year, children have been well grounded in how independent work in literacy centers is conducted, and have had practice with it, they will likely be willing and able to continue literacy center activities on their own while the teacher is occupied with guided reading instruction or conferences later in the year.

I have noticed that when teachers participate in literacy center time, they are generally relaxed because they do not feel the pressure of having to hold the attention of all the students at once. In my observations they were usually friendly and pleasant toward the students and generally more flexible than during recitation periods.

Teachers' Evaluation of Literacy Center Time

Teachers acted as facilitators, instructors, and participants during literacy center time. They helped children get organized, they gave instructional assistance when asked for, they participated with children and read their own books. They participated socially, interacting in a friendly manner with students.

Teachers' interview comments were extremely consistent. They reported that at first they were concerned about having enough time for literacy center periods but that they gradually figured out how to make time. They came to see literacy center periods as an integral part of their reading instruction program. Teachers were initially skeptical about getting children to work on-task independently, but they were able to work through most problems. When asked what they had learned from participating in literacy center time, their responses were interesting and revealing:

- Center time during guided reading gives me a chance to attend to individual students' needs.

- Children are capable of cooperating and collaborating voluntarily and independently in reading and writing activities and learning from each other.

- In an atmosphere that provided choice of activity and work partners, children of all ability levels chose to work together, which did not normally occur. There was something for everyone in this program.

- It is the first time I realized that independent reading and writing periods are crucial for learning to read and write.

- It is the first time I realized how important it is for me to model reading and writing for children and to interact with them during literacy center time.

- It made me more flexible and spontaneous and a facilitator of learning rather than always teaching.

- It taught me how to make reading and writing more appealing for children.

- I learned that commercial instructional materials served to organize children's skill development, specifically in the area of word recognition. The literacy center program emphasized the practice of word recognition, vocabulary, and comprehension. Both programs complemented each other and should be used simultaneously.

- Children who don't readily participate in reading and writing did so during literacy center time. I think it is because they are the ones making the decisions about what they do.

When asked what students liked about the literacy center program, and what they had learned from it, teachers responded as follows:

- Students liked choices and self-directed activities, such as whether to read or write alone or with others and whether to use story manipulatives such as felt boards or taped stories alone or with others.

- Students liked teacher-directed literature activities: being read to by the teacher, and the teacher's demonstrating creative storytelling with puppets and music.

- Students liked the comfort of the literacy center—the rocking chair, the rug, the pillows, the stuffed animals—and being comfortable while reading.

- Students learned many literacy skills. Vocabulary, comprehension, and sense of story structure were improved. Skills that had been taught were reinforced. Their knowledge about authors and illustrators increased.

- Students displayed a positive attitude toward reading. They said they like to read, and they participated in literacy center time voluntarily and with enthusiasm.

I have received many letters from children in classes where teachers have literacy center time. I'd like to conclude this book by sharing some with you:

Dear Dr. Morrow,

Thank you for telling my teacher about literacy center time. It makes reading more fun than it really is. I always look forward to it every day. We don't get to have it every day, but I ask anyway.

From

Thomas Smith

Dear Dr. Morrow,

Thank you for giving us the idea for literacy centers and literacy center time. A lot of kids like it. I am doing a report on a story about *The Haunted Well* book, it is going to be a felt story. I am also helping my friend she is doing a stick puppet show on *Elizabeth Blackwell*. I have not done my characters yet but I am going to do them soon. Most of the time I help my friend and sometimes I work on my story.

From

Michelle Highland

Dear Dr. Morrow,

Thank you for teaching my teacher about literacy centers and literacy center time. It is very interesting and fun. Please tell these teachers how to do it too, Mrs. Riger, Mrs. Minor, and Mrs. Mitchille, they really need it in their classrooms. Do you have any more ideas like that for school? If you do, then please, please tell them to my teacher and the other ones I mentioned too.

Sincerely,

Michael Toffey

Organization and Management of the Literacy Center

This section provides early childhood and elementary education teachers (pre-K–5) with resources and suggestions for organizing and managing children's independent collaborative work both during literacy center time and while the teacher is occupied with guided reading instruction. The lessons include specific ways to organize materials and to encourage the use of the literacy center to promote children's voluntary reading and writing.

The lessons and materials provided are as follows:

1.1 Introduction to literacy center time
   A1.1 Book checkout form on index card
1.2 Checking books out of the classroom library
1.3 Keeping a record of books read
1.4 Using activity cards
   A1.2 Activity cards to develop comprehension
   A1.3 Activity cards for word study
   A1.4 Log forms for completed activities
1.5 Using a center chart
   A1.5 Additional icons for center chart
   A1.6 Accountability forms for completed work
1.6 Sharing completed tasks
   A1.7 Bookmark for children

RESOURCE
1.1 Introduction to Literacy Center Time

Purpose

- To introduce materials in the literacy center
- To establish rules for literacy center time

Materials

See "Materials for Creating a Literacy Center" below.

Activity

1. Bring children into the literacy center. Explain that they will have the opportunity to engage in daily literacy activities using the many books and materials available.
2. Introduce and demonstrate a limited number of activities for use during literacy center time. Explain that they can work alone or with others.
3. Go over the following rules with the class:

    - Handle materials carefully.
    - Select only one or two items at a time.
    - Put completed books away before selecting another.
    - Treat each other with respect.

4. Allow students to explore the materials. If necessary, assist children in using materials. Be prepared to closely supervise literacy center time during the first several days. When the class has mastered using the materials independently, begin to model reading behavior by practicing silent reading. Add new activities and model their use. When children work alone without difficulty, take small groups for guided reading.

Materials for Creating a Literacy Center

When designing the literacy center, keep in mind that it should be a comfortable place where students with a variety of interests and abilities can gather to engage in literacy activities. The following suggested materials have been proven to intrinsically motivate children toward reading and writing.

rug
pillows
rocking chair
table and chairs

quiet place for reading (e.g., beneath a counter or in a box)
posters that advertise reading and writing
"Library Corner" and "Literacy Center" signs
mural paper hung on wall for impromptu writing

open-faced bookshelves
bookshelf labeled "Literacy Center Books Only"
bookshelf labeled "Books That Can Go Home"
approximately 100 books
library book check-out/check-in system

literature-based videos, television set, and video player
tape recorder
headsets
audiotaped stories, including musical stories

puppets
stuffed animals and props that are associated with books
felt board with figures to accompany various books
materials for children to create their own felt board figures: felt strips, construction paper, markers, scissors, glue
roll movie box
materials for making roll movies: shelving paper, pencils, crayons
popsicle stick figures to accompany various books
materials for children to make their own popsicle stick figures: popsicle sticks, construction paper, scissors, markers, glue
materials for children to write, illustrate, and publish their own books: construction paper, writing paper, stapler, pencils, crayons, scissors, glue

magnetic, wooden, foam, cube, and sandpaper letters
flashcards with phonograms, prefixes, suffixes, and roots
board games that promote use of phonics skills
puzzles for matching uppercase and lowercase letters, rhymes, onsets with rimes, etc.
word wheels to create words with onsets or rimes
pocket chart to build words, sequence sentences, etc.
word wall for high-frequency words

RESOURCE
1.2 Checking Books Out of the Classroom Library

Purpose

- To establish a checkout system for books in the classroom library
- To encourage daily reading

Materials

Index Card Option

two different colored 5-by-8-inch index card file boxes (labeled "Books Out" and "Books In")
colored index cards (two per child, one for each box)
white index cards (see A1.1)

Log Option

loose-leaf binder, clipboard, or spiral notebook with a separate page for each child, headed with child's name and having the columns "Title," "Date Out," and "Date In"

Both Options

stickers used as rewards for book returns
bookshelf of books marked "Take-Home Books"

Activity

1. Show the bookshelf marked "Take-Home Books." Explain that books can be checked out of the classroom library to be read at home. Circulate about one quarter of your books at a time.
2. Show the two index card boxes or the log. Explain the procedure for checking books out.
3. If using the file card system, children take a blank white index card from the "Books Out" box, write their name, the title of the book they are borrowing, and the date. Then they put the card behind the colored index card with their name on it in the "Books Out" box. When the book is returned, they remove the white index card from the "Books Out" box, write the date returned, and place it in the "Books In" box behind the colored index card with their name on it.
4. If using the log, students have their own page in a loose-leaf binder or spiral notebook. When checking out a book, they turn to the page with their name on it, and write the title of the book and the date in the "Date Out" column. When the book is returned, the date is written in the "Date In" column.

A1.1 Book Checkout Form on Index Card

Your Name	Book Title	Date Out	Date in

1.3 Keeping a Record of Books Read

Purpose

- To motivate voluntary reading by keeping track of books read

Materials

3-by-5-inch index cards
one index card box, plastic bag, or spiral note-
    book per child
markers

Activity

1. Let children know that they should keep track of books they read throughout the school year.
2. Once children finish a book, encourage them to write the book's title and the date completed in a notebook or log or on an index card.
3. Tell children to write about and illustrate their favorite part of the story or favorite characters. If using index cards, children should place them in the box or plastic bag when completed.
4. The teacher should review students' logs or cards weekly or at least every other week. This system can serve as an authentic assessment of literacy development.

1.4 Using Activity Cards

Purpose

- To help children organize themselves to accomplish goals in collaborative groups

Materials

an activity card, for instance, Use a Felt Story
accompanying materials, for instance, a felt
    board and story characters
accompanying book
log form for completed activity

Activity

1. Activity cards that have already been introduced by the teacher are available to the children (see A1.2, A1.3).
2. The teacher may choose to organize groups of children and assign an activity card to each group.
3. The teacher may choose to organize groups of children and allow each group to select an activity card.
4. The teacher may display four or five activity cards to choose from and ask the children to decide what they would like to do.
5. When groups and activities are selected, children go to the designated area in the classroom to carry out the task.
6. The children follow the steps outlined on the activity card by assigning tasks to everyone in the group and carrying out the activity.
7. When the activity is complete, the children fill out log forms (see A1.4). Younger children who are not yet able to write circle the activity they have completed. Others write on the form.
8. Photocopy and enlarge activity cards onto colored paper, laminate, and place in a convenient spot for children to select and use.

Variation

- For word study activity cards, the materials consist of an implement (e.g., word wheel or game board), the appropriate letter cards (e.g., onsets/rimes), and an accountability form.

A1.2 Activity Cards to Develop Comprehension

Use a Felt Story

Goal: Retell a well-formed story

1. With a partner or group, choose a felt story to use.
2. Get the book, felt board, and characters.
3. Read the book and practice telling the story with the felt pictures.
4. Be ready to tell the story to the class at sharing time.
5. Record your activity in your literacy log.
6. Check your work:
   How well was your project done?
   Were you able to recall the story and its main events without using the book?
   How well did you work as a group?

Make a Felt Story

Goal: Retell a well-formed story

1. With a partner or group, choose a book to make into a felt story, or write your own story for a felt story.
2. If this is your own story, begin by writing the story. Decide which characters and what other things will be in the felt story.
3. If this is from a book, read the book and look carefully at the pictures. Decide which characters and what other things will be in your felt story.
4. Get the things you'll need: paper, drawing and coloring materials, glue, felt.
5. Be sure everyone has a job: writer, drawer, colorer, gluer, storyteller.
6. Draw the pictures you want to have in the story. Glue felt on the back of them.
7. When you are done, practice telling the story with the felt pictures.
8. Be ready to retell the story and its main events to the class at sharing time.
9. Record your activity in your literacy log.
10. Check your work:
    How well was your project done?
    How well did you work as a group?

Use and Make a Prop Story

Goal: Sequence events

1. With a partner or group, get the props and the book that goes with them.
2. Read the story.
3. In sequential order, retell the story using the props. Be sure everyone has a job. Take turns telling the story and holding the props.
4. Try new things:
   Tell your own story with the props.
   Make new props to add to this story.
   Make new props for a story you wrote.
5. Be ready to tell the prop story, in the correct sequential order, to the class at sharing time.
6. Record your activity in your literacy log.
7. Check your work:
   How well was your project done?
   Were you able to remember the correct sequence of events from the story?
   How well did you work as a group?

Use and Make a Puppet Story

Goal: Find the main idea

1. With a partner or group, choose a story to make into a puppet show, or write your own story for a puppet show, and choose the puppets you'd like to use.
2. If this is your own story, begin by writing a story with a moral or main idea. Decide which characters will be in the puppet story and what they will do and say.
3. If this is from a book, read the book. Decide which characters will be in your puppet story and what they will do and say.
4. Get the things you'll need: paper, drawing and coloring materials, glue, sticks.
5. Be sure everyone has a job: writer, drawer, colorer, gluer, storyteller, puppeteers.
6. Make the puppets for the story.
7. When you are done, practice telling the story with the puppets. Take turns using the puppets and telling the story.
8. Be ready to tell the story to the class at sharing time.
9. Record your activity in your literacy log.
10. Check your work:
    How well was your project done?
    Did you remember to include the main idea or moral in your puppet story?
    How well did you work as a group?

Use and Make a Chalk Talk

Goal: Follow directions

1. With a partner or group, choose a book to make into a chalk talk, or write your own story for a chalk talk.
2. If this is your own story, begin by writing the story. Decide which parts of the story will be in the chalk talk.
3. If this is from a book, read the book and look carefully at the pictures. Decide which parts of the story will be in your chalk talk.
4. Get the book and the materials you'll need: paper, markers or chalk.
5. Be sure everyone has a job: planner, drawer, storyteller, materials maker.
6. Read the book and look carefully at the pictures. Decide which parts of the story will be in your chalk talk.
7. Draw the pictures you want to have in the story. Make any other materials you'll use.
8. When you are done, practice telling the story while you draw the pictures on the chalkboard or paper. Take turns drawing and telling or reading.
9. Be ready to tell the story to the class at sharing time.
10. Record your activity in your literacy log.
11. Check your work:
    How well was your project done?
    How well did you work as a group?

Listen to a Taped Story

Goal: Create a story ending

1. With a friend or by yourself, choose a taped story to listen to.
2. Get the things you'll need: paper, writing and drawing materials, storybook, tape recorder, tape, headsets.
3. Listen to the story and follow along in the book.
4. After the story, draw a picture of your favorite part or favorite character.
5. Decide how you would change this story to have a different ending. If you are working with a friend, decide together on one character that you will write down. Take turns writing and sharing ideas from that character's perspective.
6. Be ready to write your ideas down or share them with the class at sharing time.
7. Record your activity in your literacy log.
8. Check your work:
    How well was your project done?

Use and Make a Roll Movie

Goal: Include setting, theme, plot episodes, and resolution in a story retelling

1. With a partner or group, choose a story to make into a roll movie, or write your own story for a roll movie.
2. If this is your own story, begin by writing the story. Decide which main parts of the story will be in your roll movie.
3. If this is from a book, read the story and look carefully at the pictures. Decide which parts will be in your roll movie.
4. Get the things you'll need: paper, drawing and coloring materials, roll movie box.
5. Be sure everyone has a job: writer, illustrator, storyteller, reader, roll movie turner.
6. Make the pictures for your story on the roll paper. Remember to include the elements of story structure in your story.
7. Put the paper into the roll movie box. Tape the ends of the paper onto the dowel.
8. When you are done, practice telling the story with the roll movie. Take turns reading, telling, and turning the roll movie.
9. Be ready to tell the story to the class at sharing time.
10. Record your activity in your literacy log.
11. Check your work:
    How well was your project done?
    Did you remember to include the setting? theme? plot episodes? resolution?
    How well did you work as a group?

Quiet Reading

Goal: Visualize story episodes

1. With a friend or by yourself, choose something to read: a book, a magazine, a newspaper.
2. Picture the story in your mind as you read. Think about what the characters look like and about the main parts of the story.
3. If you are reading the same book or article with a friend, take turns reading.
4. When you are done reading, talk about the story with your friend.
5. If you and a friend are reading different stories, tell them to each other when you are done.
6. If you are working alone, try some ideas after you finish reading:
   Find some friends and tell them the story.
   Find some friends and read to them, or listen to them read to you.
   Retell the story you read to some friends.
7. Record your activity in your literacy log.
8. Record the main idea in the story you read.
9. Record if you liked or did not like the story, and why.

Partner Reading

Goal: Retell from character's perspective with appropriate expression

1. With a partner, choose a book to read.
2. Take turns reading the book. One person can read one page, then the next person reads the next page.
3. When you're done reading, take turns retelling the story to each other or to a stuffed animal.
4. Be ready to tell the class about the book at sharing time.
5. Record your activity in your literacy log.
6. Record the major idea in the book.
7. Record if you liked or did not like the book, and why.

What Will Happen Next?

Goal: Predict outcomes

1. With a partner, choose a book to read that you haven't heard of or read before.
2. Take turns reading the first few pages.
3. Stop reading and talk about what you think will happen next. Take turns talking.
4. Write your ideas down on paper.
5. Finish reading the book, taking turns.
6. At the end of the book talk about what you thought would happen and what really happened. Which way do you like the story better?
7. Tell the class about the story during sharing time.
8. Record your activity in your literacy log.
9. Check your work:
   How well did you read and write?
   How well did you work with your partner?

Favorite Character Book

Goal: Relate story to background knowledge

1. With a partner or group, look through the classroom library and choose a favorite character from one of the books. Here are some ideas, or you can choose your own:
   Clifford   Harold
   Frog and Toad   Curious George
   Miss Nelson   Miss Frizzle and the Magic
   Berenstain Bears   School Bus
2. Read the book you've picked out. Plan a new story with this character. Think about: Who else is in the new story? Where and when does the new story take place? What is the problem the main character has? What will happen to the characters? How will the problem be solved? How will the new story end?
3. When writing your story, use your own life experiences and your knowledge about the character to help you create the plot in the story.
4. Write the words to your story and make pictures for your book. Make a title page with the name of the book and the name of the authors and illustrators (you!).
5. Be sure everyone has a job. Take turns telling the story, writing the words, and making the pictures.
6. When you are done, staple your pictures together to make a book. Show the class your book during sharing time, then put it in the literacy center for others to read.
7. Record your activity in your literacy log.
8. Check your work:
   How well was your project done?
   How well did you work as a group?

Journal Writing

Goal: Write with substantiating details

1. Get the materials you'll need: journal, pencil, crayons.
2. Write about an experience you have had recently that made you happy or sad.
3. Write in your journal. Add pictures if you want to.
4. Read your entry to be sure you have included all details.
5. Record your activity in your literacy log.
6. Check your work:
   How well did you think of ideas?
   Does your journal entry contain a lot of detail?
   How well did you write?

Create an Original Book

Goal: Write using figurative language

1. With a partner or group, decide on an idea for a book to write.
2. Plan the story:
   Who is in it?
   Where and when does the story take place?
   What is the problem the main character has?
   What will happen to the characters?
   How will the problem be solved?
   How will the story end?
3. Include some similes and metaphors in your book.
4. Write the words to your story and make pictures for your book. Make a title page with the name of the book and the name of the authors and illustrators (you!).
5. Be sure everyone has a job. Take turns telling the story, writing the words, and making the pictures.
6. When you are done, staple your pictures together to make a book. Show the class your book during sharing time, then put it in the literacy center for others to read.
7. Record your activity in your literacy log.
8. Check your work:
   How well was your project done?
   How well did you work as a group?

A1.3 Activity Cards for Word Study

Word Wall

Goal: Recognize high-frequency words

1. Get the materials you will need: pencil, word wall book or folder, newspaper, magazines, scissors, glue.
2. Look at the words posted on the word wall.
3. Write the words from the word wall in your book or folder.
4. Check your work for spelling errors.
5. Search through the magazine and newspaper for the word wall words.
6. When you find the specific words, cut them out and glue them into your word wall book or folder.
7. Be ready to show the class the words you have found during sharing time.
8. Record your activity in your literacy log.
9. Check your work:
   How well did you stay with the activity?
   Did you spell all the word wall words correctly?
      If not, did you correct them?

Puzzle for Rhyming Words

Goal: Identify words that rhyme and create rhymes

1. With a partner, get the materials you will need: puzzle pieces for rhyming words, paper, pencil.
2. Take turns trying to match the puzzle pieces. Match the words that rhyme with another rhyming word. If you are correct, the puzzle pieces will fit together.
3. When you are finished matching all the puzzle pieces, create a rhyming poem with your partner. You can use the rhyming words from the puzzle pieces or think of some new ones.
4. After you create the poem, proofread your work for errors and make corrections if needed.
5. Be ready to read the poem to the class during sharing time.
6. Check your work:
   Does your poem use rhyming words?
   Does your poem make sense?
   Did you and your partner take turns putting the puzzle pieces together?
   How well did you work with your partner when you made the poem?

Bingo with Alphabet Letters

Goal: Identify letters of the alphabet

1. With a group, get the materials you will need: lowercase letter Bingo cards, uppercase letter cards, Bingo markers (counters, beans), paper, pencil.
2. Have one student be the caller; the other students are the players.
3. Caller gives out the Bingo cards and Bingo markers.
4. Caller turns over the uppercase letter cards. Caller calls out a letter.
5. Players put a marker on the card if the letter that was called is on their Bingo card.
6. First person to put five markers in a row, wins.
7. After each game, players write on paper all the letters (uppercase and lowercase) from their Bingo card that have markers on them. Caller writes all the letters (uppercase and lowercase) that he called during the game.
8. Record your work in your literacy log.
9. Check your work:
    Are your letters written correctly?
    Have another student from your group check your work.
    How well did you work as a group?

Jeopardy! with Consonant Blends

Goal: Identify consonant blends

1. With a group, get the materials you will need: Jeopardy! board, die, pencil, paper.
2. One player is the host of the game.
3. All the other players roll the die to see who will go first.
4. The first player picks a cateogory.
5. The host reads the clue, for example, "Use this instead of tape when you want to hold something together."
6. The player gives an answer, for example, "What is *glue*?" If the answer is correct, the player receives the card. Remember, every answer will begin with a consonant blend.
7. Each player totals the numbers written on all the cards she has won. The largest sum wins.
8. Each player sorts the cards he has won according to their consonant blends.
9. Record your work in your literacy log.
10. Check your work:
    How well did you do? How well did you work with your group?

The Jeopardy! activity card is adapted from D. R. Bear et al., *Words Their Way* (Englewood Cliff, NJ: Prentice Hall, 1996).

Pocket Chart for Making Words

Goal: Use onsets and rimes to create words

1. With a partner, get the materials you will need:
    * cards with onsets (beginning consonants)—for instance, *c, m, ch, th,*
    * cards with rimes (endings)—for instance, *-at, -ip, -in, -op,*
    * pocket chart, paper, pencil.
2. Put one of the onset cards in the top left pocket of the pocket chart.
3. Put one of the rime cards in the top right pocket of the pocket chart.
4. Mix all the other cards together.
5. One person chooses a card and reads aloud what is printed on the card.
6. The other person decides which side of the pocket chart the card belongs on.
7. Then, together, decide whether the card is on the correct side.
8. Do this until all the cards are used up.
9. Now take some cards from each side of the pocket chart. Try to match onset and rime cards to make real words.
10. If both agree that the words are real, write them on paper.
11. Record your work in your literacy log.
12. Check your work:
    Were all the cards on the correct sides of the pocket chart?
    Did you spell all the real words correctly?
    Did you and your partner work well together?

Making Little Words Out of a Big Word

Goal: Identify letter patterns

1. With a partner, get the materials you will need: letters in a plastic bag, pencil, paper.
2. The letters in the bag make a big word, such as *Rain Forest.*
3. Write the big word on paper.
4. Use the letters to make little words, such as *ran, fan, tan, for.*
5. Now write the little words under the big word on the paper.
6. How many little words did you make?
7. Compare your words with your partner, and see who came up with the most words.
8. Record your work in your literacy log.
9. Check your work:
    How well did you complete your work?
    Did you check your spelling?
    How well did you work with your partner?

Memory with Picture Cards

Goal: Learn short and long vowel sounds

1. With a partner or group, get the materials you will need: picture cards, pencil, paper.
2. Place the cards face down in rows.
3. Each player turns over two cards at a time.
4. Each card has a picture on it. The player says the name of each picture aloud and tells whether the name has a long or short vowel in it, for example, *cake* or *pen.*
5. If the two cards have the same picture, the player keeps them and goes again. If the two cards have different pictures, the player puts them back in a row, and another player gets a turn.
6. Whoever has the most cards at the end of the game, wins.
7. When the game is over, write all the words with long vowels in one column and all the words with short vowels in another column.
8. Record your work in your literacy log.
9. Check your work:
   Were you able to make lots of matches?
   Did you know which words had long and short vowels?
   How well did you work with your partner or group?

Morning Message

Goal: Read print from left to right

1. With a partner, get the materials you will need: pencil, paper.
2. Go to the morning message.
3. Read the morning message to your partner.
4. Count the number of words in the morning message. Write a complete sentence telling how many words are in the morning message.
5. Count the number of letters in the morning message. Write a complete sentence telling how many letters are in the morning message.
6. Compare your answers with your partner's answers. If you have different answers, go back and count again. See if you can get the same answers.
7. Record your work in your literacy log.
8. Check your work:
   Were you able to read the morning message today by yourself?
   How well did you work with your partner?

Word Wheels for Prefixes and Suffixes

Goal: Identify prefixes and suffixes

1. With a partner, get the materials you will need: a prefix word wheel or a suffix word wheel, pencil, paper.
2. Make new words by sliding the wheel around.
3. After you have created some new words with the word wheel, write on paper the root word and the new words with the prefixes or suffixes.
4. Record your work in your literacy log.
5. Check your work:
   Did you write down the root word and all the new words?
   Did you check your spelling?
   Did you work well with your partner?

Literature Circles

Goal: Develop interpretive comprehension

1. As a group (four or five students), choose a book to read together.
2. Get the book, pencil, paper.
3. Decide by which date everyone has to finish reading the book.
4. Assign jobs. Make sure each person has a job.
   - *Summarizer.* Summarize the main events in the book. Write them down.
   - *Artful Artist.* Draw something you like in the story. Describe the picture you chose to draw and why you chose it.
   - *Connector.* Find connections between the book and the outside world.
   - *Word Finder.* Find special words in the story. Write what you think the words mean and the definitions from the dictionary. Write the sentences the words are in, and the page numbers, so you can share them with your group.
   - *Discussion Director.* Write down good, "fat" questions that you think your group would want to talk about.
5. Read the book independently until the finish date arrives.
6. Perform your job while reading the book, and record your responses.
7. Monitor your progress so that you can be finished on time.
8. On the finish date, meet as a group again.
9. Each person presents the job they completed.
10. Record your work in your literacy log.
11. Check your work:
    Were you prepared with your completed job by the finish date?
    How well did you work as a group?

A1.4 Log Forms for Completed Activities

Log Form for Younger Children

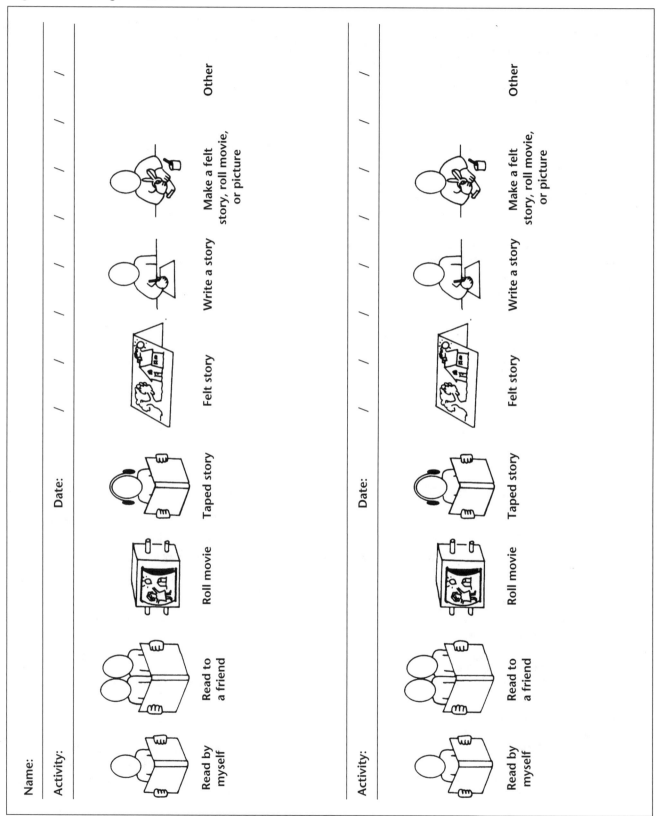

Log Form for Older Children

Name:	Read by myself	Read to a friend	Roll movie	Taped story	Felt story	Write a story	Make a felt story, roll movie, or picture	Other
Date:	The activity that I worked on today was							

RESOURCE
1.5 Using a Center Chart

Purpose

- To use the center chart to organize independent work

Materials

center chart and icons
center accountability forms

Activity

A center chart designates several independent work options for heterogeneous groups of three or four children. The chart is made of a sturdy material such as tagboard and laminated. It has a side column of several labeled icons representing center activities. Across the top of the chart are written the

work period numbers. The icons can be made movable and attached to the chart with Velcro. Additional icons are provided in A1.5.

Rules for selecting activities and moving from one center to the next are decided upon by the teacher. Students can be assigned to independent center activities when the teacher is to be occupied with guided reading instruction. The groups rotate through the various centers, moving from one to another when the teacher changes from one guided reading group to the next, or when they have completed a task. To show the order in which children move from one center to another when work periods change, movable name cards are placed into the chart grid, or the names can be written into the grid with erasable markers. The sample chart in the figure has two rows (computer center and art) left blank because the activities are optional and could be done after assigned center work is completed.

When each activity is completed, children fill in accountability forms (see A1.6).

Sample Center Chart

	1	2	3	4	5
Partner Reading	Amy, Peter, Govindh, Molly, Jane	Bella, Keisha, Sara, Tom, Jean	Claude, Zak, Helen, Bill, Joan	Dora, Ruth, Fran, Rachel, Marshall	Elgin, Leslie, Jim, Tanya, Sue
Writing	Elgin, Leslie, Jim, Tanya, Sue	Amy, Peter, Govindh, Molly, Jane	Bell, Keisha, Sara, Tom, Jean	Claude, Zak, Helen, Bill, Joan	Dora, Ruth, Fran, Rachel, Marshall
Listening Cener	Claude, Zak, Helen, Bill, Joan	Dora, Ruth, Fran, Rachel, Marshall	Elgin, Leslie, Jim, Tanya, Sue	Amy, Peter, Govindh, Molly, Jane	Bella, Keisha, Sara, Tom, Jean
Word Study Center	Bella, Keisha, Sara, Tom, Jean	Claude, Zak, Helen, Bill, Joan	Dora, Ruth, Fran, Rachel, Marshall	Elgin, Leslie, Jim, Tanya, Sue	Amy, Peter, Govindh, Molly, Jane
Computer Center					
Art Center					

OPTIONAL

The center chart is adapted from the work board described in I. C. Fountas and G. S. Pinnell, *Guided Reading: Good First Teaching for All Children* (Portsmouth, NH: Heinemann, 1996).

A1.5 Additional Icons for Center Chart

Pocket Chart Activities

Block Building Center

Word Study Center

Literacy Center: Silent Reading

Buddy Reading

Read Around the Room

Math Activities

A1.6 Accountability Forms for Completed Work

Center Recording Form

Center _____

Students _____

_____

What did you do? _____

_____

_____

_____

_____

What did you learn? _____

_____

_____

_____

_____

A1.6 *(cont.)*

Name_____ Date _____

Literacy Center: Silent Reading

Title: _____

In this story _____

_____

A1.6 *(cont.)*

Name _____ Date _____

Pocket Chart: Read and Write the Poem

Today I read the poem _____

I can write the poem!

_____

_____

_____

_____

_____

_____

_____

A1.6 *(cont.)*

Name_____ Date _____

Choice

Today I had free choice! Here is what I did!

I worked in _____

_____

_____

RESOURCE
1.6 Sharing Completed Tasks

Purpose

- To have children feel a sense of accomplishment after completing a task
- To improve children's ability to make oral presentations

Materials

bookmarks

Activity

1. Create an environment where students feel comfortable sharing their enthusiasm and concern about the literacy center program.

2. Encourage children to share their thoughts and feelings, as well as their literacy accomplishments, with the class. An excellent forum for this is through the author's chair, which is a place where students can sit and share their favorite stories or read their original published books.

3. Time should be set aside to review the day's activities as well as to remind children of materials needed for the following day (e.g., props, returned books).

4. Close the day's program by reciting as a class the rhyme "Before you go to sleep tonight, read a book, then turn off the light."

5. A pattern for making bookmarks with this rhyme is provided in A1.7. Photocopy and enlarge on colored paper, color, cut, and laminate.

A1.7 Bookmark for Children

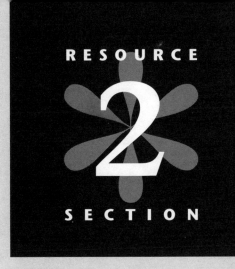

Comprehension Development

This section provides teachers with resources and suggestions for developing comprehension by the use of creative storytelling techniques. The lessons and activities are appropriate for pre-kindergarten through fifth grade. All activities engage children in enjoyable independent and collaborative projects that develop literacy and promote participating in reading and writing.

In each lesson a sample story is given to assist the teacher in becoming familiar with each storytelling technique. The stories are labeled as suitable for grades pre-K–2 or grades 3–5. However, all the activities can be used at any grade level by substituting a more appropriate story. Suggestions for additional books for grades pre-K–2 and grades 3–5 are provided at the end of each lesson.

Before assigning children to work independently with these activities, the teacher should model each storytelling technique and have children practice it by retelling a favorite or original story. When older children choose a chapter book to retell, they should choose only a portion of the book—a favorite scene or chapter, a plot summary, or the part liked most or least—as the basis for retelling. (See also Resource Section 1, A1.2, Activity Cards to Develop Comprehension.)

The lessons and materials provided are as follows:

2.1 Felt board story

    A2.1 Making a felt board

2.2 Prop story

2.3 Puppet story

    A2.2 Puppet patterns—Old lady and the
            animals she swallows

    A2.3 Puppet patterns—Face puppets

    A2.4 Puppet patterns—People and animals

2.4 Chalk talk stories

    A2.5 Chalk talk prop

2.5 Photo story

2.6 Sound and music stories

2.7 Song story

2.8 Roll movie stories

    A2.6 Making a roll movie box

2.9 Movie or television stories

2.10 Food story

2.11 Cut story

2.12 Origami story

    A2.7 Origami fish

    A2.8 Origami crane

RESOURCE
2.1 Felt Board Story

"A Bunny Called Nat" (grades Pre-K–2)

Purpose

To have students:

- Learn how to use a felt board to tell a story
- Retell the teacher's sample story including story structure elements (characters, theme, resolution)
- Create and tell a felt board story using the characters and plot of a favorite book
- Write, create, and tell an original felt board story

Materials

felt board (A2.1)
felt characters: five bunnies, one each in gray, blue, yellow, green, and orange (A2.1)

Activity

1. Tell the children that you are going to model how to tell a story using a felt board.
2. Introduce ("walk through") the story. Ask, "Who can tell me what the plot episodes of a story are?" Show the felt characters: "While I'm telling you this story, pay attention to when I put these characters on the felt board." (See Directed Listening Thinking Activity—DLTA—in Chapter 3.)
3. As you tell the story, model how to use the felt board, particularly how the pieces stick to the board and how the characters are placed on it at appropriate times.
4. After telling the story, discuss with children the plot episodes of the story and fill in a story map. Then discuss how the felt characters were used during the plot episodes.
5. Have students work with a partner to retell the teacher's sample story.
6. Students can re-read a favorite book alone or with a partner, then create a felt board presentation to share with the class.
7. Students can write, create, and tell an original felt board story.

Sample Story: "A Bunny Called Nat"

(adapted from an anonymous tale)

Once upon a time there was a little gray rabbit and his name was Nat. One day he looked around and saw that all his brothers and sisters, cousins and

friends were gray, too. He thought he would like to be different from them. So he said:

(*Chorus:*) I'm a bunny called Nat,
I'm funny and fat,
And I can change my color
Just like that (*snap your fingers*).

And suddenly Nat was a blue bunny. He was blue like the sky and blue like the sea. He was blue like the twilight and blue like the dawn. It felt nice and cool to be blue. He decided to take a look at himself in the pond. He hurried to the edge and admired his reflection in the water. He leaned over so far that SPLASH! He fell into the pond. Nat fell deep into the blue water and he couldn't swim. He was frightened. He called for help. His friends heard him, but when they came to the pond they couldn't see him because he was blue like the water. Fortunately a turtle swam by and helped Nat get safely to shore. Nat thanked the turtle. He decided that he didn't like being blue. So he said: (*Chorus*)

And this time, what color did he change himself to? Yes, he was yellow—yellow like the sun, yellow like a daffodil, yellow like a canary. Yellow seemed like such a happy color to be. He was very proud of his new color, and he decided to take a walk through the jungle. Who do you think he met in the jungle? He met his cousins the lion and the tiger. The lion and the tiger looked at Nat's yellow fur and said, "What are you doing in that yellow coat? We are the only animals in this jungle that are supposed to be yellow." And they growled so fiercely that Nat the bunny was frightened and he ran all the way home. He said: (*Chorus*)

And this time, what did he change his color to? Yes, he was green. He was green like the grass and green like the leaves of the trees. He was green like a grasshopper and green like the meadow. As a green bunny, Nat thought he'd be the envy of all the other bunnies. He wanted to play with his other bunny friends in the meadow. But because he was the color of the grass in the meadow, he could not be seen, and his friends just ran and jumped about him not seeing him at all or mistaking him for a grasshopper. So Nat the bunny had no one to play with while he was green. Being green wasn't much fun. So he said: (*Chorus*)

And what color was he then? Right, he was orange. He was orange like a carrot, orange like a sunset, orange like a pumpkin—he was the brightest color of all. He decided he would go out and play with all his brothers and sisters and friends. But what do you suppose happened? When his friends saw him, they all stopped playing and started to laugh, "Ha, ha, whoever heard of an orange bunny?" No one wanted to play with him. Nat didn't want to be orange anymore. He didn't want to be a blue bunny because if he fell into the pond, no one could see him to save him. He didn't want to be a yellow bunny and be frightened by the lion and the tiger. He didn't want to be a green bunny because then he was just like the meadow and none of his friends could see him. And so he said: (*Chorus*)

Do you know what color Nat the bunny changed himself into this time? Yes, you're right. He changed himself back to gray. And now that he was gray, all of his friends played with him. No one growled or laughed at him. He was gray like a rain cloud, gray like an elephant, gray like pussy willows. It felt warm and comfortable being gray. From that time on, Nat the bunny was always happy being a gray bunny, and he decided that it's really best being just what you are.

Books Appropriate for Felt Board Stories for Grades Pre-K–2

The Artist and the Architect (Demi). Chinese folktale about a rivalry between an artist and an architect. Felt board figures: emperor, architect, artist, parchment, castle, house connected by tunnel, smoke.

The Great Kapok Tree (Cherry). A hunter falls asleep in the rain forest and is visited by the creatures who live there. Together they convince him not to cut down the great kapok tree. Felt board figures: kapok tree, man, boa constrictor, bee, monkey, toucan, macaw, cock-of-the-rock, tree frog, jaguar, porcupine, anteater, three-toed sloth, child.

How the Camel Got Its Hump (Kipling). Classic fable about the consequences of laziness. Felt board figures: camel with no hump, camel with hump, genie, horse, ox, dog.

Books Appropriate for Felt Board Stories for Grades 3–5

Choose the introduction or a favorite scene or chapter, or do a plot summary. Some main characters have been listed.

Freckle Juice (Blume). Andrew Marcus is obsessed with Nicky Lane's freckles and gets caught counting them in school. Sharon explains that the more juice Andrew drinks, the more freckles he can get. Felt board figures: boy without freckles, boy with freckles, girl, glass of juice.

James and the Giant Peach (Dahl). James, an orphaned boy, is sent to live with his mean and terrible aunts. But James is able to escape into a giant peach filled with funny characters. Felt board figures: boy, peach tree, one giant peach, skinny woman, heavy woman, grasshopper, ladybug, centipede.

Mr. Popper's Penguins (Atwater). Mr. Popper, a house painter, adds twelve penguins to his family. He gets larger food bills, some messy situations, and a lot of laughs. Felt board figures: man, woman, girl, boy, twelve penguins.

A2.1   Making a Felt Board

1. Lay the piece of corrugated cardboard flat. Prebend all flaps.
2. Set up front panel. Line up A slots with matching B slots on bottom panel.
3. Insert tabs C from last panel through both A and B slots.
4. Pull through and lock into D slots. Your easel is set up.
5. Cover front of board with felt.

This board can be used as a felt board, as a Big Book stand, and for stick puppet shows (scenery can be made on the felt and the puppets held from the back top of the board).

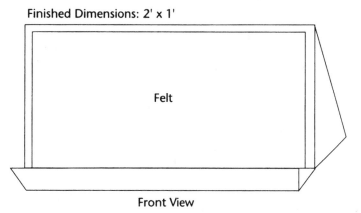

Finished Dimensions: 2' x 1'

Felt

Front View

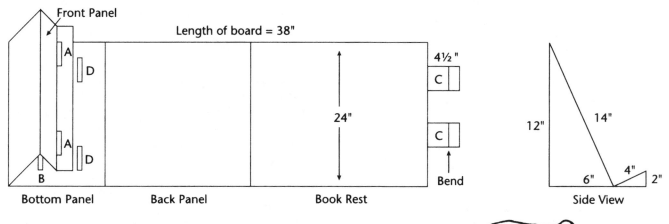

Front Panel

Length of board = 38"

A   D   A   D   B

24"

4½"   C   C   Bend

12"   14"   6"   4"   2"

Bottom Panel   Back Panel   Book Rest   Side View

* A readymade Story Center that can be used as a felt board is available for purchase from the author, <www.mmmeducational@msn.com/>

STORY CENTER

Front of Story Center Felt Board

Use this template to make felt board characters. Photocopy to enlarge as needed. Make five bunnies: one for each color discussed in the story.

RESOURCE
2.2 Prop Story

The Chocolate Touch (grades 3–5)

Purpose

To have students:

- Identify details when retelling the teacher's sample story
- Use a web to organize details for retelling
- Criticize and evaluate materials in choosing props for retelling a favorite story

Materials

yellow pencil
brown pencil
silver coin
coin painted brown
red apple
apple painted brown
white glove
brown glove

Activity

1. Introduce the story. Ask students to listen carefully for the details of the story that make it a good story (without them the story would not be as interesting or make sense). Explain that these details help you choose what props to use in the retelling. (See DLTA, Resource 2.1.)
2. As you tell the story, model how to use the props.
3. Discuss with the class what the important details of the story were. Use a web to organize the details:

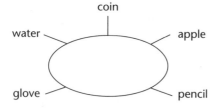

4. Have students retell the teacher's sample story using the props in correct sequence.
5. Have students choose a favorite book, re-read the book alone or with a partner, choose the props, and retell the story to the class. Remind students to pay attention to the details in the story and to use a web to help them organize the information.

Sample Story: The Chocolate Touch

by Patrick Skene Catling

Summary of favorite scenes:

John Midas loved chocolate. One day he found a mysterious old coin and used it to buy a box of chocolate from a strange candy store. John was upset to see that there was not a lot of chocolate in the box. But after he ate it, he found that everything he ate turned into chocolate.

John always chewed on his gloves (*show white glove*). His mother told him not to, but John didn't listen. Except this time something was different. Something tasted weird. His glove did not have the familiar leathery taste. He pulled his thumb out of his mouth and saw that the glove had turned into chocolate (*show brown glove*). John was so excited that he chewed and chewed until he ate the whole glove.

John's friend Susan was overjoyed about her birthday present. She ran to John to show him her new silver dollar (*show silver coin*). John had forgotten the strange things that had been happening and asked Susan if he could see if it was real silver. She replied yes, thinking that John was being silly, but challenged him to bite it. When John bit Susan's silver dollar, it too turned to chocolate in his mouth (*show brown coin*). John could not believe what was happening.

During school, John put a pencil in his mouth (*show yellow pencil*). When he pulled it out, he was shocked. Not only did the part his mouth touched turn to chocolate, but the rest of the pencil did as well (*show brown pencil*).

When Susan and John went bobbing for apples (*show red apple*), they put their faces into the bucket. The water turned a muddy brown (*show brown apple*). Susan and John pulled their heads out of the water and found they were drenched in chocolate syrup. Now everything John touched turned to chocolate. It was getting frustrating.

Books Appropriate for Prop Stories for Grades Pre-K–2

Dear Mr. Blueberry (James). During summer vacation, Emily writes to her teacher, Mr. Blueberry, about a whale who ends up in the pond in her backyard. Props: girl, man, blue whale, envelopes, mailbox.

How to Eat Fried Worms (Rockwell). Two boys compete to prove that worms can make delicious meals. Props: frying pan, gummy worms.

Paddington Bear (Bond). A small bear found at Paddington Station becomes a family member.

Props: stuffed bear with hat and coat, man, woman, girl, boy.

Books Appropriate for Prop Stories for Grades 3–5

Aunt Flossie's Hats (and Crab Cakes Later) (Howard). Sara and Susan share tea, cookies, crab cakes, and stories about hats when they visit their favorite relative, Aunt Flossie. Props: hats of various styles, as described in book.

Mr. Rabbit and the Lovely Present (Zolotow). A girl asks Mr. Rabbit to help her choose a birthday present for her mother. Props: apples, bananas, pears, purple grapes, and a basket to put them in.

Wilfrid Gordon MacDonald Partridge (Fox). A boy helps an elderly friend rediscover her memories by sharing things that are meaningful to him. Props: egg, shell, medal, puppet, football, basket.

2.3 Puppet Story

"I Know an Old Lady Who Swallowed a Fly" (grades Pre-K–2)

Purpose

To have students:

- Sequence characters and events when retelling the teacher's sample story
- Retell a favorite story using puppets created by children
- Write and present an original puppet story

Materials

old lady and the animals she swallows (A2.2) for other stories, use puppets of various types: hand, stick, finger, and face puppets (A2.3–2.4)

Activity

1. Introduce the story. Ask students to pay attention to the order of the characters and events. (See DLTA, Resource 2.1.)
2. Model how to tell the story using puppets. As the old lady swallows each animal, drop it into her stomach. (The spider can be made to wiggle by using a string attached to it.)
3. Discuss the animals the old lady swallowed and the order in which they were swallowed.
4. Have children practice retelling the sample story. When they feel comfortable with the technique, they can select a favorite book, re-read the book alone or with a partner, create puppets for it, and retell the story.
5. Students can write and create an original puppet story to share with the class.

Sample Story: "I Know an Old Lady Who Swallowed a Fly"

(an anonymous song)

I know an old lady who swallowed a fly.
I don't know why she swallowed a fly, I guess she'll die.

I know an old lady who swallowed a spider
That wiggled and jiggled and tickled inside her.
She swallowed the spider to catch the fly.

I don't know why she swallowed the fly, I guess
she'll die.

I know an old lady who swallowed a bird.
How absurd to swallow a bird!
She swallowed the bird to catch the spider
That wiggled and jiggled and tickled inside her.
She swallowed the spider to catch the fly.
I don't know why she swallowed the fly, I guess
she'll die.

I know an old lady who swallowed a cat.
Now fancy that, she swallowed a cat!
She swallowed the cat to catch the bird.
How absurd to swallow a bird!
She swallowed the bird to catch the spider
That wiggled and jiggled and tickled inside her.
She swallowed the spider to catch the fly.
I don't know why she swallowed the fly, I guess
she'll die.

I know an old lady who swallowed a dog.
What a hog to swallow a dog!
She swallowed the dog to catch the cat.
Now fancy that, she swallowed a cat!
She swallowed the cat to catch the bird.
How absurd to swallow a bird!
She swallowed the bird to catch the spider
That wiggled and jiggled and tickled inside her.
She swallowed the spider to catch the fly.
I don't know why she swallowed the fly, I guess
she'll die.

I know an old lady who swallowed a cow.
I don't know how she swallowed a cow.
She swallowed the cow to catch the dog.
What a hog to swallow a dog!
She swallowed the dog to catch the cat.
Now fancy that, she swallowed a cat!
She swallowed the cat to catch the bird.
How absurd to swallow a bird!
She swallowed the bird to catch the spider
That wiggled and jiggled and tickled inside her.
She swallowed the spider to catch the fly.
I don't know why she swallowed the fly, I guess
she'll die.

I know an old lady who swallowed a horse.
She's dead, of course.

Books Appropriate for Puppet Stories for Grades Pre-K–2

Brown Bear, Brown Bear, What Do You See? (Martin). Brown Bear sees a variety of animals, each one a different color. Face puppets: bear and other animals.

The True Story of the Three Little Pigs (Scieszka). The wolf tells his own version of what really happened when he tangled with the three little pigs. Finger puppets: three pigs and wolf.

The Very Hungry Caterpillar (Carle). The life cycle of a butterfly. From an egg hatches a caterpillar. He eats a great deal of food and goes into a cocoon. In time, out comes a butterfly. Puppet: caterpillar and food cutouts.

Books Appropriate for Puppet Stories for Grades 3–5

Catwings (Le Guin). Four young cats with wings leave the city slums in search of a better place to live. Stick puppets: four tabby cats with wings.

Charlotte's Web (White). Wilbur is a very lonely pig until a friendly spider teaches him about the meaning of friendship. Hand puppets: pig, spider, rat, and other barn animals.

The Wind in the Willows (Grahame). The adventures of four animal friends who live on a river bank in the English countryside. Face puppets: toad, mole, rat, badger.

A2.2 Puppet Patterns—Old Lady and the Animals She Swallows

Figures are made of oaktag, colored and laminated or covered with clear vinyl plastic.

1. Enlarge the figure of the old lady or make a transparency and project it onto a piece of white oaktag. Adjust the projection to the size you want your old lady to be. Trace her outline.
2. Color in the old lady's hair and dress. Leave the rectangular area for her stomach white.
3. Tape a piece of heavy clear plastic over the front of the old lady and cut a slit in the oaktag near her shoulders to create a pocket with an opening in the back.
4. Make the other animal figures to fit inside the old lady's stomach and color them.
5. When telling the story, place animal figures into the pocket using the slit in the back of the old lady.

A2.3 Puppet Patterns—Face Puppets

Make transparencies from the figures. Tape oaktag on the wall. Project the transparencies on an overhead projector onto the oaktag to get the size you want. Face puppets should be large enough for the children to stand in back of them and show their faces through the cutout portion. Draw the image and color it. Cover with clear contact paper or laminate, and then cut out. Attach tongue depressors or popsicle sticks to the back of the face puppets to provide a handle.

A2.4 Puppet Patterns—People and Animals

These universal characters can be used to illustrate hundreds of stories. Make a transparency and project on an overhead projector onto oaktag on the wall to the size you want. Color figures, adding special touches for specific stories. Cover with clear contact paper or laminate, and then cut out. Attach sandpaper to the back to adhere to a felt board, or attach tongue depressors or popsicle sticks if you wish to use as stick puppets instead of felt figures.

RESOURCE
2.4 Chalk Talk Stories

"The North Wind and the Sun" (grades 3–5)

"The Surprise in the Playhouse" (grades pre-K–2)

Purpose

To have students:

- Retell the teacher's sample story
- Respond to, evaluate, and draw conclusions about the story in a literature circle

Materials

Any of the following can be used:

chalkboard and chalk
whiteboard, mural paper, or chart paper with markers or crayons
overhead projector with transparencies
prop or character from book to wear on your hand as you draw

Activity

1. Introduce the story. Tell the children that when the story is over, they will evaluate the text and draw conclusions about its moral in a literature circle. (See DLTA, Resource 2.1.)
2. Model telling the story as a chalk talk. Usually, children have copies of the book to record page numbers to help them remember issues to discuss. (Younger children may use sticky notes to mark pages.) In this case, it may be helpful for them to take notes, as the story is being told, on issues that will be discussed in the literature circles.
3. Have the children work with a partner to retell the story using paper and crayons. Each child should take turns telling the story and drawing it.
4. Children then re-read a favorite story, alone or with a partner, and create their own chalk talk.

Sample Story: "The North Wind and the Sun"

(adapted from an Aesop fable)

The North Wind and the Sun were fighting all day about who was the strongest. (*Draw Sun and North Wind.*)

To end their argument, they decided to see who could be the first to get a man out of his clothes. (*Draw man.*)

First the North Wind blew as hard as he could to blow the clothes off the man. However, this only made the man pull his clothes closer to him. So the North Wind gave up and told the Sun to give it a try. (*Draw North Wind blowing.*)

So the Sun beamed its warm rays and heated the air with bright sunshine. (*Erase Wind and draw Sun rays.*)

The man became very warm and took off his clothes. He decided to bathe in the sun. (*Erase man's scarf and top button. Draw shorts.*)

The moral of the story is: Persuasion is better than force.

Sample Story: "The Surprise in the Playhouse"

(adapted from an anonymous tale)

(In this story, the underlined words indicate when to draw.)

There was once a little girl named Lori, and there is an L for Lori. Lori found a great big empty refrigerator box one day outside a neighbor's house; it was left for the garbage man to pick up. Lori decided that the refrigerator box would make a terrific playhouse. She dragged the box home and set it in her backyard, and it looked like this.

The house needed a lot of work. The first thing Lori did

was to <u>cut out two squares to make windows,</u> like this. Then she drew some <u>pretty shutters</u> that looked like these.

When she finished with the windows, <u>she cut out a door</u> just like this.

Lori wanted a way to get in and out of her house from the back. She thought about it a while and decided to make the back all open so it would feel bigger inside and a lot of light could shine in. To do this, <u>she cut the sides of the box, on both sides, down the middle and pulled the flaps open.</u> It made the house look like this.

Lori found some tiny garden fencing in her garage. <u>She put the fence in front of her playhouse</u> and planted seeds behind the fence.

Now that her house was finished, she thought she'd go get her friend Linda. That's another <u>L</u> for Linda.

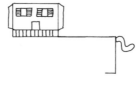

Linda lived across the street and down the block. So Lori skipped <u>across the street and went down the block</u> to Linda's house. <u>She went to the front door</u> and rang the bell.

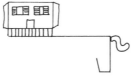

Linda's mother came to the door and said that Linda was upstairs in her room playing. <u>So Lori went upstairs</u> and asked Linda if she would like to see her new playhouse.

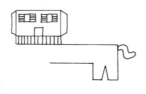

Linda said yes, so the <u>two girls hurried down the stairs.</u> Linda forgot her sweater so <u>she ran back up again</u> to get it. Now the girls were ready to go. <u>They went across the street</u> and were on their way back to Lori's house.

Lori stopped a minute and <u>bent down to look</u> at a caterpillar. Linda looked, too. <u>The girls got up and hurried along.</u> Then they pretended they were bunnies and <u>jumped up and down as they went. Lori fell down and Linda helped her up.</u>

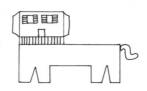

Soon they were at Lori's house. The girls were excited about playing in the playhouse. Just as Lori was about to say to Linda, "How do you like the house?" Linda stepped back and said, "Oh my, do you see the cute dog? Do you see it, Lori?"

Books Appropriate for Chalk Talks for Grades Pre-K–2

The Birthday Tree (Fleischman). A special tree reflects the events in a young man's life as his parents watch. Chalk talk: Draw the tree and its branches, fruit, leaves, etc., as it goes through the changes in the story.

The Carrot Seed (Krauss). Despite his family's lack of faith, a boy clings to his belief that the seed he has planted will grow. Chalk talk: Draw a line for the ground, a watering can sprinkling water, and seedlings above the ground. Then gradually draw the shape of a carrot underground.

Harold and the Purple Crayon (C. Johnson). Harold uses his purple crayon to draw, and everything he draws comes to life. Chalk talk: Use hand prop to tell the story (A2.5).

The Very Busy Spider (Carle). An industrious spider continues to spin his web as the other farm animals try to distract him. Chalk talk: Draw the spider's web as he spins it in the story.

Books Appropriate for Chalk Talks for Grades 3–5

Choose the introduction or a favorite character, scene, or chapter from the book, or do a plot summary. Allow students to read a portion from the book or retell it in their own words. Some suggested characters for chalk talk drawings are listed here.

The Borrowers (Norton). An eccentric family keeps to itself until the daughter ventures out into the world and makes a friend. Chalk talk: Draw a girl and her friend.

Bunnicula (Howe). A cat tries to warn his human family that their newfound baby bunny is a vampire. Chalk talk: Draw a bunny.

The Cat Who Wished to Be a Man (L. Alexander). A wizard turns a cat into a man, who begins to question humanity. Chalk talk: Draw a cat.

A2.5 Chalk Talk Prop

This figure of Harold, from *Harold and the Purple Crayon* by
Crockett Johnson, can be slipped onto the chalk talk storyteller's hand to show Harold drawing his own story, or to be
used as a symbol for chalk talks generally. The back of the
figure has a strip of oaktag, fabric, or elastic to slip onto your
hand.

Front

Back

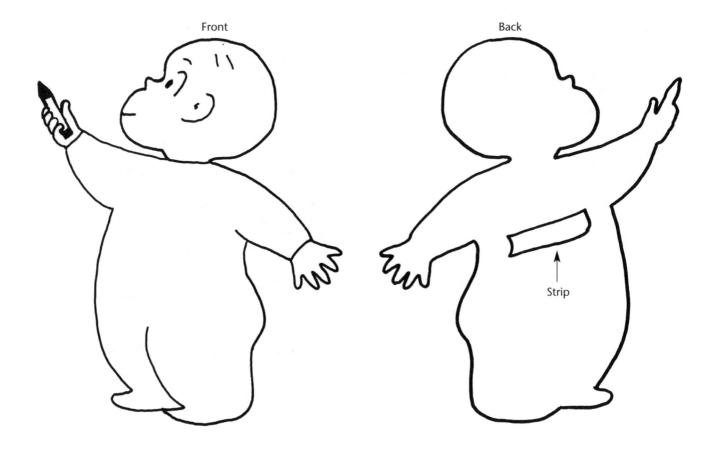

Strip

RESOURCE

2.5 Photo Story

The Snowy Day (grades K–2)

Purpose

To have students:

- Use visual imagery to help retell the teacher's sample story
- Use mental imagery to help picture the episodes
- Retell a favorite story using photographs
- Write, illustrate (with photos), and present an original photo story

Materials

camera
film
props needed to act out story

Activity

1. Introduce the story. Explain that taking photographs or slides of the children acting out scenes from the story are visual representations of the story's plot episodes. If a video camera is available, you can videotape the students acting out the story. Then have the photographs or slides developed. Specify that the students should use mental imagery to visualize the story's episodes while the story is read so that they are able to critically evaluate the appropriateness of the photographs. (See DLTA, Resource 2.1.)

2. Model how to tell a photo story. As you tell the story, show the photos, slides, or video. Show illustrations from the book side by side with the photos.

3. Have students retell the sample story using the photos, slides, or video.

4. Have children re-read a favorite book, alone or with a partner, and create a photo story. Remind them to make photographs that represent the story's plot episodes. Remind them to use the mental imagery and the think-aloud strategy to decide on appropriate photographs and present the story.

5. Students may write and create an original photo story.

Sample Story: *The Snowy Day*

by Ezra Jack Keats

Peter, the main character in the book, goes out into the snow and makes angels, builds a snowman, throws snowballs, and slides down a hill. If you live where it snows, have a child dress in winter clothes and act out these scenes. Props needed: jacket, boots, hat, scarf, mittens, stick.

Books Appropriate for Photo Stories for Grades Pre-K–2

Caps, Hats, Socks, and Mittens: A Book About the Four Seasons (Borden). Simple text and illustrations describe some of the pleasures of each season.
Hold My Hand (Zolotow). Two little girls take a walk on a snowy day.
Summer Is . . . (Zolotow). The beauty of summer, winter, fall, and spring.

Books Appropriate for Photo Stories for Grades 3–5

Choose the introduction or a favorite scene or chapter from the book, or do a plot summary.

Amelia Bedelia (Parish). A clumsy yet lovable maid takes all her job instructions literally.
The Cybil War (Byars). Simon learns about friendship when his friend Tony's stories get him into trouble with Cybil, a girl he has a crush on.
Harriet the Spy (Fitzhugh). Harriet M. Welsh is an only child who doesn't get along with the other sixth graders. Forced to grow up with the loss of her nursemaid, she uses a notebook to record her thoughts.

A child reenacting scenes from *The Snowy Day* by Ezra Jack Keats; making snow angels and a snowman.

RESOURCE
2.6 Sound and Music Stories

Charlie and the Chocolate Factory
(grades 3–5),
"The Grouchy Queen and the Happy
King" (grades Pre-K–2)
The Three Little Pigs (grades Pre-K–2)

Purpose

To have students:

- Retell the teacher's sample story with appropriate sounds or music
- Make associations between the main characters' descriptions and the sounds that represent them

Materials

tape recorder

Activity

1. Read the story without using sounds or music. Tell the children to pay attention to the way the characters are described. (See DLTA, Resource 2.1.)
2. Create a character map for each character. Explain that this story can also be told using sounds and music to represent each character and that they are used when the characters' names are read in the story.
3. Model how the sounds or music represent each character.
4. Review the names and sounds, and practice making the sounds. It will help to have the names and sounds written on a chart.
5. Tell the story and record it for use in the listening center.
6. Have children retell the teacher's sample story.
7. Have children re-read a favorite book, alone or with a partner, and create a sound or music story. Remind them to choose sounds that represent the story's characters.

Sample Story: *Charlie and the Chocolate Factory*

by Roald Dahl

When the underlined words are mentioned, the following sounds are made:

Mr. Wonka: Ha-ha-ha (he is always laughing and jolly).
Charlie Bucket: A sigh (he sighs a lot).
Augustus Gloop: Slurp-slurp (the sound of a dog lapping up water) (he gets into trouble drinking the chocolate river).
Veruca Salt: Cha-ching (the sound a cash register makes) (she is a spoiled little rich girl).
Violet Beauregarde: A chewing sound (she is always chewing gum).
Mike Teavee: Bang-bang (he always wears a holster with toy guns).

The following is a summary of Chapter 29:

"I wonder what happened to the others," said Mr. Wonka. The elevator neared the ground by the entrance of the chocolate factory. As Charlie looked out, he could see Augustus, Veruca, and Violet, and all of their parents. "But I only see three of them," said Charlie. "I expect Mike Teavee will be out very soon," replied Mr. Wonka. "Do you see the trucks, Charlie?"

Charlie answered yes and asked what they were for. Mr. Wonka replied, "The golden tickets said that each winner would get a lifetime supply of chocolate. The trucks will carry it home for them. Can you see Augustus Gloop?" continued Mr. Wonka. "There he is, getting into the truck with his parents."

"So he's really all right," asked Charlie, "even after going up the pipe?" "He's better than ever and skinnier than ever," replied Mr. Wonka.

"And there's Violet Beauregarde!" exclaimed Charlie. "I guess they were able to de-juice her. But what's wrong with Veruca Salt?" asked Charlie. "She's covered in garbage. Oh wait!" continued Charlie in amazement. "There's Mike Teavee. What did they do to him? He's so tall and thin."

"Oops!" replied Mr. Wonka. "They must have over-stretched him on the gum-stretching machine."

"That's terrible," said Charlie.

"Not true, Charlie," responded Mr. Wonka. "He's quite lucky. All of the professional basketball teams will want to recruit him."

"But now it's time we left these children," said Mr. Wonka. "I have something important to show you, Charlie." Mr. Wonka pressed another button and the elevator swooped up toward the sky.

Sample Story: "The Grouchy Queen and the Happy King"

(adapted from an anonymous tale)

When the underlined words are mentioned, the following sounds are made:

Queen Grace the Grouch: Grrrrr.
King Happy Herman: Ha-ha-ha.
Whistling Wilbur: Whistling sound high to low.
Singing Sam: La-la-la (first few notes of "Mary Had a Little Lamb").
Tired Tim: Ahhhhh (yawning sound).
Lively Lorraine: Ah-ha.

Once upon a time there was a queen named <u>Grace the Grouch.</u> She had this name because she growled most of the time. <u>Queen Grace the Grouch</u> was married to <u>King Happy Herman</u>. He was called <u>Happy Herman</u> because he laughed most of the time. Together they made a perfect couple. <u>Queen Grace the Grouch</u> and <u>King Happy Herman</u> had three sons. The first son's name was <u>Whistling Wilbur</u>. He had this name because he whistled almost all the time. The second son's name was <u>Singing Sam</u>. He had this name because most of the time he sang. The third son's name was <u>Tired Tim</u>. He had this name because most of the time he was sleeping, and when he was awake he was doing almost nothing but yawning.

There was a princess from the next kingdom named <u>Lively Lorraine</u>. She couldn't sit still for a moment. She bounced around from dawn till dusk looking for things to do. Each time the princess would find a job to be done, she'd lift her hand in the air and say, "Ah-ha." When most people spoke of Lorraine, they could not help but say, "Ah-ha."

<u>Lively Lorraine</u> decided she'd like to marry. She knew of <u>Queen Grace the Grouch</u> and her husband, <u>King Happy Herman</u>. She also knew about their three sons, <u>Whistling Wilbur</u>, <u>Singing Sam</u>, and <u>Tired Tim</u>. <u>Lively Lorraine</u> decided to take a look at the three princes to see if one might be suitable for her as a future king. She saddled her horse one day and away she galloped to the kingdom over the hill.

When she arrived, she was greeted by <u>Queen Grace the Grouch</u> and her husband, <u>King Happy Herman</u>. <u>Lively Lorraine</u> decided to stay a while to get to know each prince and to see if there was one that best suited her.

First, <u>Lively Lorraine</u> played tennis with <u>Whistling Wilbur</u>. But he whistled so much throughout the game that <u>Lively Lorraine</u> could not concentrate and kept missing the ball.

The next day, Lorraine went sailing with <u>Singing Sam</u>. Sam was nice, but he never stopped singing. Instead of talking, he'd find an appropriate song and sing what he had to say. For a while it was fun, but Lorraine tired of it quickly.

<u>Lively Lorraine</u> felt sad. She decided that she would not meet the prince of her dreams here in this kingdom. But suddenly <u>Tired Tim</u> came yawning down the garden path. Lorraine took one look at him and said, "Ah-ha." Somehow <u>Lively Lorraine</u> and <u>Tired Tim</u> made the perfect couple—something like <u>Queen Grace the Grouch</u> and <u>King Happy Herman</u>.

So <u>Lively Lorraine</u> and <u>Tired Tim</u> trotted off to the kingdom over the hill to be married. Of course, they lived happily ever after.

Sample Story: *The Three Little Pigs*

by Tadasu Izawa and Shigemi Hijikata

Retells the episode in the lives of two foolish pigs and how the third pig managed to avoid the same fate. A flute can be used for the sound of the pigs. Roll fingers across a keyboard or piano for the wolf.

Books Appropriate for Sound and Music Stories for Grades Pre-K–2

Clicky, Clack, Moo: Cows That Type (Cronin). Story about cows who rebel against a farmer and make requests using typewriter.

Mister Brown Can Moo! Can You? (Suess). As Mr. Brown makes various sounds, children are encouraged to repeat them.

The Noisy Book (M. W. Brown). Muffin, the dog, is blindfolded for a day and tries to identify things by the sounds they make.

Over the River and Through the Woods (Child). Illustrated version of a well-known song describing the joys of a visit to grandmother's house.

The Three Little Billy Goats Gruff (M. Brown). Tale of how three billy goats outwit a hungry troll.

Tingalayo (Raffi). Illustrated version of a calypso song about a jovial donkey who befriends a girl at a Caribbean carnival.

Books Appropriate for Sound and Music Stories for Grades 3–5

Max Malone and the Great Cereal Rip-Off (C. Herman). Max is upset when the prize is missing from his cereal box, so he decides to investigate.

Mrs. Frisby and the Rats of Nimh (O'Brien). Mrs. Frisby, a widowed mouse, turns to the wise rats for help in raising her children.

Peter and the Wolf (Prokofiev). Tale of a boy who, ignoring his grandfather's warnings, proceeds to capture a wolf. You can play the accompanying tape as you tell the story.

Play Me a Story (Rosenberg.) Children are introduced to classical music through various stories and poems.

Superfudge (Blume). A young boy, Peter, describes the ups and downs of life with his younger brother, Fudge.

Zin! Zin! Zin! a Violin (Moss). Children meet the orchestra: trumpet, french horn, and other instruments.

RESOURCE
2.7 Song Story

Old MacDonald Had a Farm (grades Pre-K–2)

Purpose

To have students:

- Retell the teacher's sample story
- Notice syllables in the musical beat
- Create story songbooks

Materials

copies of *Old MacDonald Had a Farm* (Quackenbush), *Go Tell Aunt Rhody* (Quackenbush), *and Chicken Soup with Rice* (Sendak)
white paper
colored construction paper
stapler
felt tip pens and crayons

Activity

1. Read *Old MacDonald Had a Farm*.
2. Sing the song and show the pictures in the book.
3. Do the same with *Go Tell Aunt Rhody* and *Chicken Soup with Rice*.
4. Discuss other songs that children could make into books.
5. Have children work in pairs to create their own songbooks.

Books Appropriate for Song Stories for Grades Pre-K–5

The Erie Canal (Spier)
Over in the Meadow (Keats)
She'll Be Coming 'Round the Mountain (Quackenbush)

RESOURCE
2.8 Roll Movie Stories

Little Red Riding Hood (grades Pre-K–2)
"The Lion and the Rat" (grades Pre-K–2)

Purpose

To have students:

- Identify plot episodes when retelling the teacher's sample story
- Use the "think, pair, share" strategy to summarize and find the main idea of each plot episode
- Write and illustrate a roll movie story of a favorite book

Materials

white drawing or shelving paper
pencils, markers, crayons
roll movie box (A2.6)

Activity

1. Show the roll movie box and how it works. Explain that a roll movie story is a shortened version of an original book. The story is retold in the storyteller's own words and with illustrations that the storyteller chose in order to illustrate important details and plot episodes. Ask students to think about (as the story unfolds) why each episode was chosen for illustration. (See DLTA, Resource 2.1.)
2. Model how to tell the roll movie story by changing scenes as appropriate. The pertinent story part should be written below each illustration or on the back.
3. With a partner, students discuss their observations. Then they meet in a whole group and share them.
4. Read the actual book so that students can compare the two stories.
5. Have students work in groups of three or four to choose a favorite book and create a roll movie. Remind them to include details and the main idea when choosing pictures and words for the roll movie.

Sample Story: *Little Red Riding Hood*

by the Grimm Brothers

A classic fairy tale of a little girl, her grandmother, and a wily wolf. Roll movie scenes:

1. Little Red Riding Hood in front of her cottage.
2. Mother giving Red Riding Hood a basket of food.
3. Red Riding Hood encountering wolf in forest.
4. Red Riding Hood picking flowers.
5. Red Riding Hood finding wolf in grandmother's bed.
6. Wolf in grandmother's clothes chasing Red Riding Hood.
7. Hunter chasing away wolf.
8. Red Riding Hood, grandmother, and hunter drinking tea.

Sample Story: "The Lion and the Rat"

(adapted from an anonymous tale)

1. A big lion who lived in the jungle claimed he was the king!

2. The lion got sleepy and took a nap.

3. A quiet little mouse walked along and came up close to the lion.

4. The lion was about to eat the mouse but the mouse begged the lion to let him go.

5. The mouse tried to be the lion's friend but the lion didn't want that.

6. Later that night, the lion got caught in a net.

7. The mouse came along and saved the lion by setting him free.

8. The lion and the mouse became friends from that day on.

Enlarge slides to size of roll box opening, color, and tape together to make a roll movie.

Books Appropriate for Roll Movie Stories for Grades Pre-K–2

Cat, You Better Come Home (Keillor). Puff, the cat, leaves home seeking a more extravagant lifestyle, but returns when she discovers life isn't greener on the other side.

The Girl Who Loved Wild Horses (Goble). Though she is fond of her people, a girl prefers to live among the wild horses, where she is happy.

The Paper Bag Princess (Munsch). A princess outsmarts a dragon and gets rid of him for good. In the process she finds out it is better to be a smart princess than a well-dressed one.

Where the Wild Things Are (Sendak). Max sails off in a private boat to where the wild things are and becomes their king.

A2.6 Making a Roll Movie Box

A roll movie box is an important piece of equipment for the classroom. With this device the child can write and illustrate an original story and present it to the class.

1. Select a strong cardboard box about 18" high by 14" wide by 10" deep (45 cm x 35 cm x 25 cm).
2. Remove the cover or flaps of the box, leaving the sides and bottom.
3. Cut a rectangular shape out of the bottom of the box, leaving about 2" (5 cm) as a border on all sides.
4. Cut two holes on both sides of the box, close to the opening, yet far enough away to fit the roll of paper that will contain the illustrations.
5. Obtain two wooden dowels about 20" (50 cm) long and place them through the holes in the box.
6. Cover the outside of the box with self-adhesive vinyl.
7. Draw each picture for the story on white shelving paper the right size to fit and show through the opening in the box. Write the text of the story under each illustration.
8. Turn the roll movie box to its back side, and attach the beginning of the roll to the top wooden dowel with masking tape. Roll up the pictures onto the top dowel and then attach the other end of the paper roll to the bottom dowel. Now roll the strip to its beginning position, and it is ready to be rolled and told.

The movie box may be used horizontally, with the strip rolling onto the right-hand dowel. However, this may be more difficult, since the box cannot sit flat but must be held by someone or be placed on the edge of the table or desk. If you are lucky enough to have an old wooden TV frame, bore some holes and use it to show movie strips.

* A readymade Story Center that can be used as a roll movie box is available for purchase from the author, <www.mmmeducational@msn.com/>

Books Appropriate for Roll Movie Stories for Grades 3–5

Choose the introduction or a favorite scene or chapter from the book, or do a plot summary.

Bridge to Terabithia (Paterson). A ten-year-old Virginia boy loses his new friend when she meets an untimely death trying to reach Terabithia, their hideaway, during a terrible storm.

The Hundred Dresses (Estes). A young girl tells her classmates about the many dresses she owns.

Island of the Blue Dolphins (O'Dell). A courageous Indian girl lives alone on an island for eighteen years, after her tribe emigrates and leaves her behind.

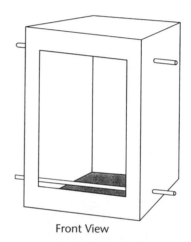

Front View

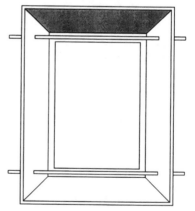

Back View

Back of Story Center Roll Movie

RESOURCE
2.9 Movie or Television Stories

The Indian in the Cupboard (grades 3–5)
Madeline (grades Pre-K–2)

Purpose

To have students:

- Retell stories that are movies or television shows made from books
- Compare and contrast the similarities and differences between a book and the corresponding television program or movie using a Venn diagram
- Become motivated to read books after seeing television show or movie
- Discuss how books activate your imagination

Materials

> television
> VCR
> video of movie
> copy of book

Activity

1. Explain that many popular movies and television shows have been created from books.
2. After students have finished reading the book, tell them that they will watch the movie or television show. Show the video, or find out when the movie will be shown on television, and encourage children to watch.
3. Ask the children to pay attention to the similarities and differences between the book and movie. After the show, complete a Venn diagram to compare and contrast them. Discuss how books leave more to the imagination.

Sample Story: *The Indian in the Cupboard*

by Lynne Reid Banks

In this story, a nine-year-old English boy accidentally brings his three-inch-tall Indian toy to life.

Sample Story: *Madeline*

by Ludwig Bemelmans

Madeline charms her classmates with funny pranks. But when Madeline needs her appendix out, she's the one who needs charm and humor for a speedy recovery.

Appropriate Books That Are Also Movies for Grades Pre-K–5

Black Stallion (Farley). A young orphan boy is shipwrecked on a deserted island with a horse.

Harry Potter and the Sorcerer's Stone (Rowling). An orphaned boy learns he is a wizard and attends a special school to improve his magical powers.

The Lion, the Witch, and the Wardrobe (Lewis). Four children discover an empty wardrobe that leads to a magical kingdom filled with heroes and villains.

The Secret Garden (Burnett). An orphan goes to live with her cold, unfeeling uncle. Behind his house she finds an abandoned garden.

The Wizard of Oz (Baum). After a cyclone lands Dorothy in Oz, she must avoid the wicked witch and find her way back to Kansas.

Appropriate Books That Are Also Television Programs for Grades Pre-K–5

Bringing the Rain to Kapiti Plain (Aardema). A cumulative rhyme of how Ki-pat brought rain to the drought-stricken Kapiti Plain.

The Magic School Bus Inside the Earth (Cole). Mrs. Frizzle and her magic school bus take her students into the earth for some real hands-on science explorations.

The Magic School Bus Inside Ralphie (Cole). Mrs. Frizzle and her magic school bus take her students into Ralphie's body to explore where his fever and sore throat are coming from.

RESOURCE
2.10 Food Story

"The Little Round Red House" (grades Pre-K–2)

Purpose

To have students:

- Retell the teacher's sample story
- Retell a favorite story using food as prop
- Follow directions in a recipe to make food
- Write and present an original food story

Materials

apples
knife

Activity

1. Tell the story "The Little Round Red House." Cut the apple in half crosswise at the end to reveal the surprise.
2. Tell the students that food can be used as a prop to tell a story.
3. Have students retell the sample story; have apples for snack.
4. Brainstorm a list of stories that can be told with food. Ask children to pick a story to retell with food. Depending on the food used for the story, have them retell the story using food as a prop, or making the food and eating it after listening to the story. When making the food, stress the importance of following the directions on the recipe.
5. Have children write and present an original food story.

Cut apple on the dotted line.

Sample Story: "The Little Round Red House"

(adapted from an anonymous tale)

School had ended for the summer. Stephanie was wandering around the house trying to find something to do. She colored for a while, cut and pasted, and looked at some books; but nothing seemed like much fun today. She looked for her mother. Her mother was at her desk, busy with some important work.

Stephanie said to her mother, "What can I do today? I just can't seem to find anything."

Her mother thought for a while and said, "Stephanie, I know what you can do. Go outside for a walk and see if you can find a little round red house that has no windows and no doors, a chimney on top, and a star inside."

Stephanie wasn't really sure what her mother was talking about, but since it sounded interesting she decided to give it a try. First, Stephanie walked down Elm Street. Then she tried Heritage Lane. But not one house fit the description her mother had given. She could not find a little round red house that had no windows and no doors, a chimney on top, and a star inside. All the houses had windows and doors. None of the houses was even red.

When she was about to give up and go home, she met her friend Darren. He was looking for something to do. Stephanie asked him to help her with her search. The two children decided to ask Mr. and Mrs. Mandel if they knew of this little round red house. Mr. and Mrs. Mandel owned the candy shop in town, and they knew everything about the town in which Stephanie and Darren lived. If there was anyone who would know about such a strange house, it would be the Mandels.

Stephanie ran into the candy shop. She immediately asked Mrs. Mandel if she knew of a little round red house that had no windows and no doors, a chimney on top, and a star inside. Mrs. Mandel thought for a while and then said, "Stephanie, go down to the shady pond where the wind blows through the trees. Sit down a while to enjoy the summer day and the breeze rippling through the trees, and maybe you will find what you are looking for."

Darren and Stephanie hurried down to the shady pond. It was a long walk and the day was hot, so they were happy to sit down and rest by the pond in the shade of the trees. Before long, a lovely cool breeze blew through the branches of the trees. The leaves rustled, and something fell out of one of the trees.

Whatever fell bounced first on Stephanie's head and then fell to the ground. It had split into two pieces. Stephanie picked up the two pieces and put them back together again. Then she began to laugh. "My goodness," she said, "I've found it! This is the little round red house that has no windows and no doors, a chimney on top, and a star inside." Hungry from their experience, Darren and Stephanie each took a piece and enjoyed the apple (*show cut apple*) that had fallen from the tree.

Books Appropriate for Food Stories for Grades Pre-K–2

Blueberries for Sal (McCloskey). A bear cub and a little girl wander off from their mothers to pick blueberries and end up confusing each other's mothers for their own.

If You Give a Mouse a Cookie (Numeroff). A boy meets a mouse who will do anything for a cookie.

Lunch (Fleming). A very hungry mouse eats a large lunch composed of colorful foods.

Books Appropriate for Food Stories for Grades 3–5

Chicken Soup with Rice (Sendak). A nonsensical rhyming book about the months of the year and chicken soup.

Cloudy with a Chance of Meatballs (Barrett). Life is delicious in the town of Chewandswallow, where it rains soup and juice, snows mashed potatoes, and blows storms of hamburgers, until the weather takes a turn for the worse.

Favorite Stories for the Children's Hour (Bailey and Lewis).

"How Maple Sugar Came," an Indian legend, and "The Wonderful Porridge Pot," a fairy tale.

Books with Accompanying Recipes

The Big Snow (Hader). As the geese fly south, the animals recognize this as a sign that winter is coming. A big snow falls and covers the ground. The animals can no longer find food. Then a little old woman scatters seeds, nuts, and bread crumbs for them. *Recipe: Pine Cone Bird Feeder.* Each needs a large pine cone. Also needed are a large jar of peanut butter, birdseed, and string. Spread the peanut butter into the open spaces of a pine cone. Stick birdseed into the peanut butter. Tie a string to the pine cone and hang it on a tree at home or outside the classroom.

Charlie and the Chocolate Factory (Dahl). Everyone, especially those who have seen the movie, will enjoy the adventures of Charlie Bucket, a poor boy who lives next to Willy Wonka's wonderful chocolate factory. Charlie wins a ticket for a tour of the factory; his adventures there are hilarious. *Recipe: Charlie's Chocolate Flake Candy.* For six dozen pieces, you will need 5 cups cornflakes; 1/4 tsp. salt; 1 lb. sweet milk chocolate; two 1-oz. squares unsweetened chocolate. Combine cornflakes and salt. Melt the chocolate in a double boiler; pour over cornflake mixture; mix well, slightly crushing the cornflakes. Drop from teaspoon onto waxed paper. Chill several hours. Keep in cool place.

Cranberry Thanksgiving (Devlin). Maggie and her grandmother live by a cranberry bog. Maggie's grandmother is famous for her cranberry bread and is said to make the best for miles around. On Thanksgiving both Maggie and her grandmother invite a guest to dinner. When the meal is over, Maggie's grandmother learns a lesson about judging people by how they look. *Recipe: Grandma's Famous Cranberry Bread.* To make one loaf of bread, you will need 2 cups all-purpose flour; 1 cup sugar; 1 1/2 tsp. baking powder; 1 tsp. salt; 1/2 tsp. baking soda; 1/4 cup butter or margarine; 1 egg, beaten; 1 tsp. grated orange peel; 3/4 cup orange juice; 1 cup coarsely chopped walnuts; 1 1/2 cups fresh or frozen cranberries, chopped. Combine flour, sugar, baking powder, salt, and baking soda in a large bowl. Cut in butter until mixture is crumbly. Add egg, orange peel, and orange juice all at once; stir just until mixture is evenly moist. Fold in cranberries and nuts. Spoon into a greased 9" x 5" x 3" loaf pan. Bake at 350°F for one hour and 10 minutes, or until a toothpick inserted in the center comes out clean. Remove from pan and cool on wire rack. Slice and serve.

Hard Scrabble Harvest (Ipcar). This story for young readers relates in rhyme the farmers' struggle against the possibility of bad weather and pesky insects, from spring planting to fall harvest. Happily, the book ends with a harvest of tomatoes, apples, pumpkins, and corn. *Recipe: Pumpkin Pie.* To make one 9" pie, you will need 1 1/2 cups cooked or canned pumpkin; 3/4 cup sugar; 1/2 tsp. salt; 1/4 tsp. nutmeg; 3 eggs, slightly beaten; 1 1/4 cup milk; 3/4 cup evaporated milk; one uncooked 9" pie shell. Combine pumpkin, sugar, salt, and spices. Add eggs and milk, and cream together. Pour into the unbaked pie shell. Bake in a hot oven (425°F) for 10 minutes, then in a moderate oven (325°F) for another 45 minutes or until the mixture does not adhere to a knife inserted in the middle.

Rabbit Hill (Lawson). A good story for middle elementary grades. The rabbit family and its friends worry if the people moving into the big house near their rabbit hill will be mean and pinching, or folks with a thought for the small creatures who have always lived there. The new folk prove their beneficence to animals by planting their vegetable garden without fences. *Recipe: Rabbit Hill Spring Salad.* If possible, use ingredients from a vegetable garden planted by the class. To make 25 servings you will need: 2 heads lettuce; 2 cucumbers; 2 stalks celery; 1 bunch carrots; 1 dozen tomatoes. Wash all vegetables. Tear lettuce into small pieces; slice cucumbers, celery, carrots, and tomatoes. Place each ingredient in its own separate bowl. Children take a dish and serve themselves salad bar-style.

The Snowy Day (Keats). On the first snowy day of winter, everyone will enjoy the adventures of a boy who goes out to play in the newly fallen snow. He builds a snowman, makes angels, throws snowballs, and takes a snowball into his house to save for the next day. *Recipe: Ice Cream Snowballs.* To make 25 snowballs you will need 1/2 gallon vanilla ice cream; 2 cups shredded coconut. Scoop 25 round ice cream balls. Roll in shredded coconut. Put into freezer.

Strawberry Girl (Lenski). Use this story with middle elementary graders. Birdie Boyer's family has moved to Florida's backwoods to raise small crops of sweet 'taters, strawberries, oranges, and the like. *Recipe: Strawberry Layer Dessert.* To make 12 servings, you will need one 10-oz. pkg. frozen sliced strawberries (thawed); one 3-oz. pkg. strawberry gelatin; 1 cup hot water; 1 cup whipping cream (whipped); one 10-inch tube angel cake. Drain strawberries, reserving 1/2 cup syrup. Dissolve gelatin in hot water. Add reserved syrup. Chill until partially set. Beat mixture till light and fluffy. Fold in whipped cream. Chill until of spreading consistency. Transfer 1 1/2 cups mixture to small bowl; fold in drained strawberries. Split cake crosswise into three equal layers. Fill between layers with strawberry mixture. Frost top and sides with remaining whipped-cream mixture. Chill and serve.

RESOURCE

2.11 Cut Story

"The Unusual House" (grades 3–5)

Purpose

To have students:

- Retell the teacher's sample story
- Retell a favorite story using the cut story technique
- Write and present an original cut story

Materials

scissors
fold drawing on colored construction paper
pencils

Activity

1. Explain that while you tell a story, you will cut out pictures of characters or figures that go along with the story.
2. Tell the story.
3. Students practice until they can retell the sample story while cutting out the figures.
4. Children work with a partner to retell a favorite story while using the cut story technique.
5. Children write and present an original cut story.

Sample Story: "The Unusual House"

(adapted from an anonymous tale)

(Take a piece of construction paper and fold it in half lengthwise; draw the outline of half a flower, as shown in the illustration. As you tell the story, cut out the flower.)

Near Susan's house was a wooded area. Once in a while Susan and her mother would walk through the woods together, exploring. Susan's mother told her never to go into the woods alone because she might get lost. Susan was allowed, however, to play in the grassy field at the edge of the woods.

While Susan was playing in the field one day, a butterfly with many colors attracted her attention. She chased it through the field, and before she realized it she was in the woods, running after the fast butterfly. Finally the butterfly landed, and Susan got a good look at it. It was pink, white, and blue. It was very beautiful. It flew off again, but this time Susan didn't chase it. She was tired from all the running she had just done. She sat down on a rock and watched the butterfly circle overhead. It finally flew farther and farther overhead, until Susan could see it no longer. (*Begin cutting, but do not unfold.*)

When she caught her breath, Susan looked around and, to her surprise, she saw that she was deep in the woods. She could not see the clearing anywhere. She got up and started for the grassy field but really wasn't sure which way to go. She began walking in the direction she thought was right. She walked straight ahead for a while, around some bushes, up a short hill, and down a path. She went around this way and that, up and down and around, but still could not find her way out. She thought she might be lost forever. She sat down on a rock and was about to cry when in the distance she noticed a house with a very strange shape. The house was most unusual; it looked something like this. (*Display the folded cutout half flower.*)

Susan was frightened but didn't know where else to go. She walked slowly toward the house and noticed that it had a most unusual chimney that was shaped something like this. (*Hold up and show cutout chimney piece.*)

Susan's curiosity got the best of her, and she continued straight for the house. She

noticed that the door of the house was as unusual as the chimney and had a shape that looked something like this. (*Hold up and show cutout door piece.*)

As she got even closer to the strange-shaped house, she could see its windows. There were only two, and they were both shaped something like this. (*Hold up and show cutout window piece.*)

Susan's curiosity again got the best of her. She moved toward the house carefully and quietly. When she was about to get to the front door, she suddenly became frightened again. At that very moment something touched her on the shoulder. She turned quickly to see what it was. It was a beautiful flower! (*Unfold the cutout.*) It smiled and said:

Happy spring day!
Don't run away.
The nice people in the house
Would like you to stay.

Susan knocked on the door of the house. The people inside the house were nice, so Susan stayed a while and played. After giving her some cookies and milk, the people told Susan how to get home. She arrived at her own house safe and sound, with a beautiful flower to give to her mother.

This same story can be told at other times of the year. Instead of cutting out a flower shape, cut an autumn leaf in the fall, a pumpkin for Halloween, a Christmas tree at Christmas time, a valentine for Valentine's Day, and a shamrock for St. Patrick's Day. As you change the item being cut in the story, change the first line of the rhyme "Happy spring day!" to "Happy Valentine's Day!" "Happy Halloween Day!" and so on.

If you develop simple fold drawings of a boy, a girl, a rabbit, a house, a tree, and so on, you will be able to tell many stories with the cut story technique.

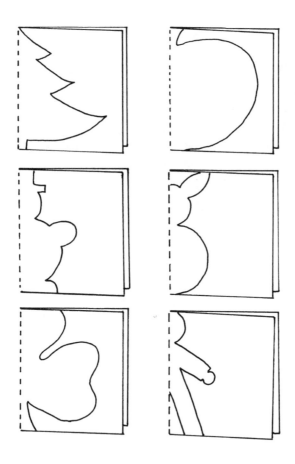

Books Appropriate for Cut Stories for Grades Pre-K–2

The Gingerbread Boy (Holdsworth). Fold, draw, and cut out half a gingerbread boy and the characters he meets along his way.

Jeanne-Marie Counts Her Sheep (Françoise). Fold eleven pieces of construction paper. On each, draw sheep with their backs on the fold. As Jeanne-Marie dreams of getting each new sheep, cut out another and open it up so that it stands.

Books Appropriate for Cut Stories for Grades 3–5

Babe the Gallant Pig (King-Smith). Draw a pig with its back on the fold. Cut it out as you tell the story so that the pig stands up. Cut out the other farm animals named in the story.

The Giving Tree (Silverstein). From a folded piece of paper, cut out a tree with branches and open up the paper. Put several pieces of red paper together and cut out apples as you tell about the boy eating the tree's apples. When the tree gives the boy its branches, cut the branches off your tree. When the tree gives the boy its trunk, cut the trunk off the tree, leaving a small stump.

Swimmy (grades Pre-K–2)

Purpose

To have students:

- Retell the teacher's sample story in order to understand and identify the story characters
- Retell a favorite story using the origami technique
- Write an original story and make an origami character

Materials

paper (newspaper, construction paper, or tissue paper)

Activity

1. Practice folding origami figures until you free confident with the technique and can fold and tell the story smoothly. (See list of books on origami and paper-folding techniques.)
2. While telling the story, fold the paper into the main character or object and display it until the story is ended.

Sample Story: *Swimmy*

by Leo Lionni

A little black fish escapes being eaten by a giant tuna and finds comfort and safety in numbers with his new friends. Origami technique: Fold paper into the shape of a fish (A2.7).

Books Appropriate for Origami Stories for Grades Pre-K–2

Have You Seen Birds? (Oppenheim). Inventively illustrated, a tale about birds of all kinds. Origami figure: bird.

Millions of Cats (G'ag). An enchanting tale of a gentle peasant who goes off in search of one kitten and returns with "hundreds of cats, thousands of cats, millions and billions and trillions of cats." Origami figure: cat.

The Owl and the Pussycat (Lear). After a courtship voyage of a year and a day, Owl and Pussycat finally buy a ring from Piggy and are blissfully married. Origami figure: boat.

Books Appropriate for Origami Stories for Grades 3–5

The Mouse and the Motorcycle (Cleary). A reckless young mouse makes friends with a boy in a motel and discovers the joy of motorcycling. Origami figure: mouse.

Sadako and the Thousand Paper Cranes (Coerr). Based on a true story of a Japanese girl who died of leukemia at the age of 12—the result of the radiation from the bomb dropped on Hiroshima, where she lived, during World War II. Legend says if sick people fold 1,000 paper cranes, the gods will make them well. Sadako folded 644 cranes before she died; her classmates folded the rest (A2.7).

Shiloh (Naylor). A boy finds a lost beagle and tries to hide it from his family and the real owner. Origami figure: dog.

Sylvester and the Magic Pebble (Steig). Sylvester Duncan, the donkey, finds a magic pebble that grants wishes. Origami figure: donkey.

Teacher Resources on Origami

Arika, Chiyo. *Origami in the Classroom,* vols. 1 and 2. Rutland, VT: Charles E. Tuttle, 1965–1968.

Harbin, Robert. *New Adventures in Origami.* New York: Harper and Row, 1971.

Honda, Isao. *The World of Origami.* Tokyo and San Francisco: Japan Publications Trading Co., 1965.

Lang, Robert J. *Origami Animals: Paper Animals from Around the World.* New York: Crescent, 1992.

Murray, William, and Francis Rigney. *Paper Folding for Beginners.* New York: Dover, 1960.

Randlett, Samuel. *The Best of Origami.* New York: Dutton, 1968.

Rojas, Hector. *Origami Animals.* New York: Sterling, 1993.

A2.7 Origami Fish

Enlarge as needed. Fold as indicated in order by number.

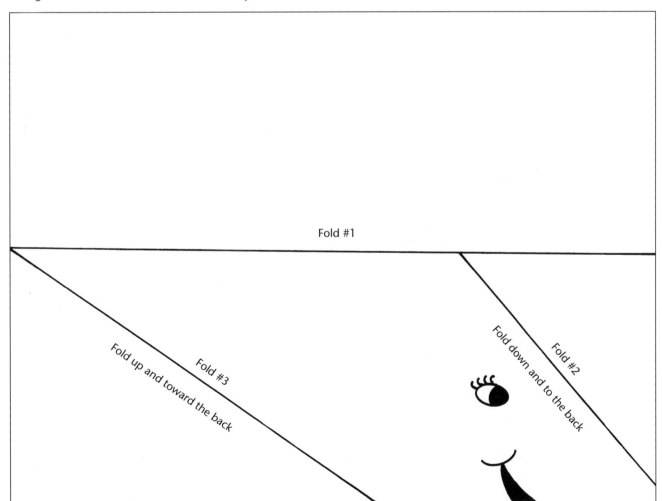

A2.8 Origami Crane

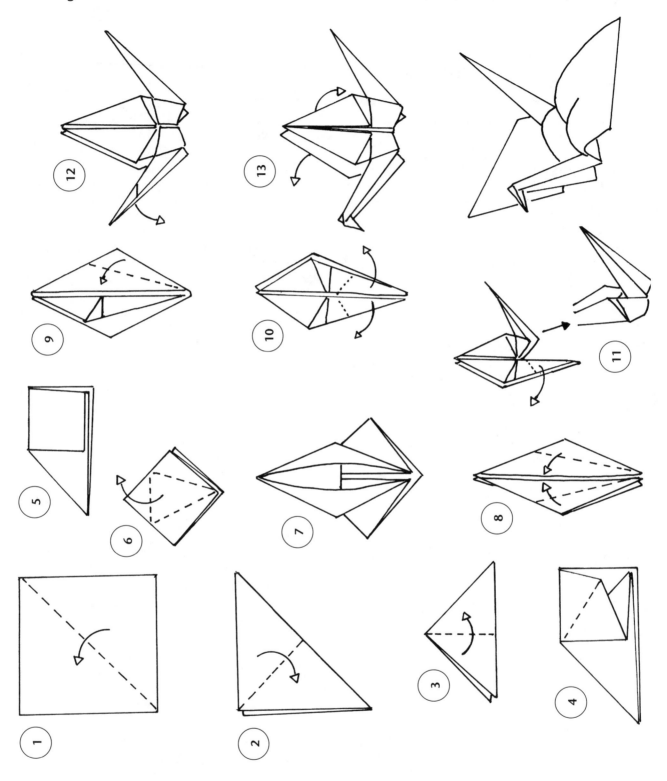

Word Study

This section provides teachers with resources and suggestions for helping children in kindergarten through fourth grade acquire word decoding skills to improve their reading ability. These word study activities may be used both during literacy center time and while the teacher is occupied with guided reading instruction.

Each lesson addresses a specific skill in such areas as phonemic awareness, letter recognition, print-sound correspondence, and using context to assist decoding. Engaging practice materials and activity/accountability forms are described. Variations on the sample lessons and appropriate children's literature are suggested.

Before assigning children to work independently, the teacher should explain the skill being taught and model the use of the materials and activity sheets. Students should be encouraged to ask questions during the modeling and have several opportunities to practice the activities before being assigned to work on their own. (See also Resource Section 1, A1.3, Activity Cards for Word Study.)

The lessons and materials provided are as follows:

3.1 Identifying letters of the alphabet by playing Bingo
   A3.1 Bingo card pattern
   A3.2 Letters of the alphabet and pictures for creating materials

3.2 Matching upper- and lowercase letters using puzzles
   A3.3 Puzzle piece patterns

3.3 Segmenting and blending phonemes using Elkonin boxes
   A3.4 Elkonin box pattern and activity sheet

3.4 Increasing sight vocabulary by reading environmental print
   A3.5 Reading environmental print activity sheet

3.5 Using semantics and syntax to decode words in the morning message
   A3.6 Morning message activity sheet

3.6 Learning letter-sound correspondence using an alphabet journal
   A3.7 Alphabet journal accountability form and letter-sound book list

3.7 Sorting words with short vowels using a pocket chart
   A3.8 Short-vowel word picture patterns and accountability form

3.8 Identifying phonograms using a game board
   A3.9 Phonogram game board and accountability form

3.9 Building words that end in silent *e* using onset/rime cards
   A3.10 Onset/rime card patterns and accountability form

3.10 Recognizing and sorting initial *l* blends by playing Memory
   A3.11 Blend picture patterns and accountability form

3.11 Building words with the *ch* digraph using word wheels
   A3.12 Word wheel patterns and accountability form

3.12 Identifying and sorting rhyming words using a pocket chart
   A3.13 Rhyming words accountability form

3.13 Making little words out of a big word
   A3.14 Making little words out of a big word

3.14 Adding prefixes to root words using a pocket chart
   A3.15 Prefixes accountability form

3.15 Identifying homophones using a flip book
   A3.16 Homophones and flip book accountability forms

3.16 Practicing high-frequency words using magnetic letters
   A3.17 High-frequency word accountability form

3.17 Sorting words according to syllables using letter/word cards
   A3.18 Syllables activity sheet

3.18 Incorporating technology into word study
   A3.19 Weather chart and temperature graph

RESOURCE
3.1 Identifying Letters of the Alphabet by Playing Bingo

Grades Pre-K–1

Purpose

To have students:

- Identify letters of the alphabet

Materials

pre-made Bingo cards (A3.1, A3.2)
letter cards (matching the case of letters on the
  Bingo cards)
Bingo markers such as dried lima beans
accountability forms
pencils

Activity

1. This game can be played by groups of four or five students. One student is the caller, and the other students are the players.

2. The caller gives each player a Bingo card and markers, and puts the letter cards in a pile.

3. Turning over one letter card at a time, the caller calls out the letter and holds up the card to help with letter identification.

4. If the players have the letter on their Bingo card, they cover it with a marker.

5. The first player to cover one row of letters on the card gets Bingo. The caller may check the players' answers by reviewing the pile of discarded cards that were called out.

Variation

- This game can be used for matching lowercase/uppercase letters, rhyming words, vowels, consonant blends, and digraphs.

Accountability

After the children have played the game, they complete an accountability form by writing on paper the letters covered (players) or called (caller) during the game.

A3.1 Bingo Card Pattern

Make five Bingo cards with all lower-case or all uppercase alphabet letters (A3.2). On each card leave one letter out, and scramble the remaining letters in different orders. Laminate. Readymade Bingo cards and letters can be downloaded from www.mcedservices.com/ESL/Bingo/AlphBing.pdf.

A3.2 Letters of the Alphabet and Pictures for Creating Materials

Photocopy to enlarge as needed

A B C D E F

G H I J K L

M N O P Q R

S T U V W X

Y Z b c d f

g h j k l m

n p q r s t

v w x y z

a e i o u

A3.2 *(cont.)*

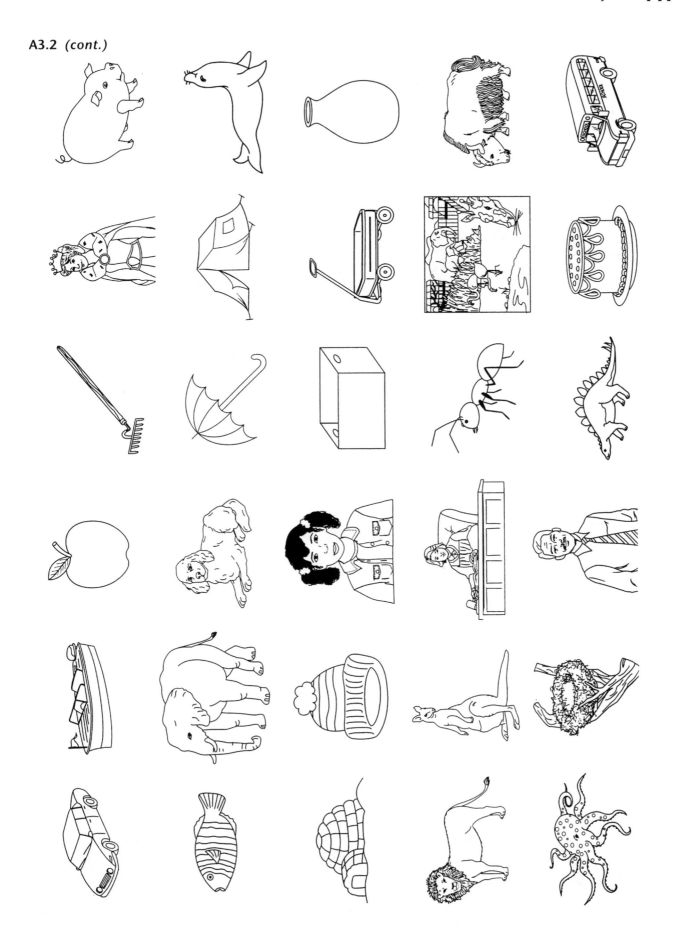

A3.2 *(cont.)*

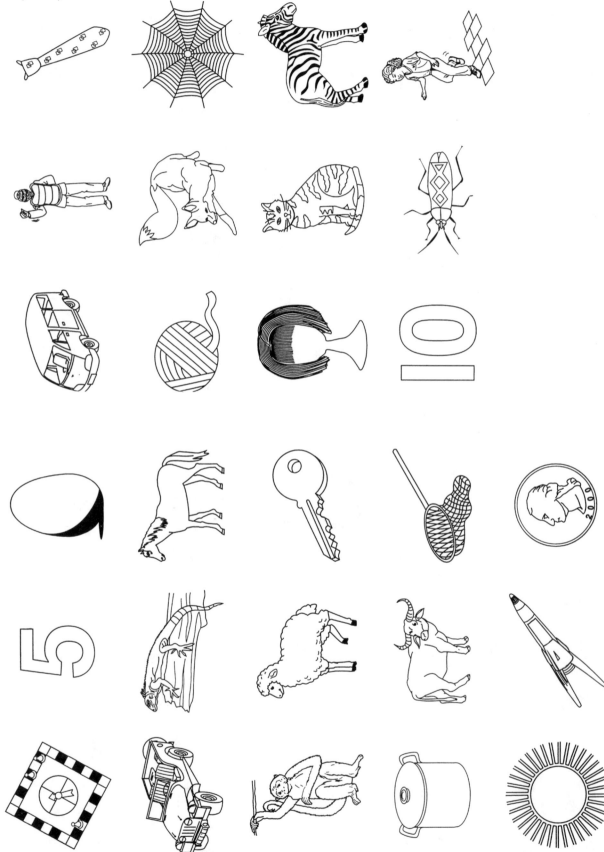

RESOURCE
3.2 Matching Upper- and Lowercase Letters Using Puzzles

Grades Pre-K–1

Purpose

To have students:

- Match upper- and lowercase letters

Materials

pre-made puzzle pieces of upper- and lowercase letters (A3.3, A3.2)

accountability forms
pencils

A3.3 Puzzle Piece Patterns

Place an uppercase alphabet letter on the left side, and the corresponding lowercase letter on the right side, of each puzzle piece (A3.2). Photocopy on colored paper. Laminate and cut. Repeat three more times, each time using different letters and different colored paper.

Activity

1. Students work alone or with a partner to match puzzle pieces.

Accountability

After the children have finished the puzzle, they complete an accountability form by writing on paper the upper- and lowercase letters they were able to match.

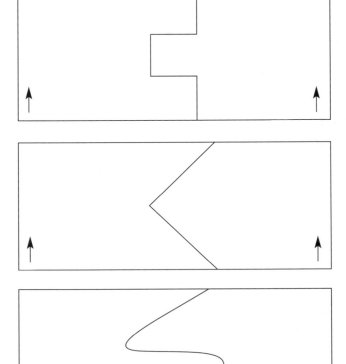
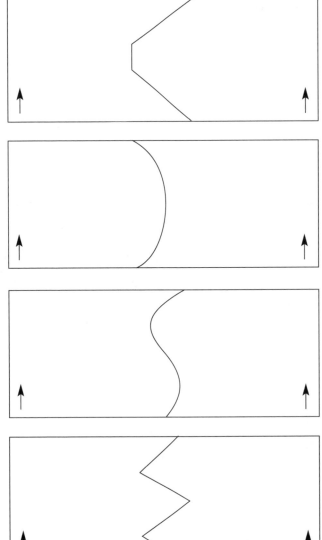

RESOURCE

3.3 Segmenting and Blending Phonemes Using Elkonin Boxes

Grades Pre-K–2

Purpose

To have students:

• Segment and blend phonemes in words

Materials

list of words being studied
wooden letters, felt letters and board, or magnetic letters and board
chips to serve as markers
laminated piece of paper divided into Elkonin boxes* (A3.4)
activity/accountability forms (A3.4)
pencils

*From the Russian psychologist D. B. Elkonin (see Clay 1985).

Activity

1. Children pick a word from the list of words being studied, such as *fish,* and spell the word with wooden, felt, or magnetic letters. They write the word on the activity sheet.
2. Give each child a laminated piece of paper divided into boxes. Have them say the word and segment the sounds. They put a chip into one of the boxes for each sound that is heard.
3. Children count the number of chips that were used (e.g., *fish* = three chips) and write the number on the activity sheet.
4. Children count how many letters are in *fish,* and record that number on the activity sheet.
5. Repeat for each word on the list.

Variation

• Instead of using a word list, use picture cards (A3.2).

Accountability

The accountability form will show all the words on the list that the children have completed.

A3.4 Elkonin Box Pattern and Activity Sheet

Photocopy on colored paper and laminate one set of boxes for each child.

Fish

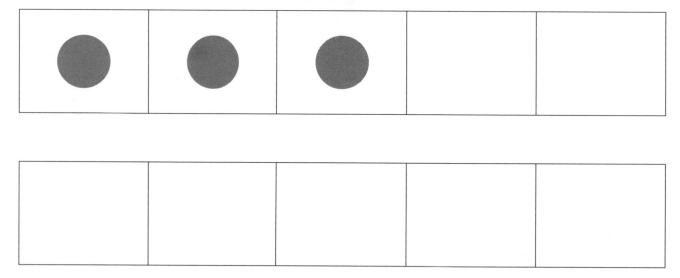

A3.4 *(cont.)*

Name _____ Date _____

For each word, write the number of sounds you hear and the number of letters in the word.

Example:

Word	Number of Sounds	Number of Letters
fish	3	4

1. _____   _____   _____

2. _____   _____   _____

3. _____   _____   _____

4. _____   _____   _____

5. _____   _____   _____

6. _____   _____   _____

7. _____   _____   _____

8. _____   _____   _____

RESOURCE

3.4 Increasing Sight Vocabulary by Reading Environmental Print

Grades Pre-K–5

Purpose

To have students:

- Increase sight vocabulary by reading environmental (classroom) print

Materials

> classroom signs
> labels
> dark felt-tip markers
> logos and trade names (e.g., from popular store chains or supermarkets)
> photographs of environmental print outside the classroom
> clipboards
> activity/accountability forms (A3.5)
> pencils

Activity

1. Fill the classroom with environmental print by posting signs around the room, such as a poster of the classroom rules. Label items in the classroom that are of interest to the class, such as content-related topics, and that serve a function, such as identifying important classroom materials. Begin each word with an uppercase letter and continue with lowercase letters. Hang labels at an easy height for children to see.

2. Carrying a clipboard and an activity sheet, children "read around the room," searching the classroom to find four words that they can decode and that they know the meaning of, and writing them down. They also list four words that they can decode but don't know the meaning of.

3. Then children write on the activity sheet a sentence using each word they knew. For words they didn't know, they use a strategy, such as asking a classmate or using context, to find its meaning and then record the strategy they used and the meaning of the word on the activity sheet.

Variation

- Students can use a newspaper from the classroom. Have them pick out three words they can decode. They can look the words up in the dictionary to find the definition if they do not know it.

Accountability

Students record their answers on an accountability sheet.

A3.5 Reading Environmental Print Activity Sheet

Name _____ Date _____

Read Around the Room

Words I knew:

1. _____

_____

_____

2. _____

_____

_____

3. _____

_____

_____

4. _____

_____

_____

A3.5 *(cont.)*

Name_____ Date _____

Read Around the Room

Words I didn't know:

1. _____

This word means _____

The strategy I used was _____

2. _____

This word means _____

The strategy I used was _____

3. _____

This work means _____

The strategy I used was _____

4. _____

This word means _____

The strategy I used was _____

RESOURCE
3.5 Using Semantics and Syntax to Decode Words in the Morning Message

Grades K–4

Purpose

To have students:

- Use semantics and syntax to decode words

Materials

chart paper, chalkboard, or dry-erase board
markers, chalk, or dry-erase pen
activity/accountability forms (A3.6)
pencils

Activity

1. Select a permanent spot for the chart paper, a chalkboard, or a dry-erase board. Every day write a message for the children at this spot, and review it with them. Use similar language each time to make the message familiar to the children. Make it part of the morning routine. Many teachers use this as part of morning meeting or circle time.
2. Write a message for the children that has sentences with blanks for omitted letters or words. Which letters or words are left out will depend on what the topic is being focused on at that particular time. For example, if the focus were on the letter *t* as an initial consonant, then all the words that began with *t* would have a blank in place of that letter.
3. During the morning routine, encourage children to use the syntax and semantics of sentences to identify words. Fill in the missing letters or words with the class.
4. Provide each student with an activity sheet showing the morning message the way it looked before it was filled in by the class.

Variation

- For younger students, it may be helpful to include a word bank to help them choose the letters or words that go into the blanks. This is similar to the cloze procedure.

Accountability

Children record the activity on an accountability sheet.

A3.6 Morning Message Activity Sheet

Name_____ Date ——————

Today's morning message is:

_____ood _____orning, Ms. Burke's class! Today _____s Mon_____,
January 13, 2001. It is the 95th day of _____, _____. Today we will go
to _____ library to read with Ms. Jones' _____. Don't forget to bring
your favorite _____.

RESOURCE
3.6 Learning Letter-Sound Correspondence Using an Alphabet Journal

Grades Pre-K–1

Purpose

To have students:

- Learn letter-sound correspondence

Materials

white paper
colored construction paper
stapler
magazines with pictures
accountability forms (A3.7)
pencils

Activity

1. Prepare blank books for each child. Use the colored construction paper for the front and back covers and 26 white pieces of paper for the inside pages. Staple the pages together.
2. Starting with the letter *A,* students write each letter of the alphabet on the top of one page.
3. On each page, children can draw or cut and paste magazine pictures that begin with the sound presented by that letter.
4. Label each picture. Each letter should have at least five pictures.

Variation

- Bare Books (books with hard covers, but no print inside), sewn books, and folded, stitched, and glued books can be used instead of blank books. To order Bare Books visit www.barebooks.com or write to Treetop Publishing, P.O. Box 085567, Racine, WI 53408-5567. For instructions on making sewn books and folded, stitched, and glued books, see Resource Section 5, A5.1.
- Paper Bag Letter-Sound Book. Give each child a brown lunch bag. Write a letter on the bottom flap of the bag. Lift the flap and draw a figure to match the letter-sound. Do this as you discuss each letter of the alphabet. Staple twenty-six letters at the top of the bag.

Accountability

Each time children complete a page, they record progress on an activity form.

Suggested Literature

For a list of books emphasizing consonant and long and short vowel sounds, see A3.7.

A3.7 Alphabet Journal Accountability Form and Letter-Sound Book List

Name _____ **Date** _____

List 3 of the words or names of pictures that you have included for each letter of the alphabet.

A	B	C	D
_____	_____	_____	_____
_____	_____	_____	_____
_____	_____	_____	_____

E	F	G	H
_____	_____	_____	_____
_____	_____	_____	_____
_____	_____	_____	_____

I	J	K	L
_____	_____	_____	_____
_____	_____	_____	_____
_____	_____	_____	_____

M	N	O	P
_____	_____	_____	_____
_____	_____	_____	_____
_____	_____	_____	_____

Q	R	S	T
_____	_____	_____	_____
_____	_____	_____	_____
_____	_____	_____	_____

U	V	W	X
_____	_____	_____	_____
_____	_____	_____	_____
_____	_____	_____	_____

Y	Z		
_____	_____	_____	_____
_____	_____	_____	_____
_____	_____	_____	_____

A3.7 *(cont.)*

Books for Letter-Sound Correspondence
Consonants

B

Crisp, M. 1995. *Buzzard Breath.* New York: Atheneum.

Gregory, V. 1993. *Babysitting for Benjamin.* Boston: Little, Brown.

Hadithi, M. 1993. *Baby Baboon.* Boston: Little, Brown.

Yee, W. H. 1993. *Big Black Bear.* Boston: Houghton Mifflin.

Yep, L. 1995. *The Butterfly Boy.* New York: Farrar, Straus, Giroux.

C (hard)

Berenstain, S., and J. Berenstain. 1972. *C Is for Clown.* New York: Random House.

Gibbons, G. 1993. *Caves and Caverns.* New York: Harcourt Brace.

Hoff, S. 1993. *Captain Cat.* New York: HarperCollins.

Owens, M. B. 1993. *Counting Cranes.* Boston: Little, Brown.

Scott, A. H. 1993. *Cowboy Country.* New York: Clarion.

C (soft)

Duqennoy, J. 1996. *The Ghosts in the Cellar.* New York: Harcourt Brace.

Ehlert, L. 1992. *Circus.* New York: Greenwillow.

Fowler, S. G. 1998. *Circle of Thanks.* New York: Scholastic.

Kuskin, K. 1994. *City Noise.* New York: HarperCollins.

Woodman, J. 1986. *Bossy Bear at the Circus.* London: Brimax Books.

D

Bunting, E. 1995. *Dandelions.* New York: Harcourt Brace.

Carmine, M. 1997. *Daniel's Dinosaurs.* New York: Scholastic.

Cole, B. 1994. *Dr. Dog.* New York: Knopf.

Moncure, J. 1984. *My "D" Sound.* Elgin, IL: Child's World Publishing.

Steig, W. 1992. *Doctor DeSoto Goes to Africa.* New York: HarperCollins.

F

Carlstrom, N. W. 1993. *Fish and Flamingo.* Boston: Little, Brown.

Littledale, F. 1987. *The Farmer in the Soup.* New York: Scholastic.

Lobel, A. 1970. *Frog and Toad Are Friends.* New York: Harper and Row.

San Souci, R. D. 1995. *The Faithful Friend.* New York: Simon and Schuster.

Silverman, E. 1994. *Don't Fidget a Feather.* New York: Macmillan.

G (hard)

Grejniec, M. 1993. *Good Morning, Good Night.* New York: North-South.

Grimm Brothers. 1995. *The Golden Goose.* New York: Farrar, Straus, Giroux.

Keats, E. J. 1969. *Goggles.* New York: Collier Books.

Kimmel, E. 1995. *The Goose Girl: A Story from the Brothers Grimm.* New York: Holiday House.

Seuss, Dr. 1960. *Green Eggs and Ham.* New York: Beginner Books.

G (soft)

Galdone, P. 1975. *The Gingerbread Boy.* New York: Clarion.

Lionni, L. 1979. *Geraldine, the Music Mouse.* New York: Random House.

Peck, J. 1998. *The Giant Carrot.* New York: Dial.

Rey, H. A. 1973. *Curious George.* Boston: Houghton Mifflin.

Silverstein, S. 1964. *A Giraffe and a Half.* New York: HarperCollins.

H

Hadithi, M. 1994. *Hungry Hyena.* Boston: Little, Brown.

High, L. O. 1995. *Hound Heaven.* New York: Holiday House.

Wormell, M. 1995. *Hilda Hen's Happy Birthday.* New York: Harcourt Brace.

Yolen, J., and M. H. Greenberg. 1995. *The Haunted House.* New York: HarperCollins.

Zion, G. 1976. *Harry the Dirty Dog.* New York: Harper and Row.

J

Grossman, B. 1997. *The Bear Whose Bones Were Jezebel Jones.* New York: Dial.

Hennessy, B. G. 1990. *Jake Baked the Cake.* New York: Viking.

Kalan, R. 1981. *Jump Frog Jump.* New York: Greenwillow.

Ogburn, J. K. 1998. *The Jukebox Man.* New York: Dial.

Saltzman, D. 1995. *The Jester Has Lost His Jingle.* Palos Verdes, CA: The Jester Company.

K

Demi. 1999. *Kites.* New York: Crown Publishing.

Ford, J. G. 1996. *A Kente Dress for Kenya.* New York: Scholastic.

Moncure, J. 1984. *My "K" Sound.* Elgin, IL: Child's World Publishing.

Senisi, E. 1994. *Kindergarten Kids.* New York: Scholastic.

Wood, A. 1985. *King Bidgood's in the Bathtub.* New York: Harcourt Brace.

L

Raimondo, L. 1994. *The Little Llama of Tibet.* New York: Scholastic.

Scheidl, G. M. 1993. *Loretta and the Little Fairy.* New York: North-South.

Shepard, A. 1993. The Legend of *Lightning Larry.* Phoenix, AZ: Scribner's.

A3.7 *(cont.)*

Yerxa, L. 1994. *Last Leaf First Snowflake to Fall.* New York: Orchard.

Zolotow, C. 1987. *I Like to Be Little.* New York: Crowell.

M

Allen, J. 1990. *Mucky Moose.* New York: Macmillan.

Brennan, H. 1995. *The Mystery Machine.* New York: Margeret McElderry.

Herman, C. 1993. *Max Malone the Magnificent.* New York: Holt.

Lyon, G. E. 1994. *Mama Is a Miner.* New York: Orchard.

Young, E. 1993. *Moon Mother.* New York: HarperCollins.

N

Masner, J. 1989. *Nicholas Cricket.* New York: Harper and Row.

Ryland, C. 1986. *Night in the Country.* New York: Bradbury Press.

Wells, R. 1997. *Noisy Nora.* New York: Scholastic.

Wezel, P. 1967. *The Naughty Bird.* Chicago: Follet.

Wood, A. 1984. *The Napping House.* New York: Harcourt Brace.

P

Ehrlich, A. 1993. *Parents in the Pig Pens, Pigs in the Tub.* New York: Dial.

Kleven, E. 1994. *The Paper Princess.* New York: Dutton.

Palatini, M. 1995. *Piggie Pie!* New York: Clarion.

Papademetriou, L. 1998. *My Pen Pal, Pat.* Brookfield, CT: Millbrook Press.

Rockwell, A. 1993. *Pots and Pans.* New York: Macmillan.

Q

Good, M. 1999. *Reuben and the Quilt.* New York: Good Books.

Harness, C. 1993. *The Queen with Bees in Her Hair.* New York: Holt.

Holtzman, C. 1995. *A Quarter from the Tooth Fairy.* New York: Scholastic.

Johnston, T. 1996. *The Quilt Story.* New York: Penguin Putnam.

Wood, A. 1997. *Quick as a Cricket.* New York: Scholastic.

R

dePaolo, P. 1992. *Rosie and the Yellow Ribbon.* Boston: Joy Street Books.

Gantos, J. 1994. *Not So Rotten Ralph.* Boston: Houghton Mifflin.

Marshall, J. 1993. *Red Riding Hood.* New York: Scholastic.

Pinkwater, D. 1998. *Rainy Morning.* New York: Atheneum.

Weeks, S. 1995. *Red Ribbon.* New York: HarperCollins.

S

Burnie, D. 1994. *Seashore.* New York: Dorling Kindersley.

Garland, S. 1995. *The Summer Sands.* New York: Harcourt Brace.

Robb, L. 1995. *Snuffles and Snouts.* New York: Dial.

Stolz, M. 1993. *Say Something.* New York: HarperCollins.

Thomson, P. 1993. *Siggy's Spaghetti Works.* New York: Morrow.

T

Biney, B. G. 1994. *Tyrannosaurus Tex.* Boston: Houghton Mifflin.

Cosgrove, S. 1984. *Tee-Tee.* Vero Beach, FL: Rourke Enterprises.

Cocca-Leffler, M. 1999. *Mr. Tannen's Ties.* Morton Grove, IL: Albert Whitman.

Gershator, P. 1994. *Tukama Tootles the Flute: A Tale from the Antilles.* New York: Orchard.

Griffing, A. 1999. *Trashy Town.* New York: HarperCollins.

V

Bovetz, M. 1993. *Machines.* Bothell, WA: Wright Group.

Cannon, J. 1997. *Verdi.* New York: Harcourt Brace.

Schweninger, A. 1990. *Valentine Friends.* New York: Scholastic.

Williams, M. 1981. *The Velveteen Rabbit.* New York: Scholastic.

Williams, S. 1998. *Let's Go Visiting.* New York: Harcourt Brace.

W

Brenner, B. 1995. *Wagon Wheels.* New York: Scholastic.

Calstrom, N. W. 1993. *How Does the Wind Walk?* New York: Macmillan.

Halpern, S. 1995. *What Shall We Do When We All Go Out?* New York: North-South.

Peet, B. 1981. *The Wump World.* New York: Scholastic.

Thomas, A. 1993. *Wake Up, Wilson Street.* New York: Holt.

X

Langen, A., and C. Droop. 1996. *Felix Explores Planet Earth.* New York: Abbeville Kids Press.

Moncure, J. 1979. *My "X, Y, Z" Sound Box.* Elgin, IL: Child's World Publishing.

Robbins, J. 1985. *Addie Meets Max.* New York: Harper and Row.

Thomas, P. 1979. *There Are Rocks in My Socks Said the Ox to the Fox.* New York: Lee, Lothrop and Shepard.

Y

Kellogg, S. 1996. *Yankee Doodle.* New York: Aladdin Paperbacks.

Marshall, J. 1973. *Yummers.* Boston: Houghton Mifflin.

Oram, H. 1997. *Baba Yaga and the Wise Doll.* New York: Dutton.

Seuss, Dr. 1958. *Yertle the Turtle and Other Stories.* New York: Random House.

Z

McDermott, G. 1996. *Zomo the Rabbit: A Trickster Tale from West Africa.* New York: Scholastic.

A3.7 *(cont.)*

Moss, L. 1995. *Zin! Zin! Zin! A Violin.* New York: Simon and Schuster.

Most, B. 1999. *Z—Z—Zoink!* New York: Harcourt Brace.

Steig, W. 1994. *Zeke Pippin.* New York: HarperCollins.

Wynne-Jones, T. 1993. *Zoom at Sea.* New York: HarperCollins.

Vowels (Long and Short)

A

Bernstein, M. 1998. *That Cat!* Brookfield, CT: Millbrook Press.

Cherry, L. 1994. *Armadillo from Amarillo.* New York: Harcourt Brace.

Karlin, N. 1996. *The Fat Cat Sat on the Mat.* New York: Harper Trophy.

Lachner, D. 1995. *Andrew's Angry Words.* New York: North-South.

Ray, M. L. 1994. *Alvah and Arvilla.* New York: Harcourt Brace.

E

Grace, E. S. 1993. *Elephants.* San Francisco: Sierra.

Johnson, S. A. 1994. *A Beekeeper's Year.* Boston: Little, Brown.

Kent, J. 1975. *The Egg Book.* New York: Macmillan.

Rockwell, A., and H. Rockwell. 1985. *The Emergency Room.* New York: Macmillan.

Wood, A. J. 1993. *Egg! A Dozen Eggs. What Will They Be?* Boston: Little, Brown.

I

Kinerk, R. 1998. *Slim and Miss Prim.* Flagstaff, AZ: Rising Moon.

Marston, H. I. 1993. *Big Rigs.* New York: Dutton.

Moncure, J. 1984. *Short i and Long i: Play a Game.* Elgin, IL: Child's World Publishing.

Oram, H. 1985. *In the Attic.* New York: Holt, Rinehart, and Winston.

Zolotow, C. 1966. *If It Weren't for You.* New York: Harper and Row.

O

Frankel, J. 1991. *Oh No, Otis!* Danbury, CT: Children's Press.

George, J. C. 1995. *There's an Owl in the Shower.* New York: HarperCollins.

Krupp, E. C. 1993. *The Moon and You.* New York: Macmillan.

Leonard, M. 1998. *Spots.* Brookfield, CT: Millbrook Press.

Machotka, H. 1993. *Outstanding Outsides.* New York: Morrow.

U

Allen, S. 1995. *The Bug and the Slug in the Rug.* Bridgeport, CT: Green Bark Press.

Andersen, H. C. 1994. *The Ugly Duckling.* New York: Dorling Kindersley.

Mitchell, M. K. 1993. *Uncle Jed's Barbershop.* New York: Simon and Schuster.

Moncure, J. 1984. *Short u and Long u: Play a Game.* Elgin, IL: Child's World Publishing.

Digraphs

CH

Martin, B. Jr., and J. Archambault. 1989. *Chicka Chicka Boom Boom.* New York: Scholastic.

Hobson, S. 1994. *Chicken Little.* New York: Simon and Schuster.

Onyefulu, O. 1994. *Chinye: A West African Folk Tale.* New York: Viking.

Shen, R. 1993. *Chicken Pox!* Boston: Little, Brown.

Tunnel, M. O. 1993. *Chinook!* New York: Tambourine.

PH

Govan, C. 1968. *Phinny's Fine Summer.* New York: World Publishing.

SH

Brown, M. 1995. *Shadow.* New York: Aladdin Paperbacks.

Cowley, J. 1990. *Mrs. Wishy Washy.* Bothell, WA: Wright Group.

Pfister, M. 1990. *Shaggy.* New York: North-South Books.

Shaw, N. 1994. *Sheep Takes a Hike.* Boston: Houghton Mifflin.

Simon, S. 1995. *Sharks.* New York: HarperCollins.

TH

Cowley, J. 1987. *One Thousand Currant Buns.* Bothell, WA: Wright Group.

Leodhas, S. 1962. *Thistle and Thyme.* Toronto: Alger.

Simms, L. 1998. *Rotten Teeth.* Boston: Houghton Mifflin.

Word Families

Brown, M. W. 1984. *Goodnight Moon.* New York: Harper and Row.

Butler, A., and P. Neville. 1987. *May I Stay Home Today?* Crystal Lake, IL: Rigby.

Cowley, J. 1990. *Dan the Flying Man.* Bothell, WA: Wright Group.

Patrick, G. 1974. *A Bug in a Jug.* New York: Scholastic.

Seuss, Dr. 1957. *The Cat in the Hat.* New York: Random House.

RESOURCE
3.7 Sorting Words with Short Vowels Using a Pocket Chart

Grades K–2

Purpose

To have students:

- Sort words according to their short-vowel sounds

Materials

laminated word or picture cards (A3.8) for each short-vowel sounds
small plastic zipper bags to store each set of cards
laminated header cards
pocket chart
accountability forms (A3.8)
pencils

Activity

1. Choose two vowels for children to sort. Begin by using vowels that have easily distinguishable sounds. As children become more familiar with short-vowel sounds, teachers may assign any of the short-vowel sounds.

2. Place the header cards of both vowels in the pocket chart. Combine and shuffle the word cards from each bag. Place them in a pile.

3. As the students turn over each card in the pile, they must decide which short-vowel sound they hear and place the card underneath the correct header.

Variation

- When picture cards are used, teachers must review the names of each picture with the children before they begin the activity.

Accountability

Students record the activity on an accountability form.

Suggested Literature

Leveled books, such as the Little Books series by William H. Sadlier, 9 Pine Street, New York, NY 10005, are appropriate for this activity because different books focus on a particular vowel and its sound.

A3.8 Short-Vowel Word Picture Patterns and Accountability Form

Name _____ Date _____

I sorted short vowel words in a pocket chart today. When I finished the activity, this is what the pocket chart looked like:

_____   _____
              Header #1   Header #2

_____   _____

_____   _____

_____   _____

A3.8 *(cont.)*

CAT

HAT

BAT

RAT

BOX

FOX

MAN

CAN

FAN

Photocopy, laminate, and cut.

RESOURCE
3.8 Identifying Phonograms Using a Game Board

Grades K–2

Purpose

To have students:

- Identify phonograms associated with short *a* vowel sound

Materials

> piece of children's literature that features the short *a* vowel sound
> game board (A3.9)
> game pieces for each player, such as small toy cars or dried lima beans
> one die
> accountability forms (A3.9)
> pencils

Activity

1. Read aloud a book that features short *a* words, such as *Green Eggs and Ham* (Seuss). Encourage students to listen for the words that have the short *a* sound. Other books featuring short *a* can be used.
2. Children recall the words they heard and write them down. Clues or picture cards can be used.
3. Students work in pairs to play the game. Each pair of students is given a game board, a die, and two game pieces.
4. A student rolls the die, moves to a space, and reads the short-vowel word.
5. The student then says two more words that are in the same family. These are the neighbors that live in the word family neighborhood.
6. The activity continues until one player reaches the end of the neighborhood.

Variation

- This game can be used for other short vowels and their corresponding phonograms. Simply adjust the book and the game board to match the objective.

Accountability

After the game, students write words from different word families in the word family houses on the accountability form.

Suggested Literature

For a list of books that have word families, see A3.7.

Common Rimes Studied in Early Literacy

-ain	-ate	-ice	-ink
-ale	-aw	-ick	-ip
-am	-eat	-ill	-op
-an	-ell	-in	-ore
-at	-est	-ing	-ump

Source: Wylie and Durrell (1970).

A3.9 Phonogram Game Board and Accountability Form

Color and laminate.

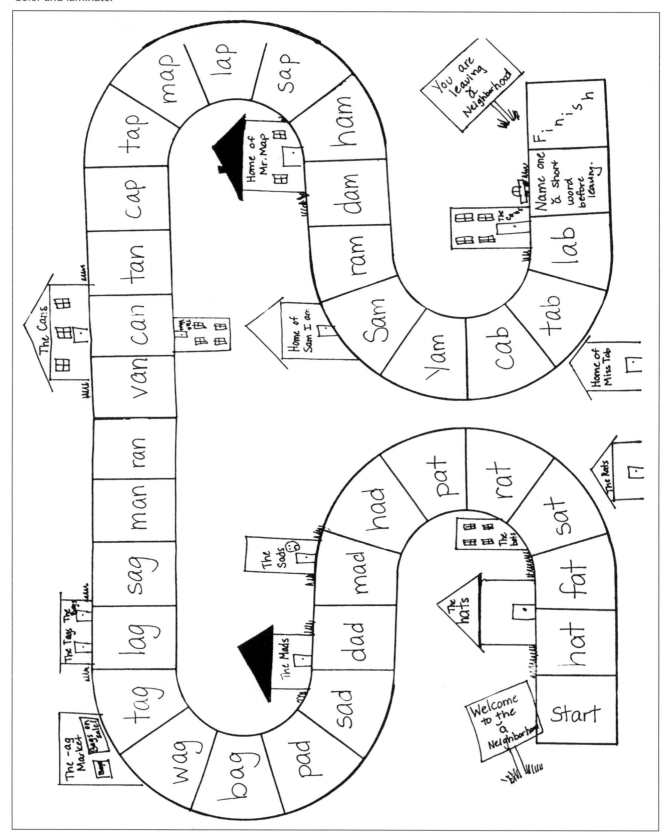

A3.9 (cont.)

Word Family Houses

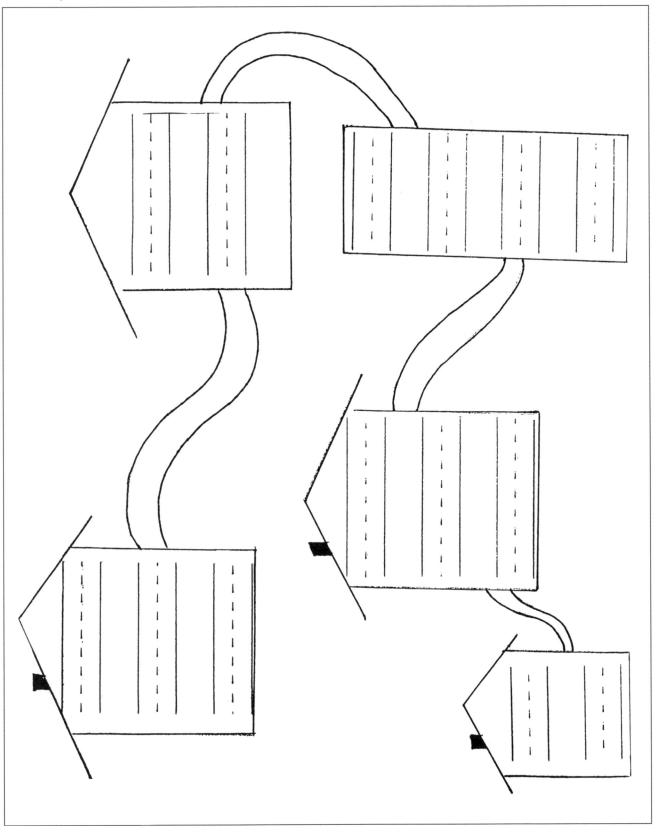

RESOURCE
3.9 Building Words that End in Silent *e* Using Onset/Rime Cards

Grades K–2

Purpose

To have students:

- Learn silent *e* rule
- Build words by blending onsets and long-vowel rimes

Materials

laminated rime and onset cards (A3.10)
accountability forms (A3.10)
pencils

Activity

1. Students pick a rime card and blend it with the onset cards to build new words, which they write down.

2. After students have used all the onset cards with the rime card, they choose another rime card and repeat the process.

Variation

- For older students, consonant blends (*st, pl, fl, sn, sp*) and digraphs (*th, ch, sh, wh*) can be used as onset cards.

Accountability

When activity is finished, students record their work on an accountability form.

Suggested Literature for –*ame* Ending

Albert's Ballgame (Tyrone)
We All Sing With the Same Voice (Miller and Greene)
Andy (That's My Name) (dePaola)

Other Rimes Ending in Silent *e*

-ate	-ose	-ike	-une
-ave	-ole	-ime	-ude
-are	-oke	-ite	-ule
-ade	-ome	-ive	

A3.10 Onset/Rime Card Patterns and Accountability Form

ake	ine
ame	ote
ute	

b	n	c	ch
sh	bl	st	

A3.10 *(cont.)*

Name _____ **Date** _____

Today I built the following words with the _____ ending:

1. _____

2. _____

3. _____

4. _____

5. _____

6. _____

7. _____

8. _____

9. _____

10. _____

3.10 Recognizing and Sorting Initial *l* Blends by Playing Memory

Grades K–2

Purpose

To have students:

- Recognize and sort words with initial *l* blends (*bl, cl, gl, fl, pl, sl*)

Materials

chart paper
piece of children's literature that features *l* blends
l blend picture/word cards (A3.11)
accountability forms (A3.11)
pencils

Activity

1. Read aloud a book that features *l* blends, such as *Blue Frogs* (Campilonga).
2. On chart paper list words that start with each of the *l* blends.
3. Students work with a partner. Each pair of players receives a laminated deck of picture/word cards.
4. Students sort the cards into piles according to their blends, and write the words on an activity sheet.
5. Students use the same cards to play *l* blend Memory:
   a. The cards are placed face down in rows on a table.
   b. Students take turns flipping two cards at a time to find a blend match, such as *black* and *blueberry*, or *plane* and *play*.
   c. If the cards do not match, they are replaced in their original position. When a match is made, the player keeps the cards.
   d. When all cards are matched, the player with the most cards wins.

Variation

- This activity can be done with other blends.

Accountability

Students list words on an accountability form according to initial blend.

Suggested Literature

Glad Monster, Sad Monster (Emberley)
Slip, Slide, Skate! (G. Herman)

A3.11 Blend Picture Patterns and Accountability Form

Photocopy to enlarge as needed. Laminate and cut.

blade	block	blouse	blanket
blindfold	clip	clap	cloud
clothes	claw	glove	globe
glue	glass	glasses	flag
flower	float	flashlight	fly
plant	plus	plum	plate
plyers	slipper	sleeve	sleep
slide	sled		

The Literacy Center: Contexts for Reading and Writing, 2d ed. Copyright © 2002 Lesley Mandel Morrow. Stenhouse Publishers.

A3.11 *(cont.)*

Name_____ **Date** _____

Bl   Cl   Gl

_____   _____   _____

_____   _____   _____

_____   _____   _____

Fl   Pl   Sl

_____   _____   _____

_____   _____   _____

_____   _____   _____

RESOURCE
3.11 Identifying the *ch* Digraph Using Word Wheels

Grades K–3

Purpose

To have students:

- Identify and build words with the *ch* digraph

Materials

chart paper
piece of children's literature that features the *ch* digraph
assembled word wheels with digraphs (A3.12)
accountability forms (A3.12)
pencils

Activity

1. Read aloud a book that features the *ch* digraph, such as *Chicka Chicka Boom Boom* (Martin).

2. On chart paper list words that contain *ch,* and underline the *ch.*
3. Students work alone or with a partner to manipulate the wheel to build words with *ch.*
4. When children build a word, they say it aloud. They self-check by lifting the flap.

Variation

- Word wheels can also be used to study other digraphs, initial consonants, consonant blends, and rimes and onsets.

Accountability

Students write the words that they built on an accountability form.

Suggested Literature

For a list of books that have digraphs, see A3.7.

A3.12 Word Wheel Patterns and Accountability Form

Name_____ **Date** —————

I used a word wheel to build the following words:

1. _____
2. _____
3. _____
4. _____
5. _____
6. _____
7. _____
8. _____
9. _____
10. _____

A3.12 *(cont.)*

First photocopy to enlarge as needed. Then cut out the top circle and cut out the indicated region. Cut out the bottom circle. Place the circle with the notch cut out on top of the other circle, and attach with a fastener.

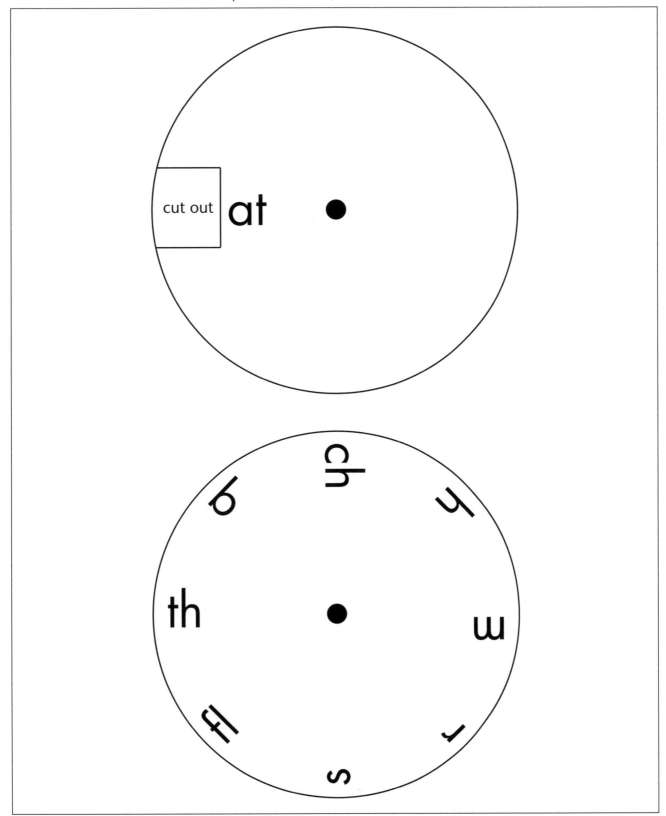

A3.12 *(cont.)*

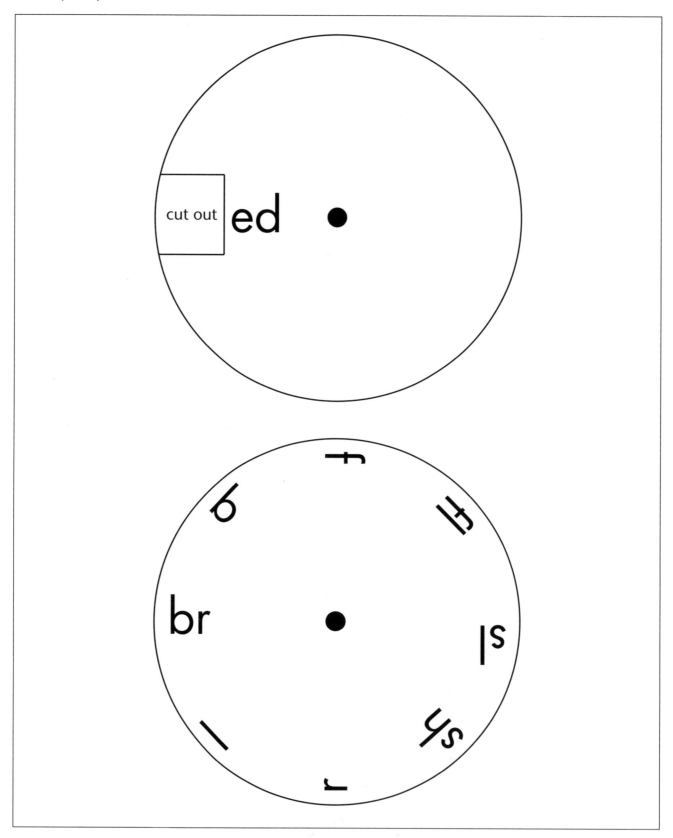

A3.12 *(cont.)*

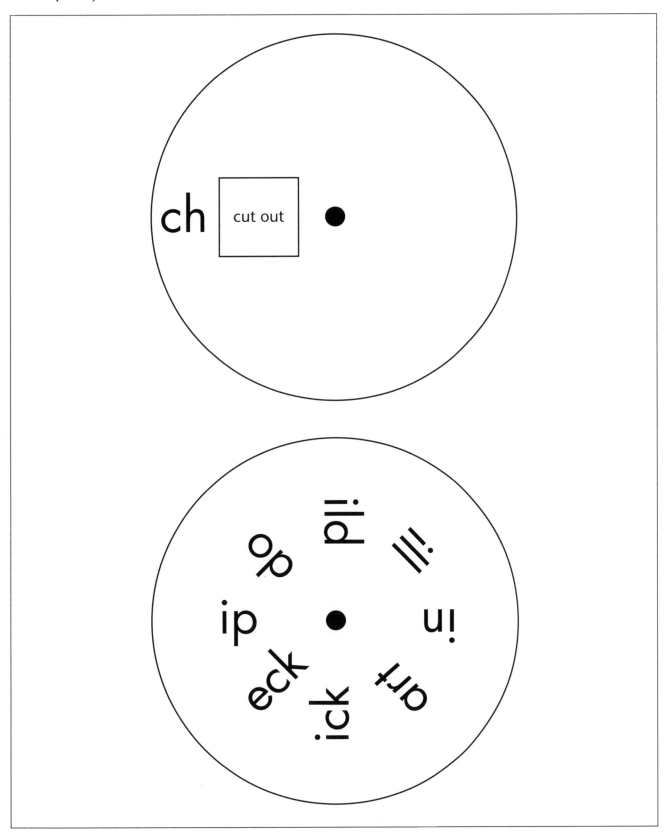

RESOURCES
3.12 Identifying and Sorting Rhyming Words Using a Pocket Chart

Grades Pre-K–2

Purpose

To have students:

- Identify rhyming words

Materials

rhyming word cards
pocket chart
accountability forms (A3.13)
pencils

Activity

1. Students are given two header cards (e.g., *–at* and *–an*) and rhyming word cards with the same endings (*hat, cat, man, fan*).
2. Students work alone or with a partner to sort the cards under the correct header on a pocket chart.

Variation

- Additional headers (such as *–ox, -ap, -ot*) can be added to increase the difficulty of the activity.

Accountability

Students record the words they sorted on an accountability form.

Suggested Literature

Animals, Animals (Carle)
The Foot Book (Seuss)
Ten Little Ladybugs (Gerth)

A3.13 Rhyming Words Accountability Form

Name _____	**Date** _____

Today, I sorted the following rhyming groups:

_____   _____

_____   _____

_____   _____

_____   _____

_____   _____

_____   _____

_____   _____

_____   _____

_____   _____

_____   _____

_____   _____

_____   _____

RESOURCE
3.13 Making Little Words Out of a Big Word

Grades Pre-K–2

Purpose

To have students:

- Look for patterns in words
- Learn how to make new words by changing one letter or more

Materials

letters in a labeled plastic bag (the letters should be only those that compose the big word)
activity/accountability form (a "word ladder") (A3.14)
pencils

Activity

1. Select a large word from content areas, vocabulary words, or thematic unit, such as *hippopotamus*.
2. Write *hippopotamus* on a sentence strip. Cut it into individual letters. Store the letters in a plastic bag labeled with the word.
3. Students manipulate these letters to form smaller words. They begin with one-letter words, then two-letter words, then three-letter words, then four-letter words.
4. Students reassemble the letters into *hippopotamus*.

Accountability

As students make a word, they record it on an activity sheet according to the number of letters in it.

A3.14 Making Little Words Out of a Big Word

Photocopy and cut into individual letters.

A3.14 *(cont.)*

Name_____ Date _____

One-letter words

_____

_____

_____

Two-letter words

_____

_____

_____

Three-letter words

_____

_____

Four-letter words

_____

_____

RESOURCE
3.14 Adding Prefixes to Root Words Using a Pocket Chart

Grades 3–4

Purpose

To have students:

- Add prefixes to root words to build new words

Materials

    copy of a poem that has an example of a prefix in it
    chart paper or overhead transparency
    pocket chart
    set of laminated index cards with prefixes
    set of laminated index cards with root words
    accountability form (A3.15)
    pencils

Activity

1. Write a poem such as "Why Not Get a Perodactyl?" (Hopkins) on chart paper or an overhead transparency. Read it aloud.
2. Model how to make a word by matching the root word and the prefix.
3. Discuss the meaning and use of the prefix by asking students to think about the root word and the meaning of the word when the prefix is added.
4. List other examples of prefixes. Model their use in sentences.
5. Using the index cards and the pocket chart, students combine the prefixes and root words to make new words and write each new word in a sentence.

Variation

- This activity can also be used for suffixes. In addition, students can do a closed sort of the words using the prefixes as headers.

Accountability

Students record their work on an accountability form.

A3.15 Prefixes Accountability Form

Name _____ **Date** _____

I built the following words and sentences using prefixes:

1. _____

_____

_____

2. _____

_____

_____

3. _____

_____

_____

RESOURCE
3.15 Identifying Homophones Using a Flip Book

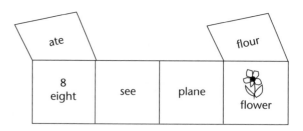

Grades 2–3

Purpose

To have students:

- Identify pairs of homophones (words that sound alike but are spelled differently)

Materials

construction paper (9" by 12")
markers
crayons
scissors
accountability forms (A3.16)
pencils

Activity

1. Fold paper in half lengthwise (4.5" by 12").

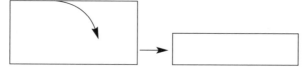

2. Fold paper in half (4.5" by 6").

3. Fold paper in half again to make quarters (4.5" by 3").

4. Open paper so that it is folded in half lengthwise (4.5" X 12").

5. On one side only, cut along the folded creases to make four flaps.

6. Students choose four pairs of homophones, such as *see/sea, ate/eight, flower/flour, plane/plain*. For each pair, they write one word on the front flap and the other word underneath with an illustration for it.

Variation

- A Flip Book is also suitable for grouping words according to their patterns, such as short *a* word families (*cat, sat, rat, mat*). Students write the word on the front flap and make an illustration underneath. Rhyming word pairs, antonyms, synonyms, contractions can also be used.

Accountability

Students complete both accountability forms provided for this lesson.

Homophones

read	red	write	right	sum	some
cellar	seller	here	hear	blue	blew
roll	role	beet	beat	which	witch
there	their	know	no	won	one
to	two	doe	dough	you're	your
flew	flu	by	buy	bear	bare
be	bee	I	eye	hi	high
see	sea	ate	eight	plane	plain
hole	whole	not	knot	jeans	genes
son	sun	flee	flea	pail	pale
so	sew	pair	pear	sole	soul
die	dye	heard	herd	rain	reign
ant	aunt	great	grate	waist	waste
its	it's	wear	where		

A3.16 Homophones and Flip Book Accountability Forms

Name _____ Date _____

Match the homophones. Use four or five homophones correctly in sentences.

read	hear
write	blew
sum	red
cellar	some
here	role
blue	right
roll	seller
beet	witch
which	their
there	beat
know	one
won	it's
to	no
doe	two
you're	dough
flew	your
by	flu
flee	buy
bear	flea
its	bare

_____

_____

_____

_____

_____

A3.16 *(cont.)*

Name _____ Date _____

My Flip Book

Today I made a Flip Book. The skill that my book focused on was

_____

The words that I used were

1. _____

2. _____

3. _____

4. _____

RESOURCE
3.16 Practicing High-Frequency Words Using Magnetic Letters

Grades K–3

Purpose

To have students:

• Learn high-frequency words

Materials

familiar text
word wall
magnetic letters and magnetic board
letter stamps
index cards
"high-frequency word" box for each student
accountability forms (A3.17)
pencils

Activity

1. When reading a book or teaching a unit, decide which high-frequency words should be featured.
2. Write the words on the word wall.
3. The students or teacher choose a familiar text, and each student looks for the high-frequency words in the text.
4. Students use magnetic letters and a magnetic board to spell each word.
5. They say the word aloud and stamp it on an index card using letter stamps.
6. Students put the card in their "high-frequency word" box and repeat the process until all the featured words have been added.

Accountability

Students record the list of featured high-frequency words on an accountability form.

High-Frequency Words

a	came	her	look	people	too
after	can	here	looked	play	two
all	come	him	long	put	up
an	could	his	make	run	us
and	day	house	man	ran	very
are	did	how	mother	said	was
am	do	I	me	saw	we
as	don't	I'm	my	see	went
asked	down	if	no	she	were
at	for	in	not	so	what
away	from	into	now	some	when
back	get	is	of	that	where
be	go	it	old	the	will
because	going	just	on	then	with
before	good	keep	one	there	would
big	had	kind	or	they	you
boy	has	know	our	this	your
but	have	like	out	three	
by	he	little	over	to	

Source: Reprinted by permission of Irene Fountas and Guy Su Pinnell: *Guided Reading: Good First Teaching for All Children* (Heinemann, a division of Reed Elsevier, Inc., Portsmouth, NH 1996).

A3.17 High-Frequency Word Accountability Form

Name _____ **Date** _____

The high-frequency words for this week are

1. _____

2. _____

3. _____

4. _____

5. _____

RESOURCE
3.17 Sorting Words According to Syllables Using Letter/Word Cards

Grades K–3

Purpose

To have students:

- Sort words according to syllables

Materials

    laminated picture/word cards
    laminated letter cards
    activity/accountability forms (A3.18)
    pencils

Activity

1. Pick a card and say the word or the name of the picture on the card.
2. Spell the word using the letter cards.
3. Clap the syllables heard in the word and manipulate the letters to divide the word into syllables.
4. Write the word on an activity sheet according to the number of syllables in it.

Accountability

Students record the activity on an accountability form.

A3.18 Syllables Accountability Form

Name_____ **Date** _____

Record the words according to the number of syllables in them:

One   Two

_____   _____

_____   _____

_____   _____

_____   _____

Three

_____

_____

_____

_____

RESOURCE
3.18 Incorporating Technology into Word Study

Grades Pre-K–4

Purpose

To have students:

- Use the Internet to find the day's weather

Materials

    computer (www.weather.com)
    weather chart (A3.19)
    temperature graph (A3.19)
    pencils

Activity

1. This activity can be used as an independent center activity or as a daily job for students.
2. Go to www.weather.com (The Weather Channel). Enter the city or zip code for the school.
3. Students locate the type of weather (sunny, rainy, cloudy, snowy) and the temperature for the day. They record the information on their weather charts.
4. At the end of the week, each student completes a graph for the week's temperatures.

Variation

- Computer programs and games are available that feature word study and comprehension activities as well as content-related themes. Games can be found in libraries, bookstores, electronic stores, and other specialty stores. The average cost of these games is twenty dollars.
    Some popular programs are
Jumpstart, 1995–96, Knowledge Adventure, Inc
Reader Rabbit, 1994–96, The Learning Company
Reading Blaster, 1997, Davidson & Associates, Inc.
The Cruncher (*Spell It 3, Kid Works 2*), 1992–94, Davidson & Associates, Inc.
Alphabet, Dinosoft Educational Software
Word Munchers Deluxe, 1997, The Learning Company
Sesame Street Letters (*Creative Wonders*), 1995, Henson Productions, Inc.
- Students can e-mail word study puzzles to one another at home. For example, one student may write, "I am thinking of a word that rhymes with *sack*. It is used to hold papers on a bulletin board. What is it?" The other student replies to the e-mail with an answer. If the answer is correct, the students switch roles. If the answer is incorrect, the first student may provide additional clues.
- Students can use word processors such as Microsoft Word to type stories or poems.

Accountability

Students turn in a completed weather chart and temperature graph.

A3.19 Weather Chart and Temperature Graph

Name_____ Date _____

Weather Chart

Date	Type of Weather	Temperature
For example:		
Monday, May 4, 2001	sunny	75°F

1._____   _____   _____

2._____   _____   _____

3._____   _____   _____

4._____   _____   _____

5._____   _____   _____

A3.19 *(cont.)*

Name _____ Date _____

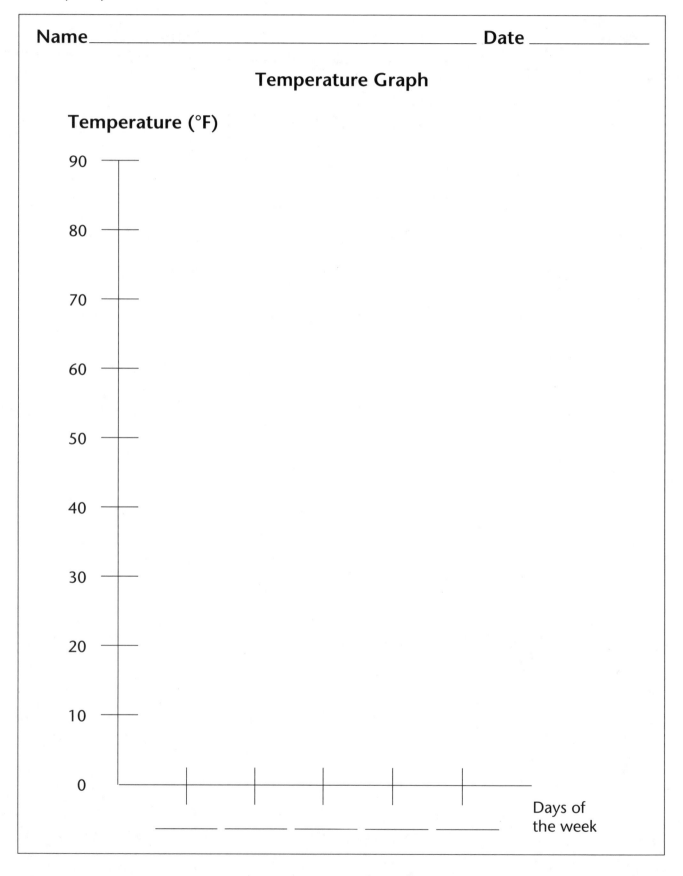

Temperature Graph

Temperature (°F)

All About Books

This section provides teachers of preschool through fifth grade with activities to develop students' literacy concepts and encourage them to apply this knowledge to reading and writing. All the storytelling techniques discussed in Resource Section 2 can be used with the activities presented in this section and serve as a vehicle for students to share their literacy learning.

The lessons are as follows:

RESOURCE
4.1 Introduction to Quiet Book Time

Purpose

To have students:

- Understand that quiet book time is a time for independent reading

Materials

classroom library's collection of books

Activity

1. Explain what quiet book time is.
2. Tell children that when it is quiet book time, they are to select one or two books from the literacy center and find a quiet place in the classroom where they feel comfortable reading or looking at their books independently.
3. Children keep a record of books read (Resource 1.3).

RESOURCE
4.2 Writing to Authors

Purpose

To have students:

- Realize authors are real people
- Extend understanding of letter writing as a means of communication

Materials

writing paper
pens, pencils, crayons
copies of familiar literature books
sample letter

Activity

1. Show children the books and read the titles.
2. Ask if anyone is familiar with the author and if anyone knows the titles of any other books by that author.
3. Explain that the authors who write the stories in books are real people.
4. Have children select one of their favorite authors and write a letter to the author telling him or her what they liked about one or more of the author's books. Remind students to include questions they would like answered about the book or the author.
5. Have children illustrate in the letter their favorite or the funniest part of the book(s) they are writing about.
6. Give a copy of the following letter to any child who cannot write independently, and allow him or her to use it.

> Dear _____,
> I have been reading many books. I like one of yours very much. The title of the book is
>
> _____.
>   How do you get ideas for books?
>   I am sending you a picture of my favorite part of the book.
>   Please answer this letter. I have never met an author.
> Sincerely,

7. Address envelopes to the publishers, and mail the letters. Share any responses with the children as they come in.

RESOURCE
4.3   Series Book Author Study

Purpose

To have students:

- Understand who authors are and what they do
- Read series books and examine authors' writing styles

Materials

copies of Ludwig Bemelmans' *Madeline,* about a young girl named Madeline as she experiences life in a boarding school, and *Madeline's Rescue,* about how Madeline's life is saved by a dog who later stirs up a great deal of trouble in her school

copies of Katherine Holabird's *Angelina Ballerina,* about a forgetful young mouse named Angelina, who dreams of becoming a ballerina, and *Angelina's Birthday Surprise,* in which Angelina discovers what a special day a birthday can be.

copies of Bill Martin's *Brown Bear, Brown Bear, What Do You See?,* in which children see a variety of animals that are different colors, and *Polar Bear, Polar Bear, What Do You Hear?,* in which children are encouraged to listen and imitate zoo animals' distinctive sounds

Activity

1. Hold a brief class discussion about what students think an author does.
2. Explain that all authors have their own writing style and some authors have particular topics they write about in what is known as a series style.
3. Read a page from four books by two different authors and ask children to guess which two books are written by the same author. Students should listen for similar character names and the general writing style of the author.
4. Allow children to look through their classroom library to find series books and share their findings with the class.

Series Books for Grades Pre-K–2

Alexander, Sue. *World Famous Muriel.* Muriel, a tightrope walker, solves the mystery of the queen's missing lanterns.

———. *World Famous Muriel and the Scary Dragon.* When a dragon becomes a threat to the kingdom, Muriel thinks up a plan to keep everyone happy.

Bridwell, Norman. *Clifford, the Big Red Dog.* Emily Elizabeth tells about her adventures with her big red dog.

———. *Clifford's Puppy Days.* Fun memories of Clifford's days as a puppy.

Brown, Marc. *Arthur's Baby.* To Arthur's dismay, his parents' big surprise is not a new bicycle, but a new baby.

———. *Arthur's Birthday.* Arthur's birthday party plans must undergo some changes when he hears that his friend Muffy's party is the same day.

Series Books for Grades 3–5

Cleary, Beverly. *Henry and Beezus.* Henry Higgins thinks his friend Beezus's sister Ramona is a pest until she helps Beezus save money for a bicycle.

———. *Ramona the Pest.* Ramona Quimby's adventures in kindergarten lead to her dropping out.

Hurwitz, Johanna. *The Up and Down Spring.* Rory and Derek's friend Bolivia plans many activities for spring break, but they end up backfiring.

———. *The Hot and Cold Summer.* Derek befriends a girl named Bolivia.

MacLachlen, Patricia. *All the Places to Love.* A young boy describes the favorite places that he shares with his family on his grandparents' farm and in the nearby countryside.

———. *Baby.* While taking care of a baby that was left with them at the end of the tourist season, a family is able to come to terms with the death of their own infant.

RESOURCE
4.4 Illustrator Study

Purpose

To have students:

- Understand what an illustrator does
- Increase their visual discriminatory skills by noticing the differences and similarities among illustrators
- Appreciate and explore different artistic media

Materials

watercolors, pastels, colored pencils
collage materials
pencils
paper
transparencies from selected books
copies of Eric Carle's *A House for a Hermit Crab,* in which a hermit crab is helped and helps others through the changes he undergoes, and *The Very Quiet Cricket,* in which a small cricket tries to greet his fellow insect friends but has a difficult time chirping (artistic style: watercolor/collage)
copies of Anthony Brown's *The Tunnel,* in which a young girl searches through a frightening tunnel to find her brother, and *Changes,* about the effects of a new baby on an older brother (artistic style: surrealist/lifelike pictures)
copies of Ann Grifalconi's *Osa's Pride,* which is set in Africa, about how the nurturing love of the grandmother helps Osa overcome her pride, and *The Village of Round and Small Houses,* in which a grandmother tells the tale of why, beyond the volcano, women live in round houses and men live in square houses (artistic style: vibrant pastels)

Activity

1. Explain that illustrators are people who draw and create the pictures seen in books and that sometimes they write the books as well. Make it clear that all illustrators have their own style or technique.
2. Read a book and follow up the reading by showing a transparency or picture from another book created by the same illustrator.
3. Encourage students to generate descriptive words that describe the illustrator's style.
4. Repeat this procedure for one or two more illustrators.

5. Have children then make an illustration modeled after their favorite illustrator.
6. Create a bulletin board or a class book with the children's pictures.

Books for Teaching About Illustrators for Grades Pre-K–5

Hutchins, Pat. *Rosie's Walk.* A rooster unknowingly sends a hen on a wild chase.
———. *Don't Forget the Bacon.* A young boy is sent to get groceries by his mother and tries to remember the shopping list.
(artistic style: lines and patterns to depict texture)
Sendak, Maurice. *Where the Wild Things Are.* A young boy named Max takes a dream trip to a far-off land of wild things.
———. *Chicken Soup with Rice.* Praises, songs, pictures, and hymns in honor of the months of the year accompany a tale about the author's favorite soup.
(artistic style: fanciful watercolor figures)

RESOURCE
4.5 Picture Storybooks

An Extraordinary Egg

Purpose

To have students:

- Enjoy reading picture storybooks
- Recognize characteristics of picture storybooks
- Create an original picture storybook

Materials

large pieces of construction paper with writing
space at the bottom
crayons, pencils
large pictures of interesting scenes
copy of Leo Lionni's *An Extraordinary Egg,* in
which three frogs befriend an alligator after
mistaking it for a chicken

Activity

1. Show the large pictures to the class. Ask them to describe what is happening in each picture and to think of words to go along with the pictures.
2. Hang the pictures on the chalkboard and write their descriptions underneath.
3. Explain that books that contain pictures with matching words like the ones on the board are called picture storybooks.
4. Reinforce the idea that the book would not be complete without its illustrations.
5. Ask students to listen while you read a picture storybook to see if the words describe the pictures, and read the Lionni book.
6. Have each student draw a picture on a large piece of construction paper and write words or sentences to describe the picture.
7. Collect all the work and bind the pages into a class picture storybook (Resource Section 5).

Picture Storybooks for Grades Pre-K–2

Pfister, Marcus. *The Rainbow Fish.* Rainbow Fish is the most beautiful fish in the entire ocean. However, his refusal to share his sparkling silver scales has made him the loneliest fish, until he learns to share and make friends.
Ross, Tom. *Eggbert, the Slightly Cracked Egg.* Eggbert is very popular in the refrigerator, until it is discovered that he is slightly cracked and is sent away.

On his journeys Eggbert comes to realize that our flaws are natural and something to be proud of.

Picture Storybooks for Grades 3–5

Bunting, Eve. *Smoky Night.* A boy, his mother, and their cat are caught in the middle of the L.A. riots when their apartment is set on fire. These events bring them together with a family of a different race.
Schimmel, Schim. *Dear Children of the Earth: A Letter from Home.* A letter from Mother Earth asks the children of the world to help protect their brother and sister animals and the environment.
Van Allsburg, Chris. *Just a Dream.* Walter is a litterbug. He never sorts his recyclables. One night his magic bed takes him into the future, where he discovers that the environment has been harmed. When Walter awakes, he rethinks his litterbug ways.

RESOURCE
4.6 Fairy Tales

Cinderella

Purpose

To have students:

- Understand and identify characteristics of fairy tales
- Retell fairy tales

Materials

chart paper
markers
storytelling technique of choice: puppets, felt board, stick puppets, etc.
copy of *Cinderella* (Perrault)

Activity

1. Describe the characteristics of fairy tales: there are usually only a few characters; some of the characters are good and some are bad; usually something bad happens to the good character; there is some unreal element, such as a fairy, an elf, magic; the main character usually winds up happy at the end of the story.
2. Ask students to listen for these characteristics as you read the story of *Cinderella*. Then read the story.
3. Ask students to recall the fairy tale characteristics. List their responses on chart paper.
4. Retell the story in your own words using a storytelling technique (to model a fairy tale retelling).
5. Explain that after a few readings and practice, students will retell their own fairy tale to the class.

Fairy Tales for Grades Pre-K–2

Grimm, Jacob. *Snow White and the Seven Dwarfs.* A princess left to die in the woods is cared for by seven little men.

Lesser, Rika. *Hansel and Gretel.* A poor woodcutter's children get lost in the forest. They find a candy house, but a wicked witch lives there and plans to eat them for supper.

Scieszka, Jon. *The Stinky Cheese Man and Other Fairly Stupid Tales.* Zany recreations of familiar fairy tales.

Fairy Tales for Grades 3–5

Hodges, Margaret. *Saint George and the Dragon.* A knight slays a dragon who has been attacking a kingdom and brings happiness to the land.

Louie, Ai-Ling. *Yeh-Shen: A Cinderella Story from China.* A young Chinese girl struggles against her stepmother and stepsisters and becomes the bride of a prince.

Young, Ed. *Lon Po Po: A Red Riding Hood Story from China.* Three sisters are left home alone and are threatened by a fierce and hungry wolf who is camouflaged as their grandmother.

RESOURCE
4.7 Fables, Folktales, and Legends

The Tortoise and the Hare

Purpose

To have students:

- Understand, identify, and describe characteristics of fables, folktales, and legends
- Write an original fable, folktale, or legend

Materials

> stuffed animals: one turtle and one rabbit
> piece of string (for finish line)
> a rock
> small treelike plant
> writing paper, pencils
> copy of *More Fables of Aesop: The Tortoise and the Hare* (Kent)

Activity

1. Describe the characteristics of a fable: characters are usually animals or other nonhumans; there are just a few characters; the story is simple and teaches a lesson.
2. Tell the story *The Tortoise and the Hare* using props.
3. Have children choose a partner to write a fable with. Have the partners work together in writing and illustrating an original fable. Encourage the teams to present their fable to the class. Be available to assist the children in writing their fables as needed. Do the same with folktales and legends.

Fables, Folktales, and Legends for Grades Pre-K–2

Lionni, Leo. *Frederick.* While several field mice gather supplies for the upcoming winter, Frederick gathers something that is irreplaceable.

Lobel, Arnold. *Ming Lo Moves the Mountain.* Unhappy with a mountain being at the foot of their house, Ming Lo and his wife consult a wise man, who shows them how they can move their house.

Young, Ed. *Seven Blind Mice.* Seven courageous mice set out to discover something that rests by the pond. Each mouse has his own opinion as to what it is.

Fables, Folktales, and Legends for Grades 3–5

Cooney, Barbara. *Chanticleer and the Fox.* A clever fox tries to outsmart a proud rooster through the use of flattery.

Showalter, Jean B. *The Donkey Ride.* Retelling of Aesop's fable about a father and son who, while on their way to market, keep taking the advice of people they meet.

Steptoe, John. *The Story of Jumping Mouse: Native American Legend.* A little mouse sets out to see the world and learns a great many things.

RESOURCE
4.8 Realistic Literature

Tight Times

Purpose

To have students:

- Recognize the characteristics of realistic literature
- Create an original realistic story

Materials

large pieces of construction paper
pencils, markers
chart paper
copy of *Tight Times* (Hazen) about a youngster
who isn't sure why a thing called "tight
times" means not getting a dog

Activity

1. Explain that realistic literature consists of stories about something that could actually happen in real life. They are about serious topics and how to deal with them.
2. Read the story *Tight Times*.
3. Ask children to identify the parts of the story that could really happen. Discuss those events.
4. During a shared writing activity, write a realistic story on chart paper about something that could happen to the whole class, such as going on a class trip and losing a member of the class while on the trip.
5. Have students work independently to construct a short creative writing piece that describes a realistic problem they had in their life.
6. Have them illustrate their stories.

Realistic Literature for Grades Pre-K–2

Alexander, Martha. *Nobody Asked Me If I Wanted a Baby Sister*. Resenting the attention and praise lavished on his new baby sister, Oliver tries to give her away to his neighbors.

Lapsley, S. *I Am Adopted*. A little boy explains what it means to be adopted.

Wolf, Bernard. *Don't Feel Sorry for Paul*. Two weeks in the life of a handicapped boy as he learns to live successfully in a world made for people without handicaps.

Realistic Literature for Grades 3–5

Durant, Penny Raife. *When Heroes Die*. Twelve-year-old Gary needs advice and guidance when he finds out that his Uncle Rob, his hero, is dying of AIDS. Uncle Rob himself is the one who gives Gary strength to face the future.

Sobol, Harriet Langsam. *My Brother Steven Is Retarded*. An eleven-year-old girl talks about the mixed feelings she has for her older, mentally retarded brother.

———. *My Other-Mother, My Other-Father*. Twelve-year-old Andrea, whose parents are divorced and remarried, discusses the problems and joys of being part of a new, larger family.

RESOURCE
4.9 Biography

If You Grew Up with George Washington

Purpose

To have students:

- Recognize the characteristics of a biography
- Write an original biography

Materials

writing paper
pencils, crayons
book-binding materials
pictures of each student
copy of *If You Grew Up with George Washington*
(Gross)

Activity

1. Ask children to name some famous people they would like to learn about and how they would go about finding information about them (TV, books, newspapers).
2. Explain that biographies tell us the story of someone's life.
3. Tell students that the author of a biography is not the actual person the book is about, just as Ruth Gross is the author of a book about George Washington.
4. Ask students to listen to or read the biography *If You Grew Up with George Washington* so that they will be able to discuss the facts about his life.
5. Have each child write a biography about someone in the class. Pair off the children and allow them to interview each other about their life histories: where they were born, where they live, their family, friends, and hobbies. Be sure each child takes notes.
6. Have children illustrate the pages of their biography; use the photographs of each child in the published bound books.

Biographies for Grades Pre-K–2

Aliki. *The Many Lives of Benjamin Franklin.*
Austin, James. Easy to Read Discovery Books. Series includes biographies of Daniel Boone, Lafayette, Theodore Roosevelt, Abraham Lincoln, George Washington Carver, Clara Barton, Paul Revere, and the Wright Brothers.

Sutton, Felix. *Master of Ballyhoo: The Story of P. T. Barnum.*

Biographies for Grades 3–5

Brown, Gene. *Anne Frank: Child of the Holocaust.*
Daugherty, James. *Daniel Boone.*
Mitchell, Barbara. *A Pocketful of Goobers: A Story About George Washington Carver.*

RESOURCE
4.10 Poetry

Blackberry Ink

Purpose

To have students:

- Listen to and understand poetry forms
- Write and illustrate an original poem

Materials

chart paper
markers, pencils, crayons
copy of *Blackberry Ink* (Merriam)

Activity

1. Recite a few poems (such as "Humpty Dumpty") to children.
2. Ask them what we call things that sound like that (poems).
3. Ask what makes them poems (rhyme or other sounds that are similar to each other, rather short length, one topic each).
4. Read poems from *Blackberry Ink*.
5. Encourage children who know poems to recite them.
6. Ask children to write a poem together. Write the word *snow* in the middle of the chart paper. Ask children what snow is like, and how it looks and feels. Write their responses to the left of the word *snow*. For example

What is it like?	*Who or what?*
white	snow
bright	
wet	
cold	
fluffy	

     Chant each pair of words together (white snow, bright snow, wet snow). Then ask children what snow does, and write their responses to the right of the word *snow*. For example,

What is it like?	*Who or what?*	*What does it do?*
white	snow	blows
bright		drifts
wet		flurries
cold		melts

Chant the poem in rhyme:

White snow blows,
Bright snow drifts,
Wet snow flurries,
Cold snow melts.

7. Have children write their own poems using the three questions (1) Who or what? (2) What is it like? (3) What does it do?
8. Share the poems with the class and bind them into a class book.

Poetry for Grades Pre-K–2

Goldstein, Bobbye S. *What's on the Menu?*
———. *Inner Chimes.*
———. *Special Times.*

Poetry for Grades 3–5

Hudson, Wade. *Pass It On: African American Poetry for Children.*
Prelutsky, Jack. *It's Thanksgiving.*
Silverstein, Shel. *Where the Sidewalk Ends.*
———. *A Light in the Attic.*
———. *Falling Up.*

Supporting the Writing Process

This section provides teachers of kindergarten through fifth grade with ways to introduce the writing process and promote daily voluntary writing. Students work through each step of the writing process: prewriting or brainstorming, composing first drafts, engaging in peer and teacher conferences, and editing, illustrating, and publishing original stories. All students are given the opportunity to discuss their works in progress and present their published books. Storytelling techniques can be used as children retell their original stories. Each child's book should include a comment page at the end where other students may write positive remarks.

The lessons are as follows:

RESOURCE
5.1 Introduction to Journal Writing

Purpose

To have students:

- Engage in the roles of author and illustrator
- Improve their existing writing abilities

Materials

notebook
pencils, crayons

Activity

1. Explain that everyone has the ability to be a reader, a writer, and an illustrator. Let students know that one way to do this is to keep a journal. Tell students that many authors and illustrators get ideas through their own journals.
2. Explain that a journal is a special and personal place to record daily thoughts, feelings, and ideas in both written and illustrative form.
3. Show children how journal pages are dated.
4. Set aside allocated time for daily journal writing.
5. Allow time for students to share journal entries with the class.
6. Encourage children to personalize their journals by decorating the cover.

RESOURCE
5.2 Creating Original Stories

Purpose

To have students:

- Understand the elements of a well-formed story
- Increase their oral language and writing abilities
- Create and present original stories through active storytelling

Materials

felt board characters
popsicle stick figures
hand puppets
(Resource Section 2)

Activity

1. After introducing students to the concept of storytelling using the felt board, popsicle stick puppets, and hand puppets, retell a familiar story using one of these techniques. At the completion of the story, ask students questions that identify story elements:

   Where did the story take place?
   Who were the main characters?
   What was the problem, and how was it solved?

2. Have students identify each story element and ask them to include them in stories of their own.
3. Have children pick their favorite part of their own story and create appropriate character props for use in a presentation of their story.

RESOURCE
5.3 Writing Stories and Making Bound Books

Purpose

To have students:

- Understand the publishing process
- Write a rough draft of a story of their own

Materials

writing paper
copies of books by various authors
materials for making bound books (A5.1)

A5.1 Making Books

Bound Books
After writing an original story, a child can illustrate and publish his or her own book. This book can be placed in the classroom library. The following are directions for one method that a child can follow to make such a book. (Dimensions can be adjusted to make larger or smaller books.)

1. Place 11" x 14" (27.5 cm x 35 cm) pieces of wallpaper (or plastic or cloth) face down. Paste two pieces of 6" x 9" (15 cm x 22.5 cm) oaktag or cardboard on the wallpaper 1/4" (0.5 cm) apart, leaving about a 1" (2.5 cm) border.
2. Fold each corner of the wallpaper from the corner points onto the cardboard to form a triangle; paste down. Fold flaps onto the cardboard and paste.
3. Next, using a large needle and strong thread, sew a running stitch down the center of 10 or more sheets of 8 1/2" x 11" (21 cm x 27.5 cm) plain white paper. Fold along the stitched line.
4. Put glue on the 1/4" (0.5 cm) space between the pieces of cardboard and also on the entire exposed area of the cardboard. Place the folded and stitched edge of the plain paper in the 1/4" (0.5 cm) glued space; paste the first and last sheets onto the cardboard and over the wallpaper border to make the inside covers.
5. Add a design to the finished cover.

Activity

1. Explain that each author has his or her own writing style. Read excerpts from several books to illustrate different writing styles.
2. Talk with children about writing their own books with their own individual style.
3. Have students write rough drafts of an original story.
4. Teach children how to make their own bound books (A5.1). Children in grades 3–5 are usually capable of making their own books; children in grades K–2 usually need assistance.

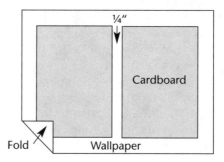

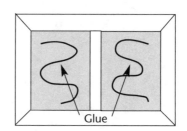

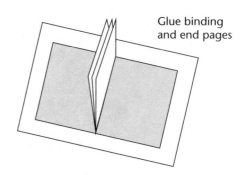

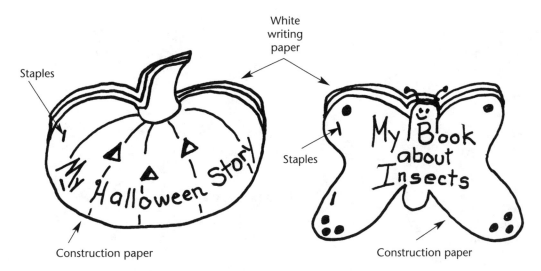

Staples

White writing paper

Staples

My Halloween Story

My Book about Insects

Construction paper

Construction paper

Class-Made Books

For special class themes or for children's own books, other types of bound books can be created.

Stapled Book

A stapled book can be made by cutting colored construction paper and white writing paper into a desired shape, and then stapling at the side.

Sewn Book

A simple sewn book can be made by punching holes into oaktag and white writing paper, and then sewing the pages together with yarn.

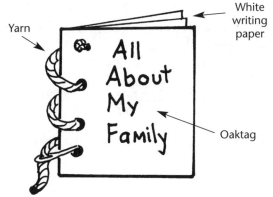

Yarn

White writing paper

All About My Family

Oaktag

Big Books

12 pieces of oaktag (20" x 30")
6 loose-leaf rings (1 1/4")
Hole punch

Punch three sets of holes in the top, middle, and bottom of the oaktag. Insert a loose-leaf ring in each hole. The Big Book should be a minimum of ten pages or as many as is manageable. The print should be 1 1/2" to 2" high.

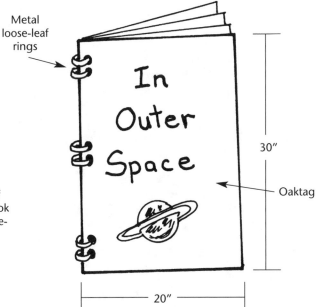

Metal loose-leaf rings

In Outer Space

30"

Oaktag

20"

5.4 Writing Series Books

Purpose

To have students:

- Understand the elements of series books
- Write sequels to existing books

Materials

writing paper
pencils
publishing materials

Activity

1. Discuss how authors may write different stories for the same characters.
2. Discuss similarities in style and illustrations within a series.
3. Talk about how readers who enjoy one book in a series often like others from that series as well.
4. Have students choose a favorite author's latest book in a series and write a new story for that series, following the same writing and illustrative styles (Resource 4.3).

5.5 Writing a Science Story

Purpose

To have students:

- Understand how to use factual information and reference books to write and illustrate an original science story

Materials

writing paper
pencils
reference books: dictionary, encyclopedia, science magazines, science books
copy of *A Seed Is a Promise* (Merril)

Activity

1. Create a K-W-L chart about plants: What do we *know* about the topic? What do we *want to learn* about the topic? What did we *learn* about the topic?
2. Brainstorm the K and W sections of the chart. Read and discuss *A Seed Is a Promise* and complete the L section.
3. Have students write original science stories about plants using information on the K-W-L chart or from additional research gathered from available reference materials and science books. Encourage them to include as many facts and new words as possible.

Pre-Service and In-Service Staff Development

This section provides a plan for a series of teachers' meetings to read this book, set goals for improving classroom management, share ideas, make materials together, and offer modeling help when necessary. The plan is for pre-service and in-service teachers.

A Plan for Staff Development Using This Book

This book may be used by both pre-service and in-service teachers. Pre-service teachers will be guided through the book by an instructor, and in-service teachers may be guided by a supervisor or each other. The following plan can be used in the college classroom or in a school district.

This book is for teachers who are interested in creating rich literacy environments for their students and in helping them enjoy reading and practice skills. The book describes motivation theory, social contexts for learning, and how to organize social learning. It emphasizes the physical design of classrooms, the materials necessary for independent work, and the management in the classroom necessary for carrying out the independent work.

If this is a plan for pre-service teachers, they should be observing or participating in an elementary school classroom to carry out the activities discussed. If in-service teachers are involved, they should be meeting at least once a month. They can meet with or without a supervisor. Participants will be reading the book, setting goals, and reporting back to the group about progress. They will collaborate by sharing ideas, making materials for others, and offering modeling help when necessary. They will visit each other's classrooms to learn from their peers.

1. Meeting One. Read Chapter 1 before the first meeting.
   A. Brainstorm major points about motivation, social learning, and the need to create independent learners.
   B. Discuss elements already included in your classroom or in the classroom where you observe.
   C. Evaluate your classroom or the one where you observe for the characteristics suggested in Chapter 1 about classrooms that motivate reading and writing in social settings and independently of the teacher.

   D. Include one or two of the elements in your room, and observe and describe the change in child behavior as a result. Suggest elements for change in the classroom where you observe and write down what you think the results would be.

2. Meeting Two. Read Chapter 2 before the second meeting.
   A. Describe the changes made in your classroom or those you would suggest in the room where you observe dealing with elements to promote motivation, social learning, independent learning. Discuss the resulting changes in child and teacher behavior.
   B. Discuss Chapter 2, specifically centers and center materials you already have in your classroom. Describe centers and center materials in the room where you observe.
   C. Brainstorm changes you could make to your existing centers for improvement as a goal for the next meeting. Consult the Introduction to Literacy Center Time in Resource Section 1.

3. Meeting Three
   A. Describe the changes made in your classroom or those you would suggest in the room where you observe dealing with center activities. Discuss the changes they caused in child and teacher behavior.
   B. Discuss Chapter 3, specifically storytelling literature activities to promote comprehension skills, independent learning, and the joy of reading. Describe these elements in the room where you observe.
   C. Brainstorm changes you could make to your existing literature activities for improvement as a goal for the next meeting. Consult Resource Section 2, Comprehension Development.
   D. Visit two classrooms of colleagues to see changes made in centers.

4. Meeting Four
   A. Describe the changes made in your classroom or those you would suggest in the

room where you observe dealing with literature activities to promote comprehension. Discuss the resulting changes in child and teacher behavior.

B. Discuss Chapter 4, specifically phonics and word study activities to promote decoding skills, and independent learning. Describe these elements in the room where you are observing.

C. Brainstorm changes you could make to improve your existing word study activities as a goal for the next meeting. Consult Resource Section 3, Word Study.

D. Visit two classrooms of colleagues to see changes made dealing with storytelling/ literature activities to practice comprehension.

5. Meeting Five

A. Describe the changes made in your classroom or those you would suggest in the room where you observe dealing with word study activities. Discuss the changes in child and teacher behavior.

B. Discuss Chapter 5, specifically activities to promote the management of independent and social literacy experiences. Describe these elements in the room where you observe.

C. Brainstorm changes you could make to your existing management systems for improvement as a goal for the next meeting. Consult Resource Section 1 again, which deals with organization and management of the literacy center.

D. Visit two classrooms of colleagues to see changes made dealing with word study activities.

6. Meeting Six

A. Describe the scene from your classroom or from the room where you observe dealing with activities that occur during literacy center time.

B. Discuss Chapter 6, Scenes from the Literacy Center, in relation to your own classroom and those you are observing.

C. Discuss the areas that continue to need work in your classroom and in the room where you observe.

D. Review all Resource Sections especially Resource Section 4 (All About Books) and Resource Section 5 (Supporting the Writing Process). Decide which areas need more work, such as the need for more word study materials. Divide responsibilities so that each teacher has an assignment to create materials. For example, one teacher could choose to make word wheels (Resource Section 3, A3.11) or puppets (Resource Section 2, A2.2–A2.4) for several classrooms. This type of cooperation cuts down on the amount of work any one teacher has to do and builds a sense of community in the school.

E. Visit two classrooms of colleagues to observe their literacy center time.

7. Continuing Staff Development

A. Continue to meet and share ideas about creating literacy centers, developing independent activities, motivating students to read and write, and creating social reading and writing communities in your classroom.

B. Continue to share materials and ideas.

C. Continue to visit each other's classrooms.

D. Read additional material about the topic.

E. Visit teachers in other school districts.

F. Attend professional conferences that address the topic.

G. When the group feels they no longer need to discuss this topic, select another of mutual concern, select reading materials, select goals, and continue to meet.

Bibliography

Professional Literature

Adams, M. J. 1990. *Beginning to Read: Thinking and Learning About Print.* Cambridge, MA: MIT Press.

Anderson, R. C., E. H. Hiebert, J. A. Scott, and I. Wilkinson, eds. 1985. *Becoming a Nation of Readers.* Report of the Commission on Reading. U.S. Department of Education. Washington, DC: Government Printing Office.

Anderson, R. C., P. T. Wilson, and L. G. Fielding. 1988. "Growth in Reading and How Children Spend Their Time Outside of School." *Reading Research Quarterly* 23: 285–303.

Ashton-Warner, S. 1963. *Teacher.* New York: Bantam.

Atwell, N. 1987. *In the Middle.* Portsmouth, NH: Heinemann.

Augustine, D., K. Gruber, and L. Hanson. 1989. "Cooperation Works." *Educational Leadership* 45: 4–7.

Bear, D. R., M. Invernizzi, S. Templeton, and F. Johnston. 1996. *Words Their Way.* Englewood Cliffs, NJ: Prentice Hall.

Beck, I. L., and C. Juel. 1995. "The Role of Decoding in Learning to Read." *American Educator* 19: 8–42.

Bergeron, B. 1990. "What Does the Term Whole Language Mean? Constructing a Definition from the Literature." *Journal of Reading Behavior* 22: 301–329.

Boorstin, D. 1984. *Books in Our Future.* Report to the Congress. Senate Report 98–231. Washington, DC: Government Printing Office.

Bossert, S. T. 1979. *Tasks and Social Relationships in Classrooms.* Cambridge, UK: Cambridge University Press.

Calkins, L. M. 1994. *The Art of Teaching Writing.* 2d ed. Portsmouth, NH: Heinemann.

Cazden, C. B. 2001. *Classroom Discourse: The Language of Teaching and Learning.* 2d ed. Portsmouth, NH: Heinemann.

Clay, M. M. 1985. *The Early Detection of Reading Difficulties.* 3d ed. Portsmouth, NH: Heinemann.

———. 1998. *By Different Paths to Common Outcomes.* Portland, ME: Stenhouse.

Csikszentmihalyi, M. 1991. "Literacy and Intrinsic Motivation." In S. R. Graubard, ed., *Literacy: An Overview by Fourteen Experts.* New York: Farrar, Straus, Giroux.

Cullinan, B. E. 1992. *Invitation to Read: More Children's Literature in the Reading Program.* Newark, DE: International Reading Association.

Cunningham, A. E., and K. E. Stanovich. 1991. "Tracking the Unique Effects of Print Exposure in Children: Associations with Vocabulary, General Knowledge, and Spelling." *Journal of Educational Psychology* 83: 264–274.

Cunningham, P. 1995. *Phonics They Use.* New York: HarperCollins.

Cunningham, P., and R. L. Allington. 1999. *Classrooms That Work.* 2d ed. Boston: Allyn and Bacon.

Cunningham, P., D. Hall, and J. W. Cunningham. 1994. *Making Words.* Torrance, CA: Good Apple.

Dahl, K. L., and P. A. Freppon. 1995. "A Comparison of Inner-City Children's Interpretations of Reading and Writing Instruction in the Early Grades in Skill-Based and Whole Language Classrooms." *Reading Research Quarterly* 30 (1): 50–74.

Daniels, H. 1994. *Literature Circles: Voice and Choice in the Student-Centered Classroom.* Portland, ME: Stenhouse.

Dewey, J. 1966. *Democracy and Education.* New York: Free Press. (Original work published 1916.)

Dickinson, D. K., and M. W. Smith. 1994. "Long-Term Effects of Preschool Teachers' Book Readings on

Low-Income Children's Vocabulary and Story Comprehension." *Reading Research Quarterly* 29 (2): 104–122.

Erickson, H. L. 1995. *Stirring the Head, Heart, and Soul.* Thousand Oaks, CA: Corwin Press.

Feitelson, D., Z. Goldstein, J. Iraqi, and D. Share. 1993. "Effects of Listening to Story Reading on Aspects of Literacy Acquisition in a Diglossic Situation." *Reading Research Quarterly* 28: 70–79.

Fitzpatrick, J. 1997. *Phonemic Awareness: Playing with Sounds to Strengthen Beginning Reading Skills.* Cypress, CA: Creative Teaching Press.

Ford, M. E. 1992. *Motivating Humans: Goals, Emotions and Personal Agency Beliefs.* Newbury Park, CA: Sage.

Forman, E., and C. B. Cazden. 1985. "Exploring Vygotskian Perspectives in Education: The Cognitive Value of Peer Interaction." In J. V. Wertsch, ed., *Culture, Communication, and Cognition: Vygotskian Perspectives,* 323–347. Cambridge, UK: Cambridge University Press.

Fountas, I. C., and G. S. Pinnell. 1996. *Guided Reading: Good First Teaching for All Children.* Portsmouth, NH: Heinemann.

Gambrell, L. B., and J. F. Almasi. 1993. "Fostering Comprehension Development Through Discussion." In L. M. Morrow, J. K. Smith, and L. C. Wilkinson, eds., *Integrated Language Arts: Controversy to Consensus,* 71–90. Boston: Allyn and Bacon.

Gardner, H. 1993. *Frames of Mind.* 2d ed. New York: Basic Books.

Goatley, V. J., C. H. Brock, and T. E. Raphael. 1995. "Diverse Learners Participating in Regular Education Book Clubs." *Reading Research Quarterly* 30 (3): 353–380.

Goodman, Y. M. 1980. "The Roots of Literacy." In M. Douglas, ed., *Claremont Reading Conference Forty-Fourth Yearbook.* Claremont, CA: Claremont Reading Conference.

Goswami, U. C., and P. Bryant. 1990. *Phonological Skills and Learning to Read.* Hillsdale, NJ: Lawrence Erlbaum.

Greaney, V., and M. Hegarty. 1987. "Correlates of Leisure-Time Reading." *Journal of Research in Reading* 10: 3–20.

Guthrie, J. T., and D. E. Alvermann, eds. 1999. *Engaged Reading: Processes, Practices, and Policy Implications.* New York: Teachers College Press.

Guthrie, J. T., and V. Greaney. 1991. "Literacy Acts." In P. Barr, M. L. Kamil, P. Mosenthal, and P. D. Pearson, eds., *Handbook of Reading Research.* Vol. 2, 68–96. New York: Longman.

Harste, J. C., V. Woodward, and C. Burke. 1984. *Language Stories and Literacy Lessons.* Portsmouth, NH: Heinemann.

Hill, S. 1997. *Developing Literacy Using Reading Manipulatives.* Cypress, CA: Creative Teaching Press.

Holdaway, D. 1979. *The Foundations of Literacy.* Portsmouth, NH: Heinemann.

IRA (International Reading Association). 1999. *Using Multiple Methods of Beginning Reading Instruction.* Newark, DE: International Reading Association.

IRA and NAEYC (International Reading Association and National Association for the Education of Young Children). 1998. *Learning to Read and Write: Developmentally Appropriate Practices for Young Children.* Newark, DE: International Reading Association.

Johns, J. L., S. D. Lenski, and L. Elish-Piper. 1999. *Early Literacy Assessments and Teaching Strategies.* Dubuque, IA: Kendall/Hunt.

Johnson, D. W., and R. T. Johnson. 1998. *Learning Together and Alone: Cooperative, Competitive, and Individualistic Learning.* 5th ed. Boston: Allyn and Bacon.

———. 1999. "The Three Cs of School and Classroom Management." In H. J. Freiberg, ed., *Beyond Behaviorism,* 119–144. Boston: Allyn and Bacon.

Johnson, N. O. 1995. Four Second-Grade Children's Responses to Literature. Ph.D. diss., Rutgers University, New Brunswick, NJ.

Juel, C. 1989. "The Role of Decoding in Elementary Instruction and Assessment." In L. M. Morrow and J. Smith, eds., *Assessment for Instruction in Early Literacy.* Englewood Cliffs, NJ: Prentice Hall.

———. 1994. "Teaching Phonics in the Context of the Integrated Language Arts." In L. M. Morrow, J. K. Smith, and L. C. Wilkinson, eds., *Integrated Language Arts: Controversy to Consensus,* 133–154. Boston: Allyn and Bacon.

Lamme, L. L., and L. Ledbetter. 1990. "Libraries: The Heart of Whole Language." *Language Arts* 67: 735–741.

Loughlin, C. E., and M. D. Martin. 1987. *Supporting Literacy: Developing Effective Learning Environments.* New York: Teachers College Press.

Marriott, D. 1997. *What Are the Other Kids Doing?* Cypress, CA: Creative Teaching Press.

McCombs, B. L. 1991. "Unraveling Motivation: New Perspectives from Research and Practice." *Journal of Experimental Education* 60 (1): 3–88.

Montessori, M. 1965. *Spontaneous Activity in Education.* New York: Schocken.

Morrow, L. M. 1982. "Relationships Between Literature Programs, Library Corner Designs and Children's Use of Literature." *Journal of Educational Research* 75: 339–344.

———. 1983. "Home and School Correlates of Early Interest in Literature." *Journal of Educational Research* 76: 221–230.

———. 1988. "Young Children's Responses to One-to-One Story Readings in School Settings." *Reading Research Quarterly* 23: 89–107.

———. 1990. "The Impact of Classroom Environmental Changes on the Promotion of Literacy During Play." *Early Childhood Research Quarterly* 5: 537–554.

———. 1992. "The Impact of a Literature-Based Program on Literacy Achievement, Use of Literature, and Attitudes of Children from Minority Backgrounds." *Reading Research Quarterly* 27: 250–275.

———. 1996. *Motivating Reading and Writing in Diverse Classrooms: Social and Physical Context in a Literature-Based Program.* National Council of Teachers of English Research Report 28. Urbana, IL: National Council of Teachers of English.

———. 2001. *Literacy Development in the Early Years: Helping Children Read and Write.* 4th ed. Boston: Allyn and Bacon.

———. 2002. *Organizing the Language Arts Block.* New York: Guilford Publications.

Morrow, L. M., E. M. O'Connor, and J. K. Smith. 1990. "Effects of a Story Reading Program on the Literacy Development of At-Risk Kindergarten Children." *Journal of Reading Behavior* 22: 225–275.

Morrow, L. M., and M. K. Rand. 1991. "Preparing the Classroom Physical Environment to Promote Literacy Behavior During Play: Implications from Research." In J. Christie, ed., *Play and Early Literacy Development.* New York: SUNY Press.

Morrow, L. M., J. K. Smith, and L.C. Wilkinson, eds. 1994. *Integrated Language Arts: Controversy to Consensus.* Boston: Allyn and Bacon.

———. 1986. "Encouraging Voluntary Reading: The Impact of a Literature Program on Children's Use of Library Centers." *Reading Research Quarterly* 21: 330–346.

Moustafa, M. 1998. *Beyond Traditional Phonics: Research Discoveries and Reading Instruction.* Portsmouth, NH: Heinemann.

National Reading Panel Report. 2000. *Teaching Children to Read.* Washington, DC: National Institute of Child Health and Human Development.

Neuman, S., and K. Roskos. 1990. "The Influence of Literacy-Enriched Play Settings on Preschoolers' Engagement with Written Language." In J. Zutell and S. McCormick, eds., *Literacy Theory and Research: Analyses from Multiple Paradigms,* 179–187. Thirty-Ninth Yearbook of the National Reading Conference. Chicago: National Reading Conference.

———. 1992. "Literacy Objects as Cultural Tools: Effects on Children's Literacy Behaviors in Play." *Reading Research Quarterly* 27: 203–225.

O'Flahavan, J. F., L. B. Gambrell, J. Guthrie, S. Stahl, J. Baumann, and D. Alvermann. 1992. "Poll Results Guide Activities of Research Center." *Reading Today* 10 (1): 12.

Ogle, D. M. 1986. "K-W-L: A Teaching Model That Develops Active Reading of Expository Text." *Reading Teacher* 39: 564–570.

Pappas, C., B. Kiefer, and L. Levstik. 1990. *An Integrated Language Perspective in the Elementary School: Theory into Action.* New York: Longman.

Piaget, J. 1959. *The Language and Thought of the Child.* 3d ed. London: Routledge and Kegan Paul. (Original work published 1926.)

Piaget, J., and B. Inhelder. 1969. *The Psychology of the Child.* New York: Basic Books.

Pittelman, S. D., J. E. Heimlich, R. L. Berglund, and M. P. French. 1991. *Semantic Feature Analysis: Classroom Applications.* Newark, DE: International Reading Association.

Pittelman, S. D., K. M. Levin, and D. D. Johnson. 1985. *An Investigation of Two Instructional Settings in the Use of Semantic Mapping with Poor Readers.* Program Report 85–4. Madison: Wisconsin Center for Educational Research, University of Wisconsin.

Rasinski, T. V., and N. D. Padak. 2000. *From Phonics to Fluency: Effective Teaching of Decoding and Reading Fluency in the Elementary School.* Boston: Allyn and Bacon.

Rasinski, T. V., N. D. Padak, W. Linek, and E. Sturtevant. 1994. "Effects of Fluency Development on Urban Second-Grade Readers." *Journal of Educational Research* 87 (3): 158–165.

Robbins, C., and L. Ehri. 1994. "Reading Storybooks to Kindergartners Helps Them Learn New Vocabulary." *Journal of Educational Psychology* 86 (1): 54–64.

Rosenblatt, L. M. 1988. *Writing and Reading: The Transactional Theory.* Report No. 13. University of California, Berkeley, Center for the Study of Writing.

Routman, R. 2000. *Conversations: Strategies for Teaching, Learning, and Evaluating.* Portsmouth, NH: Heinemann.

Salomon, G., and D. N. Perkins. 1998. "Individual and Social Aspects of Learning." In P. D. Pearson and A. Iran-Nejad, eds., *Review of Research in Education.* Vol. 23, 1–24.

Schickedanz, J. 1993. "Designing the Early Childhood Classroom Environment to Facilitate Literacy Development." In B. Spodack and O. Saracho, eds., *Language and Literacy in Early Childhood Education: Yearbook in Early Childhood Education.* Vol. 4. New York: Teachers College Press.

Sharan, Y., and S. Sharan. 1989/90. "Group Investigation Expands Cooperative Learning." *Educational Leadership* 47 (4): 17–21.

Sharkey, E. A. 1992. The Literacy Behaviors and Social Interactions of Children During an Independent Reading and Writing Period: An Ethnographic Study. Ph.D. diss., Rutgers University, New Brunswick, NJ.

Short, K. G., J. C. Harste, and C. Burke. 1996. *Creating Classrooms for Authors and Inquirers.* Portsmouth, NH: Heinemann.

Sirotnik, K. A. 1983. "What You See Is What You Get: Consistency, Persistency, and Mediocrity in Classrooms." *Harvard Education Review* 53 (1): 16–31.

Slavin, R. E. 1994. *Cooperative Learning: Theory, Research, and Practice.* 2d ed. Boston: Allyn and Bacon.

Spaulding, C. I. 1992. "The Motivation to Read and Write." In J. W. Irwin and M. A. Doyle, eds., *Reading/Writing Connections: Learning from Research,* 177–201. Newark, DE: International Reading Association.

Taylor, B. M., B. J. Frye, and G. M. Maruyama. 1990. "Time Spent Reading and Reading Growth." *American Educational Research Journal* 27: 351–362.

Taylor, D., and D. S. Strickland. 1986. *Family Storybook Reading.* Portsmouth, NH: Heinemann.

Teale, W. 1986. "The Beginning of Reading and Writing: Written Language Development During the Preschool and Kindergarten Years." In M. Sampson, ed., *The Pursuit of Literacy: Early Reading and Writing.* Dubuque, IA: Kendall/Hunt.

Turner, J. C. 1995. "The Influence of Classroom Contexts on Young Children's Motivation for Literacy." *Reading Research Quarterly* 30 (3): 410–441.

Vygotsky, L. S. 1978. M. Cole, V. John-Steiner, S. Scribner, E. Souberman, eds. *Mind in Society: The Development of Higher Psychological Processes.* Cambridge, MA: Harvard University Press.

Weinstein, C. S., and A. J. Mignano, Jr. 1997. *Elementary Classroom Management.* 2d ed. New York: McGraw-Hill.

Wood, K. D. 1990. "Collaborative Learning." *Reading Teacher* 43: 346–347.

Wylie, R. E., and D. D. Durrell. 1970. "Teaching Vowels Through Phonograms." *Elementary English* 47: 787–791.

Yaden, D. 1985. Preschoolers' Spontaneous Inquiries About Print and Books. Paper presented at the annual meeting of the National Reading Conference, San Diego.

Children's Literature

Aardema, V. 1981. *Bringing the Rain to Kapiti Plain.* New York: Dial.

Agard, J. 1989. *Calypso Alphabet.* New York: Holt.

Alexander, L. 1973. *The Cat Who Wished to Be a Man.* New York: Dutton.

Alexander, M. G. 1971. *Nobody Asked Me If I Wanted a Baby Sister.* New York: Dial.

Alexander, S. 1984. *World Famous Muriel.* Boston: Little, Brown.

———. 1985. *World Famous Muriel and the Scary Dragon.* Boston: Little, Brown.

Aliki. 1977. *The Many Lives of Benjamin Franklin.* Englewood Cliffs, NJ: Prentice Hall.

Arno, E. 1970. *The Gingerbread Man.* New York: Scholastic.

Asbjørnsen, P. C., and J. E. Moe. 1957. *The Three Billy Goats Gruff.* New York: Harcourt Brace.

Atwater, R., and F. Atwater. 1938. *Mr. Popper's Penguins.* Boston: Little, Brown.

Babbitt, N. 1975. *Tuck Everlasting.* New York: HarperCollins.

Bailey, C. S., and C. M. Lewis. 1965. *Favorite Stories for the Children's Hour.* New York: Platt and Munk.

Baker, L. 1990. *Life in the Rain Forests.* New York: Puffin.

Banks, L. R. 1980. *The Indian in the Cupboard.* New York: Avon.

Barrett, J. 1978. *Cloudy with a Chance of Meatballs.* New York: Aladdin.

———. 1980. *Animals Should Definitely Not Wear Clothing.* New York: Aladdin.

Base, G. 1986. *Animalia.* New York: H. N. Abrams.

Baum, L. F. 1982. *The Wizard of Oz.* New York: Holt, Rinehart and Winston.

Bemelmans, L. 1939. *Madeline*. New York: Simon and Schuster.

———. 1953. *Madeline's Rescue*. New York: Viking.

Berger, M. 1992. *All About Seeds*. New York: Scholastic.

Berenstain, S., and J. Berenstain. 1987. *The Berenstain Bears and Too Much Birthday*. New York: Random House.

Blume, J. 1971. *Freckle Juice*. New York: Macmillan.

———. 1980. *Superfudge*. New York: Dutton.

Bond, M. 1973. *Paddington Bear*. New York: Random House.

Borden, L. 1989. *Caps, Hats, Socks, and Mittens: A Book About the Four Seasons*. New York: Scholastic.

Bourgeois, P. 1986. *Franklin in the Dark*. New York: Scholastic.

Boynton, S. 1983. *A Is for Angry: An Animal and Adjective Alphabet*. New York: Workman.

Branley, F. 1985. *Volcanoes*. New York: Harper and Row.

Brenner, B. 1972. *Walt Disney's The Three Little Pigs*. New York: Random House.

Brett, J. 1989. *The Mitten*. New York: Scholastic.

Bridwell, N. 1963. *Clifford, the Big Red Dog*. New York: Scholastic.

———. 1989. *Clifford's Puppy Days*. New York: Scholastic.

Brown, A. 1990. *The Tunnel*. New York: Knopf.

———. 1992. *Changes*. New York: Knopf.

Brown, G. 1991. *Anne Frank*. New York: Rosen Publishing Group.

Brown, M. W. 1939. *Noisy Book*. New York: Harper and Row.

———. 1947. *Goodnight Moon*. New York: HarperCollins.

Brown, Marc. 1979. *Arthur's Eyes*. Boston: Little, Brown.

———. 1989. *Arthur's Birthday*. Boston: Little, Brown.

———. 1990. *Arthur's Baby*. Boston: Little, Brown.

———. 1990. *Arthur's Pet Business*. Boston: Little, Brown.

Brown, Marcia. 1947. *Stone Soup*. New York: Scribner.

———. 1957. *The Three Little Billy Goats Gruff*. New York: Harcourt Brace.

Brown, R. 1991. *Alphabet Times Four*. New York: Dutton.

Buller, J., and S. Schade. 1988. *Space Rock*. New York: Random House.

Bunting, E. 1994. *Smoky Night*. New York: Harcourt Brace.

Burnett, F. H. 1938. *The Secret Garden*. Philadelphia: Lippincott.

Byars, B. 1981. *The Cybil War*. New York: Viking.

Cameron, A. 1994. *The Cat Sat on the Mat*. Boston: Houghton Mifflin.

Campilonga, M. 1996. *Blue Frogs*. Circleville, NY: Chicken Soup Press.

Carle, E. 1968. *1, 2, 3, to the Zoo*. Cleveland: World Publishing.

———. 1970. *The Very Hungry Caterpillar*. New York: Collins.

———. 1977. *The Grouchy Ladybug*. New York: Crowell.

———. 1984. *The Very Busy Spider*. New York: Philomel.

———. 1990. *The Very Quiet Cricket*. New York: Philomel.

———. 1991. *A House for a Hermit Crab*. New York: Scholastic.

———. 1999. *Animals, Animals*. New York: Putnam.

Catling, P. S. 1979. *The Chocolate Touch*. New York: Morrow.

Cherry, L. 1990. *The Great Kapok Tree*. New York: Harcourt Brace Jovanovich.

Child, L. 1974. *Over the River and Through the Wood*. New York: Coward-McCann.

Cleary, B. 1952. *Henry and Beezus*. New York: Morrow.

———. 1965. *The Mouse and the Motorcycle*. New York: Morrow.

———. 1968. *Ramona the Pest*. New York: Morrow.

Coerr, E. 1977. *Sadako and the Thousand Paper Cranes*. New York: Putnam.

Cohen, I. 1998. *ABC Discovery*. New York: Dial.

Cole, J. 1987. *The Magic School Bus Inside the Earth*. New York: Scholastic.

———. 1990. *The Magic School Bus Lost in the Solar System*. New York: Scholastic.

———. 1995. *The Magic School Bus Inside Ralphie*. New York: Scholastic.

Cooney, B. 1958. *Chanticleer and the Fox*. New York: Crowell.

Cronin, D. 2000. *Click, Clack, Moo: Cows That Type*. New York: Simon and Schuster.

Dahl, R. 1973. *Charlie and the Chocolate Factory*. New York: Knopf.

———. 1988. *James and the Giant Peach*. New York: Puffin.

Daugherty, J. 1966. *Daniel Boone*. New York: Viking.

Demi. 1991. *The Artist and the Architect*. New York: Holt.

dePaola, T. 1973. *Andy (That's My Name)*. Englewood Cliffs, NJ: Prentice Hall.

———. 1975. *Strega Nona*. Englewood Cliffs, NJ: Prentice Hall.

———. 1983. *The Legend of the Blue Bonnet: An Old Tale of Texas*. New York: Putnam.

———. 1988. *The Legend of the Indian Paintbrush*. New York: Putnam.

Devlin, W., and H. Devlin. 1971. *Cranberry Thanksgiving*. New York: Parents Magazine Press.

Dorros, A. 1990. *Rain Forest Secrets.* New York: Scholastic.

Durant, P. R. 1992. *When Heroes Die.* New York: Atheneum.

Eastman, P. D. 1960. *Are You My Mother?* New York: Random House.

Emberley, E. 1997. *Glad Monster, Sad Monster.* Boston: Little, Brown.

Estes, E. 1944. *The Hundred Dresses.* New York: Harcourt Brace.

Farley, W. 1941. *Black Stallion.* New York: Random House.

Feelings, M. 1974. *Jambo Means Hello: Swahili Alphabet Book.* New York: Dial.

Fitzhugh, L. 1964. *Harriet the Spy.* New York: Harper and Row.

Flack, M. 1971. *Ask Mr. Bear.* New York: Macmillan.

Fleischman, P. 1979. *The Birthday Tree.* New York: Harper and Row.

Fleming, D. 1992. *Count!* New York: Holt.

———. 1992. *Lunch.* New York: Holt.

Florian, D. 1986. *Discovering Trees.* New York: Scribner.

Fox, M. 1985. *Wilfrid Gordon MacDonald Partridge.* New York: Kane Miller.

Françoise. 1951. *Jeanne-Marie Counts Her Sheep.* New York: Scribner.

Fujikawa, G. 1981. *Jenny Learns a Lesson.* New York: Grosset and Dunlap.

G'ag, W. 1956. *Millions of Cats.* New York: Coward-McCann.

Galdone, P. 1972. *The Three Bears.* New York: Seabury.

———. 1973. *The Little Red Hen.* New York: Seabury.

———. 1975. *The Gingerbread Boy.* New York: Seabury.

George, J. C. 1959. *My Side of the Mountain.* New York: Dutton.

Gerstein, M. 1987. *The Mountains of Tibet.* New York: Harper and Row.

Gerth, M. 2000. *Ten Little Ladybugs.* Santa Monica, CA: Intervisual Books.

Gibbons, B. 1991. *The Seasons of Arnold's Apple Tree.* Orlando, FL: Harcourt.

Goble, P. 1978. *The Girl Who Loved Wild Horses.* New York: Bradbury Press.

Golding, K. 1998. *Alphababies.* New York: DK Publishing.

Goldstein, B. 1992. *What's on the Menu?* New York: Viking.

———. 1994. *Inner Chimes.* Honesdale, PA: Boyds Mills Press.

———. 1994. *Special Times.* New York: Bantam.

Grahame, K. 1933. *The Wind in the Willows.* New York: Scribner.

Grifalcone, A. 1986. *The Village of Round and Small Houses.* Boston: Little, Brown.

———. 1990. *Osa's Pride.* Boston: Little, Brown.

Grimm Brothers. 1968. *Little Red Riding Hood.* New York: Harcourt, Brace, and World.

———. 1974. *Snow White and the Seven Dwarfs.* Boston: Little, Brown.

Gross, R. 1982. *If You Grew Up with George Washington.* New York: Scholastic.

Guarino, D. 1989. *Is Your Mama a Llama?* New York: Scholastic.

Hader, B., and E. Hader. 1948. *The Big Snow.* New York: Macmillan.

Hazen, B. S. 1979. *Tight Times.* New York: Viking.

Hennessy, B. G. 1989. *The Missing Tarts.* New York: Viking.

Herman, C. 1990. *Max Malone and the Great Cereal Rip-Off.* New York: Holt.

Herman, G. 1999. *Slip, Slide, Skate!* New York: Scholastic.

Hoban, R. 1993. *Bread and Jam for Frances.* New York: HarperCollins.

Hodges, M. 1984. *Saint George and the Dragon.* Boston: Little, Brown.

Holabird, K. 1990. *Angelina's Birthday Surprise.* Santa Barbara, CA: ABC-Clio.

———. 1992. *Angelina Ballerina.* Santa Barbara, CA: ABC-Clio.

Holdsworth, W. 1968. *The Gingerbread Boy.* New York: Farrar, Straus, Giroux.

Hopkins, L. B. "Why Not Get a Pterodactyl?" In D. Evans, comp., *Weird Pet Poems.* New York: Scholastic.

Howard, E. F. 1990. *Aunt Flossie's Hats (and Crab Cakes Later).* New York: Clarion Books.

Howe, D., and J. Howe. 1979. *Bunnicula.* New York: Atheneum.

Hudson, W. 1993. *Pass It on: African American Poetry for Children.* New York: Scholastic.

Hurwitz, J. 1994. *The Up and Down Spring.* New York: Scholastic.

———. 1995. *The Hot and Cold Summer.* New York: Scholastic.

Hutchins, P. 1968. *Rosie's Walk.* New York: Macmillan.

———. 1976. *Don't Forget the Bacon.* New York: Greenwillow.

Ipcar, D. 1976. *Hard Scrabble Harvest.* New York: Doubleday.

Izawa, T., and S. Hijikata. 1970. *The Three Little Pigs.* New York: Grosset and Dunlap.

James, S. 1991. *Dear Mr. Blueberry.* New York: Macmillan.

Johnson, C. 1955. *Harold and the Purple Crayon.* New York: Harper and Row.

Johnson, S. T. 1995. *Alphabet City.* New York: Viking.

Jordan, M., and T. Jordan. 1996. *Amazon Alphabet.* New York: Larousse Kingfisher Chambers.

Kasza, K. 1988. *The Pig's Picnic.* New York: Putnam.

Keats, E. J. 1962. *The Snowy Day.* New York: Viking.

———. 1967. *Peter's Chair.* New York: Harper and Row.

———. 1968. *A Letter to Amy.* New York: Harper and Row.

———. 1971. *Over in the Meadow. Traditional Tale by Olive A. Wadsworth.* New York: Four Winds Press.

———. 1972. *Pet Show.* New York: Macmillan.

Keillor, G. 1995. *Cat, You Better Come Home.* New York: Viking.

Kent, J. 1974. *More Fables of Aesop.* New York: Parents Magazine Press.

Kessler, L. P. 1966. *Kick, Pass, and Run.* New York: Harper and Row.

King-Smith, D. 1983. *Babe the Gallant Pig.* New York: Crown.

Kipling, R. 1994. "How the Camel Got Its Hump." In *Just So Stories.* New York: Macmillan. (Original work published 1902.)

Kirk, D. 1998. *Miss Spider's ABC.* New York: Scholastic.

Krauss, R. 1945. *The Carrot Seed.* New York: Harper and Row.

Lapsley, S. 1975. *I Am Adopted.* New York: Bradbury Press.

Lawson, R. 1944. *Rabbit Hill.* New York: Viking.

Le Guin, U. 1988. *Catwings.* New York: Scholastic.

Lear, E. 1977. *The Owl and the Pussycat.* New York: Atheneum.

Lenski, L. 1945. *Strawberry Girl.* Philadelphia: Lippincott.

Lesser, R. 1984. *Hansel and Gretel.* New York: Dodd, Mead.

Lexau, J. M. 1983. *The Poison Ivy Case.* New York: Dial.

Lewis, C. S. 1950. *The Lion, the Witch, and the Wardrobe.* New York: Macmillan.

Lillegard, D. 1984. *Potatoes on Tuesday.* Columbus, OH: Pearson Learning.

Lionni, L. 1963. *Swimmy.* New York: Knopf.

———. 1967. *Frederick.* New York: Pantheon.

———. 1994. *An Extraordinary Egg.* New York: Knopf.

Lobel, A. 1970. *Frog and Toad Are Friends.* New York: HarperCollins.

———. 1982. *Ming Lo Moves the Mountain.* New York: Greenwillow.

Louie, A. 1982. *Yeh-Shen: A Cinderella Story from China.* New York: Philomel.

Mack, S. 1974. *Ten Bears in My Bed.* New York: Pantheon.

MacLachlan, P. 1993. *Baby.* New York: Delacorte.

———. 1994. *All the Places to Love.* New York: HarperCollins.

Marshall, J. 1989. *The Three Little Pigs.* New York: Dial.

Martin, B., Jr. 1967. *Brown Bear, Brown Bear, What Do You See?* New York: Holt.

———. 1991. *Polar Bear, Polar Bear, What Do You Hear?* New York: Holt.

Martin, B., Jr., and J. Archambault. 1989. *Chicka Chicka Boom Boom.* New York: Scholastic.

McCloskey, R. 1948. *Blueberries for Sal.* New York: Viking.

———. 1957. *Time of Wonder.* New York: Viking.

McGovern, A. 1967. *Too Much Noise.* Boston: Houghton Mifflin.

McNulty, F. 1979. *How to Dig a Hole to the Other Side of the World.* New York: Harper and Row.

Merriam, E. 1985. *Blackberry Ink.* New York: Morrow.

Merrill, C. 1990. *Seed Is a Promise.* New York: Scholastic.

Miller, J. P., and S. M. Greene. 2001. *We All Sing with the Same Voice.* New York: HarperCollins.

Mitchell, B. 1986. *A Pocketful of Goobers: A Story About George Washington Carver.* Minneapolis: Carolrhoda Books.

Moore, E. 1964. *Johnny Appleseed.* New York: Scholastic.

Moss, L. 1995. *Zin! Zin! Zin! a Violin.* New York: Simon and Schuster.

Munsch, R. N. 1980. *The Paper Bag Princess.* Toronto: Annick.

Naylor, P. 1991. *Shiloh.* New York: Atheneum.

Norton, M. 1953. *The Borrowers.* New York: Harcourt Brace.

Numeroff, L. F. 1985. *If You Give a Mouse a Cookie.* New York: Harper and Row.

O'Brien, R. C. 1971. *Mrs. Frisby and the Rats of Nimh.* New York: Atheneum.

O'Dell, S. 1960. *Island of the Blue Dolphins.* Boston: Houghton Mifflin.

Oppenheim, J. 1986. *Have You Seen Birds?* New York: Scholastic.

———. 1995. *Have You Seen Trees?* New York: Scholastic.

Parish, P. 1963. *Amelia Bedelia.* New York: Harper and Row.

———. 1998. *Amelia Bedelia's Family Album.* New York: Greenwillow.

Paterson, K. 1977. *Bridge to Terabithia*. New York: Crowell.

Perrault, C. 1954. *Cinderella*. New York: Scribner.

Pfister, M. 1992. *The Rainbow Fish*. New York: North-South Books.

Piper, W. 1954. *The Little Engine That Could*. New York: Platt and Munk.

Potter, B. 1902. *The Tale of Peter Rabbit*. New York: Scholastic.

Prelutsky, J. 1982. *It's Thanksgiving*. New York: Scholastic.

Prokofiev, S. 1940. *Peter and the Wolf*. New York: Knopf.

Quackenbush, R. 1972. *Old MacDonald Had a Farm*. Philadelphia: Lippincott.

———. 1973. *Go Tell Aunt Rhody*. Philadelphia: Lippincott.

———. 1973. *She'll Be Coming 'Round the Mountain*. New York: HarperCollins.

Raferty, K. 1989. *Kidsgardening*. Palo Alto, CA: Klutz Press.

Raffi. 1989. *Tingalayo*. New York: Crown.

Ranger Rick (magazine). Vienna, VA: National Wildlife Federation.

Rockwell, A. F. 1975. *The Three Bears and Fifteen Other Stories*. New York: Crowell.

———. 1989. *Apples and Pumpkins*. New York: Macmillan.

Rockwell, T. 1973. *How to Eat Fried Worms*. New York: Franklin Watts.

Rosenberg, J. 1994. *Play Me a Story*. New York: Knopf.

Ross, T. 1993. *Eggbert, the Slightly Cracked Egg*. New York: Putnam.

Rowling, J. K. 1997. *Harry Potter and the Sorcerer's Stone*. New York: Scholastic.

Schimmel, S. 1994. *Dear Children of the Earth*. Minocqua, WI: North Word Press.

Scieszka, J. 1989. *The True Story of the Three Little Pigs*. New York: Viking.

———. 1992. *The Stinky Cheese Man and Other Fairly Stupid Tales*. New York: Viking.

Sendak, M. 1962. *Chicken Soup and Rice: A Book of Months*. New York: Harper and Row.

———. 1963. *Where the Wild Things Are*. New York: Harper and Row.

Seuss, Dr. 1957. *The Cat in the Hat*. New York: Putnam.

———. 1960. *Green Eggs and Ham*. New York: Random House.

———. 1970. *Mr. Brown Can Moo! Can You?* New York: Random House.

———. 1976. *The Foot Book*. New York: Random House.

Showalter, J. B. 1967. *The Donkey Ride*. New York: Doubleday.

Silverstein, S. 1964. *The Giving Tree*. New York: Harper and Row.

———. 1974. *Where the Sidewalk Ends*. New York: Harper and Row.

———. 1981. *A Light in the Attic*. New York: Harper and Row.

———. 1996. *Falling Up*. New York: HarperCollins.

Slobodkina, E. 1995. *Caps for Sale*. New York: HarperCollins.

Sobol, H. L. 1977. *My Brother Steven Is Retarded*. New York: Macmillan.

———. 1979. *My Other-Mother, My Other-Father*. New York: Macmillan.

Spier, P. 1970. *The Erie Canal*. New York: Doubleday.

Steig, W. 1969. *Sylvester and the Magic Pebble*. New York: Simon and Schuster.

Steptoe, J. 1984. *The Story of Jumping Mouse: Native American Legend*. New York: Lothrop, Lee, and Shepard.

Sutton, F. 1968. *Master of Ballyhoo: The Story of P. T. Barnum*. New York: Putnam.

Tompert, A. 1990. *Grandfather Tang's Story: A Tale Told With Tangrams*. New York: Crown.

Tyrone, L. 1999. *Albert's Ballgame*. Old Tappan, NJ: Simon and Schuster.

Urdy, J. M. 1956. *A Tree Is Nice*. New York: Harper and Row.

Van Allsburg, C. 1990. *Just a Dream*. Boston: Houghton Mifflin.

White, E. B. 1952. *Charlotte's Web*. New York: Harper.

Wilhelm, H. 1988. *Tyrone the Horrible*. New York: Scholastic.

Williams, V. B. 1986. *Cherries and Cherry Pits*. New York: Greenwillow.

Wither, C. 1966. *The Tale of the Black Cat*. New York: Holt.

Wolf, B. 1974. *Don't Feel Sorry for Paul*. Philadelphia: Lippincott.

Young, E. 1989. *Lon Po Po: A Red Riding Hood Story from China*. New York: Philomel.

———. 1992. *Seven Blind Mice*. New York: Philomel.

Zolotow, C. 1962. *Mister Rabbit and the Lovely Present*. New York: Harper and Row.

———. 1967. *Summer Is . . . .* New York: Crowell.

———. 1972. *Hold My Hand*. New York: Harper and Row.

———. 1972. *William's Doll*. New York: Harper and Row.